John Fowles
and Nature

John Fowles and Nature

Fourteen Perspectives on Landscape

Edited by
James R. Aubrey

Madison • Teaneck
Fairleigh Dickinson University Press
London: Associated University Presses

© 1999 by Associated University Presses, Inc.

All rights reserved. Authorization to photocopy items for internal or personal use, or the internal or personal use of specific clients, is granted by the copyright owner, provided that a base fee of $10.00, plus eight cents per page, per copy is paid directly to the Copyright Clearance Center, 222 Rosewood Drive, Danvers, Massachusetts 01923. [0-8386-3796-5/99 $10.00+8¢ pp, pc.]

Associated University Presses
440 Forsgate Drive
Cranbury, NJ 08512

Associated University Presses
16 Barter Street
London WC1A 2AH, England

Associated University Presses
P.O. Box 338, Port Credit
Mississauga, Ontario
Canada L5G 4L8

The paper used in this publication meets the requirements
of the American National Standard for Permanence of Paper
for Printed Library Materials Z39.48-1984.

Library of Congress Cataloging-in-Publication Data

John Fowles and nature : fourteen perspectives on landscape / edited by James R. Aubrey.
    p.   cm.
Includes bibliographical references and index.
ISBN 0-8386-3796-5 (alk. paper)
    1. Fowles, John, 1926– —Knowledge—Natural history.
2. Landscape in literature.   3. Nature in literature.   I. Aubrey, James R.
PR6056.O85Z72   1999
823'.914—dc21   98-47658
                                                    CIP

PRINTED IN THE UNITED STATES OF AMERICA

Contents

List of Illustrations	7
Introduction JAMES R. AUBREY	13
John Fowles's *Islands*: Landscape and Narrative's Negative Space KATHERINE TARBOX	44
"In the Sea of Life Enisled": Narrative Landscape and Catharine's Fate in John Fowles's "The Cloud" CLARK CLOSSER	60
Dialectical Aesthetics: Interrelations between Image and Text in John Fowles's Nonfiction LYNNE S. VIETH	69
The Nature of John Fowles CAROL M. BARNUM	87
The Archetype of the Green Man in the Writing of John Fowles BARRY N. OLSHEN	96
The Corpse in the Combe: The Vision of the Dead Woman in the Landscapes of John Fowles EILEEN WARBURTON	114
The Undercliff of John Fowles's *The French Lieutenant's Woman*: A Note on Geology and Geography LIZ-ANNE BAWDEN, KEVIN PADIAN, and HUGH S. TORRENS	137
Deep Time, Evolutionary Legacy, and the Darwinian Landscape in John Fowles's *The French Lieutenant's Woman* KEVIN PADIAN	154
The Undercliff as Inverted Pastoral: The Fowlesian *Felix Culpa* in *The French Lieutenant's Woman* PATRICIA V. BEATTY	169

"Water out of a Woodland Spring": Sarah Woodruff and
  Nature in *The French Lieutenant's Woman* 181
  SUZANNE ROSS

Landscape This Side of Landscape: Transcendence and
  Immanence in the Fiction of John Fowles 195
  H. W. FAWKNER

The Geography of Ruins: John Fowles's *Daniel Martin* and
  the Travel Narratives of D. H. Lawrence 212
  LISA COLLETTA

Greek Myths and Greek Landscapes in John Fowles's *The
  Magus* 230
  KIRKE KEFALEA

The Landscape of Loss in the (Love) Poems of John Fowles 238
  DIANNE L. VIPOND

Afterword 254
  JOHN FOWLES

List of Contributors 258
Index 262

List of Illustrations

John Fowles	12
The Cobb and Undercliff, Lyme Regis	17
Belmont House, Lyme Regis	18
Steep Holm, near Weston-Super-Mare, Avon	19
Ceres, by Randolph Rogers	20
John Fowles on Spetses, Greece	21
Dartmoor, Devon, from Bittaford	22
La Primavera (detail), by Sandro Botticelli (about 1475–78)	25
Ouse River Valley, Sussex	27
Goat Island, in the Undercliff	28
Hampstead Heath, London	29
Exmoor, Devon	30
Stonehenge, Wiltshire	31
Wistman's Wood, Dartmoor	32
Scilly Isles, Cornwall	33
Belmont House and Garden, Lyme Regis	34
Kenwood House, London	35
Dornafield Farm, Two-Mile Oak, Devon	35
Tsankawi, Bandelier National Monument, New Mexico	36
Kitchener's Island, Aswan, Egypt	37
Whitechapel Rock, the Undercliff	38
John Fowles on Monhegan Island, Maine	45
Troy Town Maze, St. Agnes Island, Cornwall	50
Stonehenge, Wiltshire	51
The Old Man of Gugh, Scilly Isles	72
Large White Cloud Near Bilsington, Kent, England	74

LIST OF ILLUSTRATIONS

Seven Thuja [Juniper] Trees, by Wen Zhengming [or Cheng-Ming], 1532	79
Oak January Derbyshire, England	80
Wistman's Wood, Dartmoor	81
Untitled [Trees]	83
Cumberland Terrace, from Regent's Park, London	92
L'homme et la Forêt by René Magritte (about 1965)	between pages 96 and 97
Green Man in Leaf Bower	97
Green Man Pub, London	99
Green Man on Bench End, Somerset, 1534	102
Green Man on Respond, Wiltshire	103
Vision of St. Eustace (?) [or St. Hubert]	117
Punting on the River Cherwell, Oxford	125
Dornafield Farm House, Two-Mile Oak, Devon	128
Palmyra, Syria	131
Warmwell Heath, Dorset, May 1912	138
View along the Cliff at Lyme Regis, by George Cumberland, 1820	139
Undercliff from the Cobb, Lyme Regis, Dorset	139
Pinhay Bay, Devon	140
Underhill Farm, Devon	142
Underhill Farm house, Devon	142
The 1839 landslip in the Undercliff	144
Monmouth Beach, Dorset	147
Lyme Bay, English Channel	147
The Aristos, with ammonite	148
Petrified sea urchin	150
Tudor House, 16 Cheyne Walk, Chelsea, London	179
Lister House, Lyme Regis	185
Undercliff over Pinhay Bay	186
The Pasvik River between northern Norway and Russia	207
Tarquinia, Italy	215

LIST OF ILLUSTRATIONS 9

Tomb of the Painted Vases, near Tarquinia, Italy 217
Tsankawi, Bandelier National Monument, New Mexico 220
Hotel Poseidon, Spetses, Greece 231
Villa Yasemia, Spetses, Greece 234

John Fowles
and Nature

John Fowles. On July 11, 1996, Mr. Fowles was interviewed in the Masonic Hall of Lyme Regis, England, by scholars attending the John Fowles Symposium. Photograph by Yvonne Ou-Yang.

Introduction

JAMES R. AUBREY

> Even a bare grassy isle which I can see entirely over at a glance, has some undefined and mysterious charm for me.
> —Henry David Thoreau, *A Week on the Concord and Merrimack Rivers*

> Now I live here, another island,
> that doesn't seem like one, but who decides?
> —Elizabeth Bishop, "Crusoe in England"

WHEN JOHN GARDNER PREDICTED THAT THE WORKS OF JOHN FOWLES would "stand as literary classics" of the late twentieth century, he was thinking of Fowles as a fellow novelist—"the only writer in English who has the power, range, knowledge, and wisdom of a Tolstoi or James."[1] Another feature of Fowles's writing that should make him a spokesman for the age is the call to awareness of the natural world that has long informed his writing, nonfiction as well as fiction. Perhaps Fowles's success as a novelist has obscured his recognition as a nature writer, for by tradition prose fiction and essays about nature are very different kinds of writing. Depictions of the natural world in a novel typically provide the setting for a more important plot, whereas nature writers are typically seeking empirical truth in their essays, the kind of nonfiction associated with Charles Darwin or Henry David Thoreau. Both kinds of writing can be artful, but they are usually considered distinct. Because Fowles writes in both genres and sometimes blurs their distinctions, critical readers would be wise to consider his fiction and nonfiction comprehensively, and in relation to one another.

A comprehensive view of Fowles's writing would be in the spirit of ecology, of course, the very field whose name has been borrowed for literary studies of nature: ecocriticism. In *The Ecocriticism Reader*, Cheryll Glotfelty notes that the field of literary studies has been late to join other disciplines that have been "'greening' since the 1970s." She explains that ecocritics should continue to avoid restricting and systematizing what they do, so that the field will invite "suggestive and open" study of literature and the natural environment, of how nature is represented, understood, or ignored, and even of how the human species is constructed through literary discourse. Just as feminist critics sometimes examine the conditions of the lives of particular authors, she points out, ecocritics sometimes study the influence of place on the imagination of an author.[2] This volume of essays, taken as a whole, constitutes such a study.

The attachment to natural places is particularly strong in the imagination of John Fowles. One critic to recognize this fact is Robert Huffaker, who observed in 1980 that Fowles is "one of the few writers whom one may call a lover of nature without being trite."[3] Fowles displays his love of nature without sentimentalizing it, not only because he is tough-minded and a close observer of the natural world but also because he brings to nature considerable scientific knowledge. One need only read an essay such as "The Chesil Bank" to be reminded how informed Fowles has made himself:

> Many rare native plants such as the sea pea and sea kale, the yellow horned-poppy and shrubby sea-blite, survive this difficult environment. One of the most charming—and commonest—is the scurvy-grass, *Cochlearia danica*. Its myriad tiny flowers mist the bare shingle with an ethereal lilac-tinged ashy light in spring. Closer to, you must kneel; they are like alpine plants. Here as elsewhere the Chesil is lined at the back with groves of tamarisk. Nearby grows another "foreigner," the Duke of Argyll's tea-plant, a favourite shrub of mine because of the colour of its newly opened flowers. One *Hortus* I have describes *Lycium chinense* as "dull lilac purple," which deserves a suit for libel."[4]

Fowles knows fauna as well as flora, from butterflies and spiders to mammals; he once remarked casually that he could not bring himself to see the movie *Jurassic Park* "because I know too much about dinosaurs."[5] He recognizes, however, that knowledge forms only part of a satisfactory relationship with nature. Indeed, he has long recognized that knowledge can interfere. In a 1977 letter, Fowles observed," . . . though I suppose I can call myself a fairly good orthodox field botanist, ornithologist and the rest, the quasi-scientific approach had come to seem more and more inadequate (to me) emotionally, psychically, whatever you want to call it. I think I cannot be understood properly if this attachment to nature, and to natural history, and its disciplines, from the scientific to the 'Zen' aesthetic / poetic is not taken into account."[6] His relationship with nature is complex by his own account, then, and it has a significant bearing on his fiction writing, as he asserts in *The Tree*: "The key to my fiction, for what it is worth, lies in my relationship with nature."[7] In effect, Fowles was advising readers to take an ecocritical approach to his novels before the strategy had been named.

A novelist is not always the best judge of how to read his or her novels, but Fowles is a shrewd self-critic. To take his advice, to consider his "relationship with nature," one must consider who he is, this "I" who advises. The affection he feels for rural places seems partly to have been bred into him as a boy, during his urban childhood. When Fowles was about ten, he delighted in butterfly hunting with his uncle, away from his immediate neighborhood in a London suburb. Chasing and exploring in some pleasant, exurban "elsewhere" seems to have made a strong impression on him. Later his family joined the wartime evacuation from the London area, to Devon, so the adolescent Fowles was able to experience similar, rural pleasures when he was on leave from boarding school. His activities included shooting and trapping, but on reaching adulthood, Fowles gave up the pursuit of animals to become their protector, eventually advocating the preservation of biodiversity—not merely preservation of the rural look of the countryside.[8] In 1965, only three years after Rachel Carson sounded an environmental alarm with *Silent Spring*, Fowles published a travel piece titled "Swan Song of the European Wild," which describes "victims of an unbalanced ecology" in northern Norway, where one might suppose that inaccessibility would protect nature. At a lake in Finnmark, Fowles reports having met a hermitlike "Norwegian Thoreau" who tells him that "the cranes and the geese and the swans are all going or have gone to Russia. It's the people in Oslo. They think timber and tourism are everything and wildlife nothing."[9] In 1970 Fowles was again advocating biodiversity, this time in "Weeds, Bugs, Americans," an essay that pleads with readers to stop spraying their lawns with insecticides and weed killers.[10] Fowles's attitude today would be labeled "green," but it is evident that his views were taking that coloration well before green parties were formed in the 1980s, even before the environmental activism of the 1970s.

Fowles's later nonfiction continued to reflect his keen interest in preserving and protecting wild places and things. In his 1971 essay "The Blinded Eye," Fowles laments the decline of various species, even as he offers instruction on how to look at and be responsive to what nature remains ("with just as much science . . . as the poetry requires").[11] Roughly half of his reviews for the *New Statesman* in the mid-1970s were of books about the natural world, from *Whales, Dolphins and Seals* to *Birds, Beasts and Men*.[12] His book *The Tree*, first published in 1979, is Fowles's autobiographical tribute to wild nature, concluding with a description of a walk in the woods.[13] His 1984 essay on the Chesil Bank advocated increased care when visiting there, and increased sensitivity to the threatened Dorset coastline generally.[14] In 1987 Fowles contributed a jeremiad to the Greenpeace book *Coastline*, in which he laments that humanity's true profession has become destruction of the environment: "[Man] is a wrecker; and what he wrecks now is not just ships."[15] In the 1990s Fowles wrote a series of similarly impassioned reviews of books about nature for the *Sunday Times*, one of which prompted a reader to complain that Fowles must hate people if he hates cities so much.[16] It is fairer to say that Fowles dislikes the commercialism that he associates with cities, where people tend to see their environment as a place for making money. He disapproves of such attitudes in the country, as well, where monoculture planting reduces biodiversity and agribusiness inhibits people from feeling connected to the landscape. Fowles's 1995 work "The Nature of Nature" is a memoir testifying to the importance to him of wild nature, which he calls *la sauvage*. In the course of that essay, Fowles praises D. H. Lawrence for having "reached nearest—especially in his poetry—to penetrating that strange otherness" about nature. Like an English Thoreau, Fowles urges readers to adopt a double consciousness of feeling and knowing, art and science: "We need to institute an oscillation between the two sides, like a heartbeat; not to understand just the nature of things, but the nature of understanding them."[17]

Fowles's life, like his writing, reflects this attachment to wild nature. In 1966 he and his wife, Elizabeth, bought a derelict farm in Devon, just west of Dorset, on the edge of a coastal woodland. This adjoining tract of public, natural landscape, the now well-known Undercliff, would become, in effect, Fowles's playground—a wilderness that he might explore as he wished—"an English garden of Eden," as he calls it in *The French Lieutenant's Woman*.[18] A few years later, when he purchased nearby Belmont House in Lyme Regis, overlooking the Cobb and harbor, he was pleased to acquire with the house more than two acres of hillside, space that has since been maintained as a kind of wild garden.[19] His father, whose garden near London was carefully domesticated, was initially horrified by the wild garden at Belmont, but for the son that garden—like the Undercliff—represented independence from confining, middle-class values.[20] "We make our destinies by our choice of gods," Dr. Grogan reminds Charles in *The French Lieutenant's Woman* (151), and our choice of gardens would seem to have a similar function. When in 1977 Fowles was instrumental in establishing a nature sanctuary on the Bristol Channel island of Steep Holm, he was in a sense giving England its own wild garden, like his at Belmont.[21] It is perhaps significant that Fowles has chosen as his own garden god—the only sculpture in

The Cobb and Undercliff, Lyme Regis, Dorset. In *The French Lieutenant's Woman*, the narrator describes the Undercliff, the wooded slopes west of the artificial harbor formed by the Cobb of Lyme Regis, as "one of the strangest coastal landscapes in Southern England" (Little, Brown, 1969, page 66). The open fields just below those woods comprise Underhill Farm, where John Fowles lived when he was writing the novel. Photograph courtesy of the Lyme Regis Philpot Museum.

Fowles's garden, half hidden in the trees—a statue of Ceres, goddess of fertility and, as Demeter, a central figure in the Eleusinian mysteries, a Greek ceremony of liberation from the mundane world.

Fowles's life offers a rich store of experience to draw on for the construction of landscapes in his novels. Again Thoreau-like, Fowles has kept detailed records of his perceptions in a journal, which he began keeping about 1949 and from which he sometimes draws when he writes fiction.[22] In *Behind "The Magus,"* for example, Fowles acknowledges that the novel's descriptions of haunting pine forests and a private villa are based on his notebooks from 1952–53, when he was living in Greece.[23] His other novels appear to have similar relationships with places Fowles knows. In *The Collector*, Clegg kidnaps Miranda in Hampstead, London, where Fowles was living at the time he wrote it. In *The French Lieutenant's Woman* the main character, like the author at the time he was writing that novel, is recently arrived from London to Lyme Regis and the nearby Undercliff. Also like Fowles, the title character of *Daniel Martin* decides in middle age to

Belmont House, Lyme Regis. This late eighteenth-century house overlooking the English Channel has been the residence of John Fowles since 1968. His two acres of wild garden descend to the right, southward, almost to the breakwater known as the Cobb. Photograph by James Aubrey, 1992.

move from London to a farm in Devon, whose countryside he loved as a boy. *A Maggot*, too, chronicles a movement from London to Devon, again by characters whose lives are changed by their experiences in wild parts of the West Country. Even the setting of "The Ebony Tower," in the Brittany woods of France, is not far from Poitiers, where Fowles lived from 1950–51.[24] In fiction by Fowles generally, actual landscapes that he knows provide settings for events where characters struggle for personal emancipation. Central characters typically arrive at these rural places from urban locations and find the countryside magical. Each natural setting helps to create this sense of magic by the way a place in it exists as some kind of special case, geographically—an interruption of the surrounding topography by a cliff or a cleft, a secret valley or a dark forest, a mesa or an island, a large cave or a large rock. Sometimes the interruptions are built by humans, such as Clegg's isolated country house in *The Collector* or, in *A Maggot*, Stonehenge, whose extraordinary stones on Salisbury Plain are well known and thus likely to resonate with readers—as they evidently do with the author, who has discussed his fascination with the place in *The Enigma of Stonehenge*.[25] The contrast of such special

Steep Holm, near Weston-super-Mare, Avon. In 1976 John Fowles was instrumental in having this island in the Bristol Channel designated a nature reserve in memory of Kenneth Allsop, a promoter of environmental preservation. The photo of Tower Rock, on the southeast corner of the island, looks across the water to the town of Weston-super-Mare. Photograph by James Aubrey, 1994.

Ceres, by Randolph Rogers. A sculpture of the fertility goddess Ceres, or Demeter, holding a sheaf of grain, occupies a transitional space between the formal lawn and the wild garden of Belmont House. Fowles's fascination with the Eleusinian Mysteries makes Demeter a particularly appropriate *genius loci*, or presiding spirit for his garden. Rogers was an American sculptor who lived from 1825–92. Photograph by James Aubrey, 1996.

John Fowles on Spetses, Greece. He is writing in his notebook in the garden of the Villa Yasemia, model for the house of Maurice Conchis in *The Magus* (2nd edition, Little, Brown, 1978). After a 1996 celebration of his work in Athens, Fowles revisited the island for the first time since 1951–53, when he had lived and taught there at the Anargyrios School. Photograph by Kirke Kefalea, 1996.

sites with the surrounding landscape helps Fowles to construct in his own mind and to reconstruct in the mind of the reader an environment that conveys a sense of the sacred and the mysterious in life.

What, besides its discontinuous form, constitutes such an exceptional place? In *Daniel Martin* the narrator purports not to know, exactly: "Some skylines will not be forgotten; one from my childhood, on the southern edge of Dartmoor, is like that. It has always haunted my dreams; and the secret template of its contours still inhabits outwardly quite different vistas. . . . I have never quite understood why some places exert this deep personal attraction, why at them one's past seems in some mysterious way to meet one's future, one was somehow always to be there as well as being there in reality" (323–24). Elsewhere in that novel Fowles uses the words *sacred* to describe such places, and in a discussion of *Round About a Great Estate* he uses the word *special* to describe Burderop Park and its fictional equivalent, Okebourne Chase, as Richard Jefferies' "special land-

Dartmoor, Devon, from Bittaford. In *Daniel Martin*, Fowles's most autobiographical novel, the narrator observes, "Some skylines will not be forgotten; one from my childhood, of the southern edge of Dartmoor, is like that. It has always haunted my dreams; and the secret template of its contours still inhabits outwardly quite different vistas" (Little, Brown, 1977, page 323). Photograph by James Aubrey, 1996.

scape, in every sense: personally, historically, spiritually, aesthetically."[26] The experience of such places, which obliterates a sense of elapsed time as the place resonates with one's deepest self, can be literary as well as geographical, can be generated by verbal as well as visual stimuli. Fowles has often acknowledged having been profoundly affected in this way by reading Alain-Fournier's *Le Grand Meulnes*, whose protagonist is similarly haunted by the longing to find a magical place he once discovered in adolescence, then could not find again.[27] In each of these three instances, Fowles is revealing his own sympathy with the feelings of another character or author for a special place—feelings not easily explained. Environmental psychologist Stephen Kaplan has attempted to account for such complex responses to the natural environment in terms of "internal representations," a phrase useful for describing the way one's previous experiences help to form a prototypical experience that influences later, specific percepts—as Fowles's childhood "template" of Dartmoor haunts him in middle age.[28] Kaplan acknowledges that perception occurs "at a molecular level," so his model (derived from William James) offers only a partial understanding of this kind of mental event. Scientists working to trace correspondences across neuron pathways between what one sees and what one feels will, no doubt, eventually develop a more sophisticated model for explaining how people experience landscape.[29] For now, in unscientific language, Fowles seems especially capable of feeling deep resonances between the nature he looks at and the person he is—and he seems exceptionally aware that he is doing so. This sensitivity enables him to derive exceptional pleasure from nature. To the extent that Fowles can shape his own experiences into verbal representations, these resonances and pleasures are made available to his readers as well.

Fowles once used the traditional phrase *spirit of place* to describe what his novels typically create, the illusion that a fictional world exists and constitutes an imagined physical environment for the characters.[30] Part of the pleasure of being in nature—or in an imagined version of it—is that one senses unfamiliarity; because no two landscapes are formed exactly alike, any such experience will involve mystery. On various occasions Fowles has compared writing a novel to walking through a wood, where one pleasurably experiences a sequence of complex environmental cues and makes decisions as one moves forward.[31] One possibility is that similar brain activity is occurring when one reads a narrative, writes a narrative, or walks through the woods. For Fowles the pleasure of these analogous experiences seems to depend on the presence of the aleatory, on an unpredictableness in art like the wildness in nature that invests both inner and outer worlds with a mysteriousness that differentiates those worlds from more predictable environments—particularly from cities.

Fowles's best-known novel is *The French Lieutenant's Woman*, where wild nature is present as the Undercliff. This densely wooded, sometimes junglelike area west of Lyme Regis is physically extraordinary, of course, as the narrator explains in the first sentence of Chapter Ten, where he calls it "one of the strangest coastal landscapes in Southern England" (66). The Undercliff is constructed in the novel as a magical place, partly by means of reference to other cultural texts. For example, Fowles describes the Undercliff as "an English Garden of Eden" (67) to give it mythic resonance as well as to suggest that its Victorian counterparts to the biblical Adam and Eve are about to fall from innocence. But Fowles's Undercliff is not a morally symbolic landscape in the same way Eden is, a function of the moral character of its inhabitants. Nor does it symbolize social depravity, as Mrs. Poulteney thinks. In the novel, the Undercliff is a morally neutral landscape that is just there, not necessarily associated with either guilt or innocence. In this unsymbolic naturalness, however, the Undercliff does come to be associated with unbiblical views in the novel and thus becomes aligned with the politically charged names of Darwin, Marx, and Freud. So Fowles's Undercliff acquires a moral charge by its associations with both religious and counter-religious texts. The symbolic value of the Undercliff in Chapter Ten is further promoted by means of the allusion to Renaissance art, to "the ground that Botticelli's figures walk on," perhaps in the painting *La Primavera* (68). Even readers unfamiliar with Botticelli can infer that his ground must be solid, "real," unlike the ground in other paintings; a look at *La Primavera* reveals that the remarkable thing about the ground is that it is covered with flowers, not stylized but particular-looking. A comment by the narrator gives the allusive description a specific political dimension, as well, for we are told that the previous, medieval era in art history (when backgrounds were typically abstract) is associated with "chains, bounds, frontiers." Thus the flower-decked, natural-looking ground of a Botticelli painting links the Undercliff with cultural change, specifically with the Renaissance, described as "the green end of one of civilization's hardest winters" (68). The Undercliff is thus constructed to represent conditions that will allow the evolution of the modern self to continue in the character of Charles Smithson, and likewise in the novel's readers. Natural landscape functions this way in Fowles's fiction generally: to help enable a character, a writer, and a reader to attain heightened awareness of his or her freedom.

The idea that one can enhance one's sense of personal freedom by means of engagement with wild nature may have contributed to the formation of a central metaphor in Fowles's writing: each man is an island. The last page of *The French Lieutenant's Woman* implies this reversal of John Donne's declaration that "No man is an island," concluding as it does with an allusion to the Matthew Arnold poem "To Marguerite," quoted earlier in the novel. Arnold's poem begins with a description of the human condition, "in the sea of life enisl'd," where "we mortal millions live alone," and ends by declaring that sea to be "salt, estranging" (427). Fowles's narrator calls this "the noblest short poem of the whole Victorian era" (426), and it is also useful to Fowles at that point for the way its island metaphor anticipates the condition of existential aloneness that he wants to attribute to Charles. Another of his characters, David in "The Ebony Tower," wishfully fantasizes about becoming "locked away, islanded" somewhere in the West Country, away from London and his daily life of "getting and spending" (80). As a prominent feature in a natural setting, then, an island is nicely analogous to a Fowles protagonist in a natural landscape, or to an evolving reader or writer in that fictional world. As Fowles would later declare more explicitly, "*Every* man is an island."[32]

La Primavera (detail), by Sandro Botticelli (circa 1475–78). In *The French Lieutenant's Woman*, describing the Undercliff "prospect" in front of Charles Smithson, the narrator notes by name the presence of seven particular kinds of wildflower, then comments, "Only one art has ever caught such scenes—that of the Renaissance; it is the ground that Botticelli's figures walk on, the air that includes Ronsard's songs" (Little, Brown, 1969, page 68). Photograph by Marco Rabatti, courtesy of the Uffizzi Gallery.

Fowles's attraction to the analogy seems related to a longstanding fascination with islands in various forms, both literal and metaphorical. "Islanders" is the title of the first poem in *Poems,* whose contents date "mainly from 1951–52" when he was living on the Greek island of Spetses. The opening lines of a later Fowles poem express a view similar to Matthew Arnold's reply to John Donne, this time via Daniel Defoe's famous islander:

> Crusoes all of us
> stranded
> as solitary grains of sand.

Fowles's early novel *The Magus* is set mostly on a Greek island called Phraxos, and the crucial episode of an embedded narrative in Norway takes place on a near-island, "a long, tree-covered spit of land that ran into the river," a literally sacred place whose name, Seidevarre, readers are told, means "hill of the holy stone" (299–300). *The Collector* takes place metaphorically on an island, as Miranda is kidnapped from London and locked away in a country house, surrounded by a "sea" of open landscape near Lewes; Miranda notes the resemblance between her own situation and that of Miranda in Shakespeare's *The Tempest,* also stranded on an island by forces beyond her control, in exile from the mainland with a monster for company. In *The French Lieutenant's Woman,* the Undercliff is another metaphorical island, a Galapagos of wild nature in the sea of self-estranging culture that is Victorian England, where Charles and Sarah find refuge. In "The Enigma," in *The Ebony Tower,* Hampstead Heath is an area of wildness surrounded by London development, a relatively isolated place where the female character shows her rational detective friend how intuition might enable him to solve the case of a mysterious disappearance he is working on. In *A Maggot,* solutions to the novel's central mystery are similarly tentative, but the characters, likewise, have been affected by their experiences at distinctive sites in otherwise open landscapes of the West Country—Stonehenge on Salisbury Plain and the fictional Dollin's Cave on Exmoor. Stonehenge is particularly dramatic in appearance, standing in vertical contrast to the surrounding Salisbury Plain. Wistman's Wood, the copse of dwarf oaks that Fowles re-visits in the conclusion to *The Tree,* from a distance resembles an island of contrasting dark green foliage on the sealike expanse of Dartmoor. Fowles has written a book titled *Islands,* best described as a meditation on them, and *Shipwreck* is another book in which island life is his focus. Fowles has even rescued from obscurity the autobiography of an eccentric inhabitant of the

Ouse River valley, Sussex. This open countryside, south of Lewes, is near to where Frederick Clegg imprisons art student Miranda in *The Collector*, (Little, Brown, 1963). This particular view is from the garden of the house where Virginia Woolf—another doomed artist—was residing at the time of her suicide. Photograph by James Aubrey, 1994.

Isle of Wight, *The Book of Ebenezer Le Page*.[33] And Fowles is an islander himself, of course, not only as an inhabitant of one of the British Isles, but also as the inhabitant of his own, metaphorical "island," a two-acre garden surrounded by the town of Lyme Regis.

In *Daniel Martin*, more than in the other novels, there are various islandlike, specially-felt sites at which the main character undergoes transformative experiences: Kenwood House on Hampstead Heath, the ruins at Palmyra, the seashore at Tarquinia, the river at Oxford, the farm at Thorncombe. Tsankawi, the site in New Mexico of a former Anasazi village on top of an isolated mesa, is compared to an island by Dan himself, who is reminded of Phaestos, on Crete, by the way that the mesa rises dramatically from the terrain surrounding it. And Kitchener's Island on the Nile at Aswan, with its botanical garden, is literally an island. *Daniel Martin* includes some reflections on what and how such places mean, particularly in the chapter called "The Sacred Combe"—Fowles's label for a magical landscape, a sacred

Goat Island, in the Undercliff. Viewed from the coastal path, this face is the one that remains most visible of the large chunk of landscape that separated from the Bindon Cliffs during a dramatic landslip in 1839. Goat Island has since become surrounded by vegetation that masks its islandlike features. Photograph by James Aubrey, 1996.

Hampstead Heath, London. a relatively wild, urban oasis, this environment is the setting for a crucial scene in "The Enigma" when a female character in a natural landscape uses her imagination to solve a case of mysterious disappearance that has been baffling her more rationalistic friend, a male detective (*The Ebony Tower*, Little, Brown, 1973). Photograph by James Aubrey, 1993.

place, or a *locus amoenus*. A "combe" (pronounced to rhyme with *room*) is West Country dialect for a dell, or small valley, and Fowles illustrates his concept of "sacred combe"with reference to the French autobiography *Monsieur Nicolas*, by Restif de la Bretonne, who uses the local expression *bonne vaux* to describe a valley that is "miraculously lush, green, secret, and full of birds and animals."[34] Such a place, remarks Dan, is "outside the normal world, intensely private and enclosed, intensely green and fertile, numinous, haunted and haunting, dominated by a sense of magic that is also a sense of a mysterious yet profound parity in all existence." Examples in literature, Dan further points out, include the Garden of Eden, the Forest of Arden, and Shangri-La. Such isolated, magical places are, like islands, distinctly marked out from their surroundings, and they provide the settings for crucial, narrative developments in works by Fowles.

Perhaps because Fowles thinks of people as islandlike in their individuality, Fowles finds himself fascinated by both eccentric people and geographical sites that, like islands, stand out from their surround-

Exmoor, Devon. Naming this wild, "desert place" helps Fowles to constitute the imagined landscape of *A Maggot*, whose characters have a mysterious experience at a cave near here, "some ten miles from Barnstaple" (Little, Brown, 1985, pages 55, 212). Photograph by James Aubrey, 1988.

ings. The most important such place, for Fowles, is a twenty-foot high, vertical limestone formation in the Undercliff called Whitechapel Rock, which he has described as a "white tooth projecting from the cliff."[35] It marks a once-literally sacred site where religious dissenters held secret meetings in the seventeenth century, and Fowles seems to admire this place as a distinctive site, a metaphorical island of independent thinking in a sea of religious conformity. Evidently in part because dissent is associated with the idea of emancipation—a key word in the epigraph to *The French Lieutenant's Woman*—Fowles has said that he could not imagine some of the conversations between Sarah and Charles in that novel to have taken place anywhere else.[36] Fowles may likewise have imagined a crucial scene in *Daniel Martin* to have occurred at this place. Dornafield Farm (near Ipplepen, in Devon), Fowles's acknowledged model for Nancy's home, "Thorncombe," is more than thirty miles from the Undercliff. However, Dan and Nancy seem suddenly to be at a place very much like the Undercliff and very different from the farm country between their houses, after they leave the road and enter "a common, dense with brambles and bracken," where Dan leads her "through the trees to where the rocks

INTRODUCTION   31

Stonehenge, Wiltshire. This prehistoric, inland "island" of stones on Salisbury Plain provides a setting in *A Maggot*, whose female protagonist lies on the altar stone and sees either Satan or a space ship, if one can believe either version of events. Another character describes Stonehenge as "a place said to have special powers," a view similar to that of Fowles in *The Enigma of Stonehenge* (Summit Books, 1980) about the hold this place has exerted over others as well as himself (*A Maggot*, pages 245–47, 320–23). Photograph by James Aubrey, 1993.

rose vertically for twenty feet from the earth" (354–55). Fowles appears imaginatively to have blended two separate geographical locations in his novel so that the characters' sexual initiation could take place at a site that resembles Whitechapel Rock, with its remarkable features and associations with personal emancipation. Fowles may have worked in a similar, creative fashion in *A Maggot*, whose seemingly supernatural mysteries take place in a cave at the foot of "a scarp of stone, as high as a house;" this stone is perhaps another representation of White Chapel Rock, this time imaginatively transferred to Exmoor, where it helps to constitute a remarkable, imaginary space in the otherwise traceable landscape west of Taunton (218). Fowles seems to find it energizing as he writes to imagine crucial scenes at this real location that he considers sacred, and he helps to create in the reader a similar sense of being in a special landscape by

Wistman's Wood, Dartmoor, Devon. The copse of dwarf oak trees in the center is described in *The Tree* as an "infinitely rare fragment of primeval forest," isolated like a dark green island of foliage on the "dour wasteland" (Ecco Press, pages 80, 83). Fowles concludes the book with a narrated walk to Wistman's Wood. Photograph by James Aubrey, 1996.

marking out the location from its surrounding physical environment with an upright feature—also the essential form that an island takes as it rises out of the water.[37]

When Fowles narrates his visit to Wistman's Wood at the end of *The Tree*, he reminds readers of "the inalienable otherness of each, human and non-human" (91). Estranged I-lands that we are, this separateness from everything else provokes a desire in us to discover through literature some tenuous, verbal connection—readers like spiders casting out filaments, wishing to connect with what is not ourselves. Fowles appears to be acknowledging a need like this when he says, "I came to writing through nature, or exile from it, far more than by innate gift" (89). When he writes about natural landscapes and sacred places, he is partially recovering that "nature," a world that seems at once familiar, hence timeless, but never fully accessible. Nature may be more nearly accessible to Fowles when he walks in the woods than when he writes, so being in nature may serve to remind him that, ultimately, he cannot find language that will ade-

Aerial View of Scilly Isles, **Cornwall. This perspective emphasizes the isolation of the Scillies and serves as the first illustration of the book *Islands*, by John Fowles and Fay Godwin (Little, Brown, 1978). Photograph courtesy of Collections / Fay Godwin.**

quately represent the world outside himself. His need to engage that world and to keep trying to represent it, is surely the core "relationship with nature" that Fowles describes as the key to his fiction.

✳ ✳ ✳

Each of the fourteen essays in this volume is a new contribution to Fowles studies, and each offers a perspective on how natural landscape is represented in the writing of John Fowles. The essays originated in a call for proposals for the John Fowles Symposium on "Love, Loss, Landscape," which took place in Lyme Regis July 10–12, 1996. The fact that most of the contributions I received were

Belmont House and garden, Lyme Regis. In this view from the Cobb, John Fowles's wild garden occupies the hillside between the golf course at the bottom and his house at the top, partly visible above the trees. Photograph by James Aubrey, 1993.

Kenwood House, London. This museum and its grounds constitute figures of order on the wilder Hampstead Heath. The dining room inside contains a self-portrait by Rembrandt and provides the setting for important scenes in two Fowles novels, the character test by G. P. in *The Collector* (163–64) and Dan's meditations at the end of *Daniel Martin* (628–29). Photograph by James Aubrey, 1993.

Dornafield Farm, Two Mile Oak, Newton Abbot, Devon. This idyllic place near the village of Ipplepen, where the Fowles family lived during the war, was the model for Thorncombe in *Daniel Martin*, the "secret farm" which Fowles has remarked "was meant to be symbolic of certain landscapes of adolescence to which you're eternally attached" (James R. Baker, "An Interview with John Fowles," *Michigan Quarterly Review*, 25 [1986], page 681). Photograph by James Aubrey, 1988.

Tsankawi, Bandelier National Monument, New Mexico. Besides its physical distinctiveness, the narrator of *Daniel Martin* observes, "In some way the mesa transcended all place and frontier; it had the haunting and mysterious personal familiarity . . . but a simpler human familiarity as well, belonging not just to some obscure and forgotten Indian tribe, but to all similar moments of supreme harmony in human culture; to certain buildings, paintings, musics, passages of great poetry. . . . Tsankawi defeated time, all deaths. Its deserted silence was like a sustained high note, unconquerable" (page 325). Photograph by James Aubrey, 1987.

about landscape alerted me to the possibility that a shift might be underway in how Fowles is being read. The essays collected here, I believe, together with illustrations that add a visual referent to many of the landscapes being discussed, mark a new phase in Fowles criticism. The critical frameworks being used relate to the emerging field of ecocriticism, if one label should be applied to all, but the insights are locally informed by various critical approaches. Diverse as they are, these essays cohere thematically and provide insightful perspectives on John Fowles and nature.

Several essays draw on Fowles's fascination with islands in order to arrive at fresh insights into his writing. Katherine Tarbox explores how, for Fowles, islands metaphorically represent a valued kind of mental activity that takes place somehow apart from the narrative plot, which serves as a metaphorical mainland. Tarbox shows the

Kitchener's Island, Aswan, Egypt. In *Daniel Martin*, Dan hires a felucca to take him to this island in the Nile River, where he discovers that although "some attempt had been made to maintain the island as the great botanical garden Kitchener had initiated . . . the place had a charmingly haphazard and unkempt quality. . . . It was an Alhambra composed of vegetation, water, shadow; and perhaps nicest of all, it remained almost exactly as Dan had remembered it—one of the loveliest and most civilized few acres in his knowledge of this world, a tropical *bonne vaux*," (pages 535–36). Photograph courtesy of AA Publishing / Rick Strange.

central importance of the nonfiction book *Islands* for readers of Fowles's fiction. More than a meditation on landscape, she argues, *Islands* is also a demonstration of how to read like an islander and an invitation to become that kind of reader—Fowles's ideal reader, who can feel magic in the island space outside the mainland narrative. Clark Closser uses a related analogy between landscape and consciousness to help generate a new interpretation of events in "The Cloud," the final story in *The Ebony Tower*, which has often left readers in perplexity or disagreement. His suggestion that chunks of narration from various points of views are like metaphorical islands in a sea of narrative can be applied to much of Fowles's other fiction, as can his suggestion that, for Fowles, birds are often narrator-like, a kind of natural chorus. Based on such considerations, Closser offers a plausible way to understand Catherine's enigmatic behavior—and disappearance—at the end of the story. Lynne Vieth explores relationships between

Whitechapel Rock, the Undercliff, Devon. The toothlike outcropping in the center marks a densely foliated dell that was a gathering place for religious dissenters in the seventeenth century. Its history, the extremity of its isolation, and its rich wildness all seem to have made this a supremely important place for Fowles, who says in *The Tree* that he could not have imagined the crucial encounters between Charles and Sarah in *The French Lieutenant's Woman* to have taken place anywhere else (page 75). In the 1981 screen adaptation Charles is shown at the base of Whitechapel Rock when he first observes Sarah walking in the Undercliff. In this photograph, to the left, Undercliff warden Norman Barns is lopping some branches. Photograph by James Aubrey, 1991.

image and text in several Fowles books that have included photography or woodcuts by other artists. Vieth sees a development in Fowles's work of increasing value placed on the written over the spoken word, and a shift away from valuing the painterly arts over the graphic arts. With particular attention paid to Fowles's collaborative work with landscape photographer Fay Godwin and to variations among illustrated editions of *The Tree*, Vieth employs some of Walter Benjamin's ideas about art to explain the evolution of Fowles's attitudes in both verbal and visual domains.

Several other essays work with psychological theory. Carol Barnum uses Jungian thought to establish the nature of Fowles's relationship with nature and its profound effect on his writing process. Barnum shows that archetypal analysis can help to account for images of nature in Fowles's fiction and traces the evolution of Fowles's novel-writing as a personal quest for individuation. Barry Olshen examines a particular archetype, the Green Man, both as a symbol of the boundary between inner, psychological nature and outer, wild nature and as an image with a history, particularly in England. Drawing on the psychological views of D. W. Winnicott, among others, Olshen shows that the image of the Green Man serves Fowles as an important, personal symbol of the private, wild aspect of the self. Eileen Warburton sees psychological significance in the way the image of a dead woman in a natural landscape recurs in various writings by John Fowles. Paying particular attention to *Daniel Martin* and drawing on unpublished correspondence between Fowles and a psychoanalyst, Warburton links this pattern of reviving a fictional dead woman with insights that include the author's wish to restore the lost, paradisial landscape of early childhood.

Several other essays focus on the role of natural landscape in *The French Lieutenant's Woman*. Although the novel itself provides vivid descriptions of the Undercliff, readers will better appreciate this landscape when they also have read "The Undercliff of John Fowles's *The French Lieutenant's Woman*: A Note on Geology and Geography," an introduction to the features of this unique locale written by three experts: Liz-Anne Bawden, Kevin Padian, and Hugh Torrens. Although their historical information ranges from tens to millions of years ago, their perspective reveals yet another dimension of that complex character Sarah Woodruff. In the essay "Deep Time, Evolutionary Legacy, and the Darwinian Landscape in John Fowles's *The French Lieutenant's Woman*," Kevin Padian explores what kind of nature the name Darwin represents, both in the popular mind and in the mind of Fowles who, like Thomas Hardy, has a deep understanding of Darwinian thought. In "The Undercliff as Inverted Pastoral: The Fowlesian *Felix Culpa* in *The French Lieutenant's Woman*," Patricia Beatty contrasts the Undercliff with conventional, pastoral landscapes in order to show the richer mental life that results from a less convention-bound view of nature. Seen as a stage in Jung's process of individuation, the expulsion of Charles and Sarah from their paradise in the Undercliff is, Beatty points out, a fortunate fall. For Suzanne Ross, likewise, the Undercliff is a place where personal liberation is represented as a primal event. Ross cautions, however, against reading the characters of Sarah and Charles with the traditional view linking nature with the female and culture with the male, but instead urges the more ecological perspective on the Undercliff as a place where both males and females may be comprehended and transformed. In "Landscape This Side of Landscape: Transcendence and Immanence in the Fiction of John Fowles," H. W. Fawkner uses phenomenology to examine representations of landscape in *The French Lieutenant's Woman* and *The Magus*. Fawkner's discussion extends the meaning of *landscape* to include one's orientation to the world, and he concludes that the pre-Modernist outlook that occasionally emerges in the novels is not valued deeply enough by Fowles, or widely enough by his readers.

The essays by Lisa Colletta and Kirke Kefalea emphasize the importance of landscapes elsewhere, that is, away from England. In "The Geography of Ruins: John Fowles's *Daniel Martin* and the Travel Narratives of D. H. Lawrence," Colletta discusses a similarity in ways that Lawrence and Fowles both regard traveling as instrumental in the discovery of who one is. Lawrence is a felt presence in *Daniel Martin*, particularly, where travel by Dan to various historical sites in Italy, Egypt, New Mexico, and Syria—as well as to a site rich with personal history in the West Country of England—engages him with his past and enables him to understand his present. Kirke Kefalea discusses Fowles's use of the literary past and the geographical present to construct an engaging, personal mythology from a feminized Greek landscape.

In the last critical essay, focused on Fowles's poetry, Dianne Vipond extends the discussion of Greece as an important theme, along with several others, in "The Landscape of Loss in the (Love) Poems of John Fowles." Like some other contributors, Vipond uses the word *landscape* to refer to mental representations as well as to external places. Poetry has long been a form of writing Fowles values highly, even if it is not the form for which he has become so well known, and Vipond helps to establish why his poems, both collected and uncollected, deserve critical attention.

In an afterword composed for this collection, John Fowles reflects on the symposium that led to the writing of these essays. In addition to some personal reminiscences, Fowles writes about his hopes for gynecocracy and expresses concern that his life has become too fragmented.

When Fowles wants solace from such doubts, he probably goes for a walk in his garden. His relationship with nature has long been one involving personal need and deep respect, as he himself pointed out in 1971: "However strange the land or the city or the personal situation, some tree, some bird, some flower will still knit us into this universe all we brief-lived things co-habit; will mesh us into the great machine. That is why I love nature: because it reconciles me with the imperfections of my own condition, of our whole human condition, of the all that is."[38] Fowles's attitude has not changed in essentials since he wrote this passage, but he has intensified his attention to the problem of humans in their environment. Although he continues to work on fiction projects, he has published only nonfiction, mostly about nature, since 1985. This shift from fiction writing to nature writing is not so dramatic a shift as it might seem, however, for as the contributors to this volume collectively establish, John Fowles has for most of his career been an important nature writer as well as an important novelist.

James R. Aubrey

Notes

1. John Gardner, "In Defense of the Real," review of *Daniel Martin*, in *Saturday Review*, 1 October 1977, page 22.
2. Cheryll Glotfelty and Harold Fromm, *The Ecocriticism Reader: Landmarks in Literary Ecology* (Athens: University of Georgia Press, 1996), pages xxii–xxiv.
3. Robert Huffaker, *John Fowles*, Twayne English Authors Series 292 (Boston: G.K. Hall, 1980), page 15.
4. John Fowles, "The Chesil Bank," in *Britain: A World by Itself: Reflections on the Landscape by Eminent British Writers: With Commentaries by Dr. Franklyn Perring* (Boston: Little, Brown, 1984), page 26.
5. Interview with James R. Aubrey, 8 July 1993.
6. Huffaker, page 17.
7. John Fowles, *The Tree* (New York: Ecco Press, 1983), page 31.
8. The biographical sketch is condensed from James R. Aubrey, "Life of John Fowles," in *John Fowles: A Reference Companion* (Westport, Conn.: Greenwood Press, 1991), pages 4–13.
9. John Fowles, "Swan Song of the European Wild," *Venture: The Traveler's World*, October 1965, pages 136, 141. The "victims" are trees devastated by caterpillars, but the analogy with logging, later, is evident. The "Norwegian Thoreau" is probably a source for the episode in *The Magus* at Seidevarre, where Henrik Nygaard also lives alone by a lake, not blind but similarly bitter (2d ed., Boston: Little, Brown, 1977).
10. John Fowles, "Weeds, Bugs, Americans," *Sports Illustrated*, 21 December 1970, page 88.
11. John Fowles, "The Blinded Eye," *Animals* 13, no. 9 (January 1971), page 89.
12. John Fowles, "Voices of the Deep," *New Statesman*, 15 June 1973, pages 892–93, and "All too Human," *New Statesman*, 20 July 1973, pages 90–91. Fowles contributed twenty reviews to this publication, from March 1973 to February 1977.
13. Fowles, *The Tree*. This book has been reprinted in various forms since it originally appeared in 1979, with color photographs by Frank Horvat, without pagination, from Aurum Press in London and Little, Brown in Boston. Ecco Press in New York published an unillustrated but paginated version in 1983, the one generally cited in this volume. The Sumach Press in London published a paperback edition in 1992. The Nature Company in Seattle published an abridged version with photographs by William Neill in 1994. The Yolla Bolly Press in Covelo, California, published a limited edition with woodcuts by Aaron Johnson as *"The Tree" and "The Nature of Nature"* in 1995. Excerpts from the middle of *The Tree* are included in *Second Nature*, ed. Daniel Halperin (New York: Antaeus, 1986), pages 244–51; in *The Norton Book of Nature Writing*, ed. Robert Finch and John Elder (New York: Norton,

1990), pages 657–70; in *The Oxford Book of Nature Writing*, edited by Richard Mabey (New York: Oxford University Press, 1995), pages 232–34; and in *The Nature Reader*, eds. Daniel Halperin and Dan Frank (Hopewell, N.J.: Ecco Press, 1996), pages 132–34.

14. Fowles, "The Chesil Bank," page 27.

15. John Fowles, "South Cornwall, Devon and Dorset," in *Coastline: Britain's Threatened Heritage* (London: Kingfisher Books, 1987), page 153.

16. Review of *Collecting*, by Werner Muensterberger, *Sunday Times*, 6 February 1994, pages 6.1–2; review of *The Oxford Book of Nature Writing*, by Richard Mabey, *Sunday Times*, 5 March 1995, pages 7.8–9; review of *The Song of the Dodo*, by David Quammen, *Sunday Times*, 18 August 1996, page 7.5; review of *Flora Britannica*, by Richard Mabey, *Sunday Times*, 20 October 1996, pages 7.8–9; review of *The Killing of the Countryside*, by Graham Harvey, *Sunday Times*, 2 March 1997, pages 8.6–7. The reply was from A. Krouwel, *Sunday Times*, 16 March 1997, page 8.2.

17. John Fowles, *"The Tree" and "The Nature of Nature"* (Covelo, Calif.: Yolla Bolly Press, 1995), pages 84, 96.

18. John Fowles, *The French Lieutenant's Woman* (Boston: Little, Brown, 1969), page 67. Most works by Fowles have been published in both the United Kingdom and the United States, in hard- and soft-cover. In general, citations in this book are to the American hardcover editions.

19. In 1996 Fowles expressed an interest in seeing his house and garden preserved as a retreat for "'young people inquisitive about nature and art'" in remarks to the *Sunday Times*, 15 September 1996, page 7.8.

20. Fowles, *The Tree*, page 22.

21. Rodney Legg has speculated that acquisition of Steep Holm for a nature reserve would not have occurred without the support of John Fowles, in various ways (interview with James R. Aubrey, 23 August 1994). A history of the island, including this development, has been written by Stan and Joan Rendell, *Steep Holm: The Story of a Small Island* (Dover, N.H.: Allan Sutton, 1993). John Fowles has edited and contributed to *Steep Holm: A Case History in the Study of Evolution* (Sherborne, United Kingdom: Kenneth Allsop Memorial Trust).

22. James R. Baker, "The Art of Fiction 109: John Fowles," *Paris Review* 111 (1989), page 48.

23. John Fowles, *Behind "The Magus"* (London: Colophon Press, 1994), pages 15, 22.

24. John Fowles, *The Collector* (Boston: Little, Brown, 1963); *The Ebony Tower* (Boston: Little, Brown, 1974); *Daniel Martin* (Boston: Little, Brown, 1977); *A Maggot* (Boston: Little, Brown, 1985).

25. John Fowles discusses his fascination with the site in *The Enigma of Stonehenge*, co-authored with photographer Barry Brukoff (New York: Summit Books, 1980), page 5.

26. John Fowles, introduction to *Round About a Great Estate*, by Richard Jefferies (1887; reprint, Bradford on Avon, United Kingdom: Ex Libris Press, 1987), pages 9–10.

27. John Fowles, afterword to *The Lost Domain (Le Grand Meaulnes)*, by Alain-Fournier, trans. Frank Davison (New York: Oxford University Press, 1986), page 285.

28. Stephen Kaplan, "Perception of an Uncertain Environment," in *Humanscape: Environments for People*, eds. Stephen Kaplan and Rachel Kaplan (Ann Arbor, Mich.: Ulrich's Books, 1982), pages 30–35. This topic is also discussed in Scott Slovic, *Seeking Awareness in American Nature Writing: Henry Thoreau, Annie Dillard, Ed-*

ward Abbey, Wendell Berry, Barry Lopez* (Salt Lake City: University of Utah Press, 1992), pages 7–8.

29. See, for example, L. H. Snyder, et al., "Coding of Intention in the Posterior Parietal Cortex," *Nature,* 13 March 1997, pages 167–69.

30. Eileeen Warburton, "Fowles Takes a Risk for 'Minor' Work," *Los Angeles Times,* 29 September 1982, page 5.19. In this interview Fowles points out that his novel *Mantissa* (Boston: Little, Brown, 1982) is different from his other novels in that it has "'no spirit of place really.'" The name of his protagonist, Miles Green, suggests that the novel does have an interior landscape, for "miles of green" describes a forest, and *Mantissa* is an exploration of the metaphorical woods of a creative mind.

31. The analogy between writing and walking in woods is developed explicitly (and more elegantly) in *The Tree,* pages 53–54. Fowles often uses the word *fork* to describe diverging paths or roads that can represent the choices to be made as one writes, for example, in his interview with Robert Foulke, *Salmagundi* 68–69 (1985–86), page 374. In *The French Lieutenant's Woman,* there may be metafictional weight in the moment when, just before Charles discovers Sarah sleeping in the Undercliff, he determines his own future as a character by choosing the lower path when his route forward, "in the unkind manner of paths—forked without indication" (69).

32. In *Islands* (Boston: Little, Brown, 1978), page 12, Fowles writes, "In terms of consciousness, and self-consciousness, every individual human *is* an island, in spite of Donne's famous preaching to the contrary." He puts the reversal more boldly, quoted here, in "Such Darling Dodos," *Sunday Times,* 18 August 1996, page 7.5.

33. John Fowles, introduction, *The Book of Ebenezer Le Page,* by G. B. Edwards (New York: Moyer Bell, 1981), pages vii–xiv.

34. *Daniel Martin,* page 272; a longer excerpt from *Monsieur Nicolas* is quoted in Fowles's introduction to *Land,* by Fay Godwin (Boston: Little, Brown, 1985), page x. Restif explains the phrase *bonne vaux* parenthetically as an *"expression du pays, qui signifie un endroit abondant en quelque chose que ce soit"* (1793–97; reprint Paris: Jonquière, 1924), volume 1, page 57.

35. Letter to James R. Aubrey, 30 December 1996.

36. *The Tree,* page 75. In the 1981 screen adaptation of *The French Lieutenant's Woman,* Charles is shown hammering flints at the base of Whitechapel Rock when he first observes Sarah walking in the Undercliff, twenty minutes into the film.

37. In *The Magus,* likewise, a crucial episode takes place at Seidevarre, whose name we are told is Lapp for "'hill of the holy stone,' the dolmen" (300) but which in the novel is "not a true dolmen but simply a tall boulder that wind and frost had weathered into a picturesque shape" (304) on a spit of land jutting—almost an island—into the Pasvik River; however, Fowles may have written this description before he developed his particular attachment to Whitechapel Rock.

38. John Fowles, "The Blinded Eye," *Animals* 13.9 (January 1971): 392. An earlier version of this essay concludes with almost the same passage, less only the phrase "or the personal situation," in "'Your Blinded Eyes, Worst Foes to You,'" *The Traveler's World,* June/July 1966, page 84.

John Fowles's *Islands*: Landscape and Narrative's Negative Space

KATHERINE TARBOX

> Every text situates itself at the junction of several texts of which it is at once the rereading, the accentuation, the condensation, the displacement, and the inwardness.
> —Philippe Sollers

> It is important to consider not only what a narrative is, but what it is for, and what its stakes are: why it is told, what aims it may manifest and conceal, what it seeks not only to say but to do.
> —Peter Brooks

SEVERAL YEARS AGO I WENT OUT TO MONHEGAN, A WILD ISLAND TWENTY miles off the Maine coast, to interview the few year-round inhabitants and write about the strange magic the island possesses. I brought John Fowles's book *Islands* with me, because in his introduction he announces that he too wants "to analyse this attraction to something rather more than just place."[1] But as I read into this strange book that is only ostensibly about the Scilly Isles, I got farther and farther away from anything that might be called analysis or explanation. It moves wantonly, without regard for recognizable coherence relations, from vortices of etymology to literary criticism to fragments of arcane histories. In the space of just a few pages the text moves from a commentary on *The Tempest*, to the fortification problems of the Scillies in the seventeenth century, to a pebble maze on the Baltic island of Gotland, to a third millennium B.C. pot Fowles owns, to an etymology of the root *labrys*, to Odysseus, and on to a comment on an illustration in Quarles's *Emblems* of 1635. All through the book I kept wondering: How did I get here? Where am I now? What does this have to do with anything? Confused and failing to extract from the book the golden nugget that would explain why we are mysteriously and gorgeously seduced by islands, I put it down unfinished.

This spring I brought John Fowles himself out to visit this magic island, and after he left I returned to his book and knew it for the first time. I saw that the reading habits I had previously brought to the

John Fowles on Monhegan Island, Maine. In his book *Islands*, Fowles remarks, "It is this aspect of islands that particularly interests me: how deeply they can haunt and form the personal as well as the public imagination. This power comes primarily, I believe, from a vague yet immediate sense of identity" (Little, Brown, 1978, page 12). Photograph by Jack Tarbox, 1996.

book were incommensurate with its peculiar logic. In the ten years between my first and second encounters with *Islands*, I had undertaken an odyssey of reading through a maze of seditious texts, most notably Fowles's own novels, which redefined my ideas about what reading *is*. In fact I came to the conclusion that *Islands* is *about* reading and is an enactment of Fowles's own subversive reading process. This book is about the odyssey that every reader must take to learn how to read, especially to learn to read what is not said, what can never be said. Philippe Sollers, who theorizes reading and writing at such limit situations, says that every trained reader must undergo deconstructive processes to "develop the capacity to read what is written," and what is written is the "attempt to discover what everyone knows and no one can say." He continues, "*We believe we know how to read and write.* . . . Are we so sure that we weren't taught to no longer know how to read and write from the day we were told we know how to read and write?"[2] This essay is my own labyrinthine meditation on how *Islands* relates the mystery of reading—and its hinged activity, writing—to the mystery of islands; on how the landscape of islands stands for, spatializes, and reifies the negative spaces in any narrative text.

Islands dramatizes a perceived mainland as a space defiled by the depredations of capitalist greed. It works on the "dominant syllogism" that "profit is life, tourists bring profit, therefore let us sacrifice everything to tourism" (1). Human beings are "mere smoke in the wage-labour wind" (19). Their desire, that unregulated flow of libidinal energy generated by the unconscious, is regulated, directed, and controlled by a capitalist signifying system that tells them "where to go, what to enjoy, how to enjoy, when to enjoy" (105); it makes "endless exhortation to pleasure, endless attempts to tell the individual in what his pleasure consists and to guide him through the labyrinth whose deepest values can only be self-discovered" (106). The text shows how easily the mainland absorbs true desire into the hyperreal, simulatory universe of fun.

Fowles calls mainland corruption a male story, and he reads Odysseus as the archetype of the imperialist who spreads its contagion. He is a compulsive liar, driven by "suspiciousness . . . infidelity . . . vindictive anger . . . greed . . . pointless aggression." His "quintessential maleness" is a product of "biological conditioning," and his tale is the tale of "male stupidity and arrogance" (54–58 passim). What he wanted was "*Lebensraum* . . . power of some kind. His voyage was done in what he already possessed . . . and towards what he wanted to possess in addition" (19, first ellipsis in original). Odysseus learns nothing from his ten-year quest, and, in the end, dragged on by his unreflecting linearity, he reveals only "his incapacity to do anything but undergo the experience" (73).

Throughout the mazy course of *Islands,* Fowles reads many other histories as recurring versions of the *Odyssey* paradigm. The Norman Conquest, the attack on the English coast by privateers, the assaults from the Spanish fleet, the Nazi atrocities, the English colonization of America—all stories of "brute male greed for prestige and property" (56)—become the same story that re-volutes through several millennia of Western history and that appears today as the profit motive, where human desire and spirit seem to be the victims of the quest. It is a well-defined narrative that repeats, and changes, in Theodor Adorno's words, only in its refinement of the techniques of domination as we progress "from the slingshot to the megaton bomb."[3]

According to this text, narrative consciousness itself accounts for why this quest plot becomes so profoundly deterministic, for why it spawns these clone-plots. The work of contemporary cognitive psychology, and its newest branch, narrative psychology, can help to explain the phenomenon the text dramatizes. James Mancuso, for example, says that we can only process incoming experience if it can be assimilated to "an acquired, internal representation of narrative grammar structure," the structure of the Western quest plot.[4] The "basic motivation of all psychological functioning" (101) is the drive to make input congruent with "semantic material representing all the properly sequenced story grammar parts of a text" (95). In turn, we emplot our lives (and our identities) according to narrative logic, with its clockwork, its protocols, and its trajectories. Thus, narrative does not mimic life, but life mimics narrative. Narrative imposes "an inexorable form upon events."[5] Psycholinguists tell us that the written transmission of narrative has *created* modern, rational consciousness and driven a wedge between us and a universe of different mental operations and dispositions.[6]

Narrative consciousness gives rise to the storytelling practices such as history and science, which create the collective memory and being out of which a sense of society emerges. But what promotes cohesion can also give rise to cultural pathologies. As Jane Flax says, our "capacity to observe and interpret present events is damaged, for they are unconsciously viewed through a prism of the past; the new is transformed into a mere replication of the old."[7] Or, as Stewart Clegg says, we need to be suspicious of the way narrative serves "to secure and stabilize circuits of power."[8] Narrative can set forth powerful and persuasive truth claims—claims about appropriate behavior and values—that are shielded from testing and debate."[9] In this light, *The Odyssey*, which Fowles calls the sine qua non of stories, appears to be the archetypal Western narrative, in both form and content. In Fredric Jameson's terms, it is the ongoing, repetitive drama of the political unconscious, the dynamic struggle between the dominant Necessity—duty, order, obedience, narrative—and Desire, those extra-narrative realities. Fowles realizes the limitations that narrative consciousness imposes on us: in "The Nature of Nature" he says, "I am distorted by science, unable to think or write outside its bias."[10]

Text we read is a kind of input that we process against the hardwired grid of narrative consciousness. Even the pleasures and satisfactions we feel are responses generated and determined by narrative shapes. In *Islands,* Fowles acknowledges that much of his personal and our collective understanding of Nature stems from the paradigm the Romantics created in their writing. He says, "the Romantics discovered nature"(19). In truth, the Romantics, through the powerful and satisfying explanatory procedures of their texts, coupled with a cathecting aestheticism, created a Nature that is less essential than culturally and historically contingent, the polar response to growing technology and urbanization.

Fowles goes on to gently implicate Jane Austen in this ongoing drama of cultural formation through writing and reading, for her role in constructing the seaside idyll. He says (and note that he suggests that her perceptions, too, have been formed by the Romantic Nature narrative): "She grows positively Wordsworthian—if not downright brochuristical—when it comes to the setting. The lift, the allegro that takes place in *Persuasion* when the action moves to Lyme is completely typical of its time. *They had discovered what we are now taught to covet and love from infancy*" (25, my emphasis). Her narrative, itself become a paradigm, dovetails quickly with William Wordsworth's and later joins with other developing cultural myths: the Victorian "holiday" and the medical discoveries about the benefits of sea bathing. In this manner the unnamed world becomes covered with stories that satisfy our need for intelligibility.

Throughout *Islands,* Fowles reads a great many narratives that have contained and stabilized unruly experience, crystallized them into consensual reality. He reproduces a long passage from the 1870s journal of one Francis Kilvert, of which the following is one sentence that describes a young naked girl on the beach: "There was the supple, slender waist, the gentle dawn and tender swell of the bosom and budding breasts, the graceful rounding of the delicately beautiful limbs and above all the soft and exquisite curves of the rosy dimpled bottom and broad white thigh" (26). Fowles notes that because we are late twentieth-century readers, the *Lolita* narrative we've collectively and individually internalized mediates our responses to this passage, determines our valuations, quite probably grids Kilvert against the Humbert archetype. Fowles goes on to wonder, sadly, what is lost, in terms of "erotic honesty" (26) because we necessarily process information in this way.

He goes on to cite an 1889 issue of *Modern Etiquette* magazine for the power it had in warning against the cosmetic consequences of tanning (26); a series of *Punch* magazine illustrations that constructed the Belle Epoque beauty (28); *Armorel of Lyonesse* by Walter Besant and Sabine Baring-Gould's *Mehalah* for their creation of the brave "new young woman" that was the prototype for Sarah Woodruff (30–31). He considers the extraordinary influence William Golding's *Lord of the Flies* has had in supporting conservative programs to make us distrust our depths and desires. This novel is taught to nearly every high school student in the United States, and my own students invariably cite it as a cautionary tale when they begin to read Friedrich Nietzsche, Gilles Deleuze, or Félix Guattari. As James Mancuso says, input "has no meaning outside of its contact with a person's existing knowledge system," which is composed of "epigenetically acquired" narratives (99). Narrative can always and only create virtual worlds, and these virtual worlds engender life-world attitudes and praxes through exchanges of literacy. The reader enters the powerful force field of the narrative space and, as Jameson says, is taught from an early age to be managed by narrative texts that say, you are this, life is this, this is what you desire. Cultural texts "connect you to spurious objects"—that is, to "the rewards and incentives for adherence to cultural ideology" (287).

Fowles acknowledges that we have no choice but to participate in these narrative transactions, because, deprived of narrative, we become "unscripted, anxious stutterers in actions as in words."[11] Yet in this book, as in all his novels, he seeks a way to access the real, unnamed, unscripted world that is eclipsed by the obfuscating presence of narrative. To attempt to disentangle himself from the system, he has to become an undirected reader, to become someone other than one who is invited to a coded practice, a game whose rules stem from narrative mentality itself; to become, in effect, like Sollers' ideal reader, to uncover aspects of writing that are obscured by narrative habits of reading, conventions that ritualize both the writer's and the reader's engagement with the text. The reader enters the game looking for satisfactions the text is required to produce. As Walter Ong points out, university courses teach us to fictionalize ourselves to be the kinds of readers allegedly demanded by certain kinds of writers (103). In his reading of *The Tempest,* Fowles laments the degree to which William Shakespeare has been overmediated by "orthodox scholarly" treatment. In his words Shakespeare has been reduced to "merely the world's greatest dramatist" (106), and we have been taught how to read him and how to recognize the pleasures he holds. Consigned to the category called Literature, Shakespeare is "safethroned on the peak of Parnassus, at a very great and alienating distance from you, me" (106).

Fowles weaves into his reading of Shakespeare the following shard: "Every child who visits St. Agnes [island] has a hop round the Troytown maze; and I hope will long continue to do so, for I should hate to see it fenced in and museumized like Stonehenge" (105). Both Stonehenge and Shakespeare have been bracketed, explained by maps, explanations, guided tours, these bookish voice-overs silencing the texts' other language. In "The Nature of Nature," he says, "Alas, the world seems determined to abolish and destroy living feeling by stifling its existence with dead knowledge" (95). "Island" is the landscape metaphor he uses to contain what he means by "living feeling."

"Island" is the metaphor for what exists in the negative space carved by narrative, "where magic takes place" (30), home of all

Troy Town Maze, St. Agnes Island, Cornwall, by Fay Godwin. This photograph from *Islands* accompanies discussion by Fowles of mazes as symbols: "The truth is that the person who always benefits and learns most from the maze, the voyage, the mysterious island, is the inventor, the traveller, the visitor . . . that is, the artist-artificer himself" (page 98, ellipsis in original). Photograph courtesy of Collections / Fay Godwin.

Stonehenge, Wiltshire. Visitors may no longer wander among the stones, but must circumambulate. The round spot on the path is one of the holes discovered in the seventeenth century by John Aubrey, whose *Monumenta Britannica* was first edited for publication by John Fowles (Little, Brown and Dorset Publishing Company, 1980–82). Photograph by James Aubrey, 1985.

subjugated knowledges and silent languages, the domain of what he calls the "pagan mind." Island signifies "what cannot be controlled by wisdom and reason; the laboratory where the guinea-pig Odysseus must run through the mazes; where the great ally of reason, the conscious, gives way to the rule of the unconscious and the libido, the eternal and oceanic unsettler of domestic peace and established order" (59). Island is a "mysterious otherness, . . . a world where things happen in different ways from our human one."[12] The deep island mind carries out mental activities with which higher-level narrative thinking is not familiar, making communication between these two mental orders difficult, if not impossible.[13] Early in *Islands,* Fowles says that the book is "about the Scillies of a novelist's mind" (2). Thus, this book is about the cognitive adventures of the novelist as he labors in the narrative space, working on the curved surface between reading and writing, all the time trying to communicate with the mental islands that are "mute, enticing, forever just out of reach" (5). As Roland Barthes might say, the line of text Fowles lays down simultaneously opens the islands to view and covers them over.

Islands are "secret places, where the unconscious grows conscious, where possibilities mushroom, where imagination never rests" (28). The Scillies—literal, geographic islands in this book—speak for all that is ineffable about the metaphoric island. Like *la bonne vaux* in *Daniel Martin*, the islands are "sacred combes" that deconstruct the mainlander and "break down the multiple alienations of industrial and suburban man."[14] "Workaday identity can be lost" (28) as "islands strip and dissolve the crud of our pretensions and cultural accretions" (105).

In the book *Islands*, ships—those of Odysseus, the Armada, the pirates, the New World explorers—represent technology, the control of nature, the juggernauts of the mainland quest and power narrative. The Siren, island dweller that she is, represents the deconstructive dismantling of this arrogance. She is a familiar figure in contemporary literature, along with witches and enchantresses, hellcats, she cats, and conjurors: formerly vilified women who are now glorified; in the postmodern scheme of things they displace rational knowledge with alternate ontologies and epistemologies; they cause their victim to "break free from its socially articulated, disciplined, semiotized, and subjectified state . . . to become disarticulated, dismantled, and deterritorialized."[15] Fowles had this sort of experience on Spetsai: "I never knew who I really was, what I lacked, . . . until I had wandered in its solitudes and emptinesses" (11).

Fowles names island reality female—everything he feels he has lost, every irrecoverable knowledge and language—as he names mainland reality male. In "The Nature of Nature," he calls her "*la sauvage*, the wild. . . . She is that aspect of wild nature beyond all we normally attach to culture and civilization, the naked reality of the *rus*" (81). An apologist for male plots and "that dimwit Adam" (19), Fowles has a nostalgia for *la sauvage* that suggests a personal search for this unrecoverable femaleness that has been written over by cultural gender narratives. Fowles locates Odysseus's painful meeting with his dead mother as "the genesis of all art: the pursuit of the irrecoverable"; he quotes Odysseus: "'As my mother spoke, there came to me out of the confusion in my heart the one desire, to embrace her spirit, dead though she was. Thrice, like a shadow or a dream, she slipped through my arms and left me harrowed by an even sharper pain'" (59).

This kind of ontological clawing is an impulse toward the greater unity we enjoyed before the world was fractured by language and narrative, and a long series of losses and disappointments began. It is a love impulse, a desperation to deconstruct the extreme I-ness produced by narrative mentality, a desire to counteract the alienating effects of consciousness. Throughout this book Fowles associates island with love, passion, desire, and sexuality—those boundary-destroying life energies. The transferences that take place between the author and the reader are also movements toward love—though on a symbolic level, devoid of empirical or metaphysical presence. Literary exchange stands for the inherent *need* to love and be loved that every text testifies to. *Island* as text represents the gesture toward intersubjectivity and transpersonality, a means for both the reader and the writer to mutually exercise their capacity for love and connectedness to islands.

Fay Godwin's photographs deepen the sense of islandness that the words develop. They are not brochuristic, cast in travel industry clichés about what constitutes stunning landscape; they are disturbing and challenging. They show "the elemental compound of sky, sea, sand, rock, the forms and textures of simplest things, the cleansing, as the sea itself will cleanse, of over-artifice, over-knowledge and over-civilization" (106). When we open this book we see an erotic confluence of texts: his title *Islands*, in towering black print, undermined by her moody photo of a stone labyrinth. The title page announces the book's two powerful metaphors and its two different languages. The photos are black and white, stripped, elemental, full of stark shapes and contrasts: voluptuous clouds swirling around jagged rocks; odd, shapely stones arising out of a flat horizon. The photos suggest absences of all kinds—an empty, broken beach chair; shells; tombs; shards of unrecognizable human detritus. Like the text, the photos are as much about what is lost, missing, as what is present.

They are interspersed throughout the text, yet at many points several full pages of photos intervene upon the text; in one case six photos come in the middle of a hyphenated word in the middle of a Fowles sentence (32–39). During a flamboyant display of etymology we are hurled into unmediated visuals, as the photos have no captions. We see gulls soaring above crumbling ruins. But ruins of what? Who made this? What was it once? Questions abound, while the photos coolly deny access to narrative explanations. We see provocative stone formations that could be tomb markers, ancient walls, or cave entrances; we see an extreme close-up of a heavily lichened tree, a line of nameless sea wrack. The reader is thrown wordlessly from one strong, indeterminate, contextless image to the next. The photos create an unnamed, nonnarrative universe close to the one the text calls "island." They intermittently silence the text with their extra-semantic claims on our attention and disrupt even further the flow of logic the text is already struggling against.

One strategy of disorientation the text uses is to deploy a narrative logic that is fundamentally at odds with a universe beyond its ability to describe and account for teleologically. Especially mazy are his often tenuous, perhaps specious—"the purest speculation" (48)—forays into etymology, "the dark and backward abysm of linguistic time" (32). He draws us through what feels like a hypertext labyrinth as he connects island-ish words: isolation, insulation, *insula, in salo,* soul, sea, sail, salt, solan, Scilly, Siluran, insulam, Sylanacim, Sully, Sullya, Syllingar, Silimnum, school, siren, Sikelia, Sicania, seal, Scylla, gulp, gull, scull, Askalon, scallion, scald, scylfe. Each of these words in turn opens backward into a network of interconnected stories, histories, and myths, such as the story of the siren's origin in the seal. In these etymologies he takes us farther and farther back into the language of the long-dead, to the brink of the silence of the unnamed universe, to the phonemes—the sea-liquids s and *l* combined with the deathly, cutting k—he posits as a possible first utterance, arising from the time of silence when we understood experience differently. "We should not take universal onomatopoeias too lightly," he says (48), because they represent Nature's voice, vestiges of which barely make it through into our human speech. The referential, workspeech skins of words become, in this text, portals to fathomless vortices of time, space, multiple ontologies, undermining seemingly solid narrative surfaces.

If art is the attempt to recover what is lost, Fowles's art is the attempt to both read and write what "is closed out of the culturally structured conscious mind of the subject."[16] But, as Sollers wonders, can we ever learn to read in this way, or, because of our seemingly unalterable cognitive habits, are we doomed to read all input back into the orthodox narrative that is our intelligibility norm? In *Islands,* Fowles dramatizes by the way he reads, his attempt to "think the unthought," as Mumbry puts it (2).

Because this text is *made* of his alter-readings of both obscure and canonical works, it becomes heuristic for *Islands'* reader. Fowles begins his reading of *The Odyssey* with an insistence that Homer was a woman and ends with the conviction that *The Odyssey* is the template for all his own novels. This suggests that, by rewriting "her" text and revivifying her voice, he becomes transferentially allied to the wisdom of *la sauvage.* As a culturally engendered male, who identifies strongly with and is an apologist for the bumbling Odysseus, his repeated writings of the Homer-woman's text are a gesture toward a lost androgyny, an attempt to recover the faculties and sensibilities he names female.

As he works through his reading of *The Odyssey,* he performs no traditional critical operations on the text. He dispenses with those episodes that do not contain magic women on islands; the Laestrygonians, Cyclops, Aeolus, Lotus-Eaters are grouped and treated dismissively in two paragraphs, as all too familiar tales of "male greed" (62). With Circe, however, he sprawls and lingers and attempts to read the episode radically, searching the text for its other language: not its "message, its ostensible affirmations," as Peter Brooks might say, but "much more its interstices," the places where "one begins to hear other voices."[17]

He looks *not* head-on at the totalized narrative edifice of the Circe episode, but he selects odd details and stirs them into a cyclonic swirl of associations. He dwells on the moly flower that Hermes gives Odysseus as a palliative against Circe's magic. From there he ponders Hermes' role as a phallic icon and his oblique relation to Hermaphroditus and Priapus, which in turn elicits a discussion of phallic garden statuary. He uses the sailors-turned-swine narrateme to make a serious inquiry into "why pigs?" during which we learn a great deal of folklore involving pigs. Next he lights on the name Circe, its possible etymology and history, a discussion that ends with a conjecture about why Shakespeare might have worn an earring. These aleatory flights suggest that, indeed, "it is in the interstices of the told that the tale unfolds its other story" (65). Because every sentence blunders over what it cannot say, Fowles reads by grasping not the thread that will lead him through the steady linear course of the narrative itself, but the Ariadne's thread that will lead him into the labyrinths of its interstices.

In his reading of the Calypso episode, "the most enigmatic . . . and most touching of [Odysseus's] adventures" (66), he alter-reads to discover his own latent desires and to journey into the mystery of his own unconscious. The story of all reading, he says, as well as of all writing, is "the voyage in the mind" (74). He notes that as a boy he felt a powerful libidinal connection to Calypso, as she seemed to represent all unsanctioned desire, at the same time as he felt drawn to Penelope, the legitimate wife. Against all logic and many centuries of scholarly opinion, he constructs Calypso as a heroine and rewrites the denouement of the episode, in which she is given a voice to defend herself. He reads *The Odyssey* not to find resolution of quandaries, not to help him find which choice to make, but to find the the aporia, the place where two contrary realities exist at the same time. He actively seeks and endorses the impasse that narrative, with its imperative to choose among forking paths, always repairs and smooths away.

Fowles says, "I know how much I owe as a writer of fiction, to the Calypso-Penelope dilemma" (72). The magic quality of his novels arises from their experiments with this illogic of oxymoron, his assault on cognitive boundaries. He says, "More and more we lose the ability to think as poets think, across frontiers and consecrated limits. More and more we think—or are brainwashed into thinking—in terms of verifiab[ility]. . . . One reason I love islands so much is that they question such lack of imagination" (105). One is reminded of Fowles's reminiscence in his commentary on D. H. Lawrence's *The Man Who Died* that the reason he became a writer was that he was "always stumbling, despite being a novelist, after the poem."[18]

Fowles seems to believe that, though much has been lost, and though ego and its cognitive habits are powerful determinants, we can achieve a more nearly whole sight by attempting to integrate narrative consciousness with an awareness of all that it occludes: what he calls in "The Nature of Nature" the "'feeling' part of our being, this other self, . . . the shadowed one . . . . We desperately need its counterweight to all the autocratic excesses, encroachments and ukases of knowing" (94). We are not to choose between equally valid but contrary realities, but to live in an evolved state of tenant truancy, in "awareness of the reality of *both* the Sideros and the Keraunos, necessity and chaos . . ." (98). "We need to institute an oscillation between the two sides like a heartbeat; not to understand just the nature of things, but the nature of understanding them . . . . The unnecessary border war [is] foolish and futile" (96). Toward the end of *Islands*, though, even though Fowles exults in the psychological, spiritual, and political benefits that might accrue to reading well, it concludes with his profound sense of failure. He fears that all of these benefits remain either purely hypothetical or temporary, lasting only during the space of the reading. Textual play and textual exchange, he fears, leave the destructive social system it critiques "unmarked, unfazed, unaltered" (Flax, 40). "Fine language," Fowles says in "The Nature of Nature," will "not save or re-orient us. . . . Unless some great change in mankind occurs (unblinds, converts, transmogrifies), our gross stupidity and apathy will one day doom the earth" (90). In *Islands*, Fowles expresses doubt that "language and literature will prompt such a change. Like Odysseus, who can only undergo the experience, the reader likewise returns fundamentally unmarked. In Fowles's view, while the text desires to incite praxis, it ends by replacing praxis. The reader has, at best, a temporary cognitive challenge, but "something in [the text's] external, objective, 'other' nature is always inherently alienating of action" (101).

Fowles reads *The Tempest* according to these same sad lights and finds corroboration from Shakespeare for his own frustration: "The play may outwardly demonstrate true culture, or moral nobility, triumphing over both false culture and culturelessness; but it throws strange doubts and shadows on its own message and on its very form. The conflict revealed is the oldest in all art, and takes place inside the artist: between the power to imagine and the use of imagining. *Cui bono*, to what purpose? What will it change?" (98). He believes that if anything were going to change, it would have changed after Shakespeare and all that catharsis; but the power narrative still self-replicates and proliferates.

Yet, when Fowles asks the question "*Cui bono?*" it seems that he himself has been caught up in the logic of political economics, which demands that everything have a use value. I end by offering a retort. Implicit in the "being" of *Islands* is a radical alternative to material measurement: the valuation of symbolic exchange—the exchange of libidinal energies and the transference of intellectual, psychic, and spiritual contents—as an alternative to capitalist logic. It will be difficult to legitimate such symbolic exchange as long as we continue to be dominated by modernist views of political agency.

Cognition studies can give us new insights into exactly what does happen inside readers. There may not be a one-to-one correspondence between the lessons of fiction and revised life-world praxes (Do we really want there to be?), but powerful things do happen to readers. A text like *Islands*, which disallows facile narrative processing, attests to the existence of island-reality and invites the willing reader to confront it. What happens? According to constructivists like Elizabeth Loftus, every time our orderly narrative files are disturbed, the whole grid is unsettled to such an uncomfortable degree that we must reconfigure the whole system to accommodate this input. If we read only orderly cultural narratives, our minds will be so constituted, and the island mind will atrophy. Island-text will seldom elicit lightning-bolt epiphanies, but it will slowly, over time, undermine the narrative processing procedures that keep the quest culture intact. Reading's greatest power might be in its ability to revise us—not materially but cognitively. Every text begins a flow of inputs into its reader, who tries to justify those inputs against existing files; but if, along with the inputs, the writer can challenge the reader's ability to process them normatively, then *that is* what good it is. *That* is a kind of praxis.

Lynne Drexler is an artist who many years ago left the New York scene to live and work on tiny, remote Monhegan, that Maine island without the normal accoutrements of civilization, isolated and battered by the North Atlantic Ocean. When I asked her what living on the island had done to her, she replied:

> I came to believe in myself and my own inner resourcefulness. Living here revealed a strength and depth in me I didn't know I had. Recognition,

fame, and applause became trappings that were no longer important, and I opted out of a competitive situation that had nothing to do with what I was trying for in my art. When you live here you learn to see who you really are. You are very close to nature, and nature clarifies you to yourself. At night I feel a sense of awe in the way the black ocean stretches out to meet the black sky, and I'm aware of what it means to live in a universe. Everything here is reduced to essentials. I've forgotten how to act on shore. On shore is the false reality. Here, is the true reality.

Notes

1. John Fowles and Fay Godwin, *Islands* (Boston: Little, Brown, 1978).
2. Philippe Sollers, *Writing and the Experience of Limits*, trans. Philip Barnard and David Hayman, ed. by David Hayman (New York: Columbia University Press, 1983), page 204.
3. Theodor W. Adorno, *Negative Dialectics* (London: Routledge and Kegan Paul, 1973), page 320.
4. James C. Mancuso, "The Acquisition and Use of Narrative Grammar Structure," pages 91–110 of *Narrative Psychology: The Storied Nature of Human Conduct*, ed. Theodore R. Sarbin (New York: Praeger, 1986), pages 91–92.
5. Didier Coste, *Narrative as Communication* (Minneapolis: University of Minnesota Press, 1989), page xii.
6. Walter J. Ong, *Orality and Literacy: The Technologizing of the Word* (London: Methuen, 1982), page 172.
7. Jane Flax, *Thinking Fragments: Psychoanalysis, Feminism, and Postmodernism in the Contemporary West* (Berkeley: University of California Press, 1990), page 62.
8. Stewart R. Clegg, "Narrative, Power, and Social Theory," *Narrative and Social Control: Critical Perspectives*, ed. Dennis K. Mumbry (London: Sage Annual Reviews of Communication Research, 1993), page 42.
9. Dennis K. Mumbry, introduction, *Narrative and Social Control: Critical Perspectives*, ed. Dennis K. Mumbry (London: Sage Annual Reviews of Communication Research, 1993), page 105.
10. John Fowles, "The Nature of Nature," in *"The Tree" and "The Nature of Nature"* (Covelo, Calif.: Yolla Bolly Press, 1995), page 93.
11. Theodore R. Sarbin, "The Narrative as a Root Metaphor for Psychology," pages 3–21, in *Narrative Psychology: The Storied Nature of Human Conduct*, ed. Theodore R. Sarbin (New York: Praeger, 1986), page 15.
12. This quotation is from *"The Nature of Nature,"* page 80; the other page references above, in this paragraph, are to *Islands*.
13. Jonathan Lear, *Love and its Place in Nature: A Philosophical Interpretation of Freudian Psychoanalysis* (New York: Farrar, Straus and Giroux, 1990), page 8.
14. John Fowles, "The Nature of Nature," page 15; the phrase *la bonne vaux* is discussed by Fowles in *Daniel Martin* (Boston: Little, Brown, 1978), pages 272–73.
15. Stephen Best and Douglas Kellner, *Postmodern Theory: Critical Interrogations* (New York: Guilford Press, 1991), pages 90–91.

16. Jean Wyatt, *Reconstructing Desire: The Role of the Unconscious in Women's Reading and Writing* (Chapel Hill: University of North Carolina Press, 1990), page 23.

17. Peter Brooks, *Psychoanalysis and Storytelling* (Oxford: Basil Blackwell, 1994), page 86.

18. John Fowles, "Commentary," *The Man Who Died*, by D. H. Lawrence (1992; reprint Hopewell, NJ: Ecco Press, 1994), page 96; "The Nature of Nature", page 92.

"In the Sea of Life Enisled": Narrative Landscape and Catherine's Fate in John Fowles's "The Cloud"

Clark Closser

> ". . . for a bird of the air shall carry the voice, and that which hath wings shall tell the matter."
> —Ecclesiastes 10:20

John Fowles's enigmatic story "The Cloud," which concludes *The Ebony Tower* collection, is set in a wooded countryside in central France on a "noble" day in late May, the combination of trees and light suggesting to the narrator a landscape by Gustave Courbet.[1] However, there is another landscape in the story, a narrative landscape that resembles the Scilly Isles as much as it does a French woodland, an insular place of shifting points of view overseen and reported on by watchful birds. The disturbing and open-ended story of the complex protagonist, Catherine, with her problematic fate, is a narrative tour de force that derives much of its effect as well as its ambiguity from the strangeness of the story's experimental technique. The narrative complexity has frustrated many readers and created more than one crux in the criticism of what Barry Olshen calls Fowles's "most difficult work to penetrate, certainly the most opaque in *The Ebony Tower.*"[2] The story must remain as indeterminate and mysterious as the ominous cloud that appears at its conclusion, but the narrative landscape of islands of consciousness and the birds that visit them do provide some clues to its meaning.

The bird as actual or potential storyteller is not new in Fowles's work. The narrator of *The French Lieutenant's Woman* pokes fun at a traditional fiction writer's ploy: "Later that night Sarah might have been seen—though I cannot think by whom, unless a passing owl—standing at the open window of her unlit bedroom."[3] In the conclusion of the lyrical opening section of *Daniel Martin*, "The Harvest," this stance is given a name: "Down, half masked by leaves. Point of view of the hidden bird."[4] The bird thus becomes a metaphor for the peculiarity of the authorial presence in narration. Nowhere else in Fowles's fiction is this metaphor applied more self-consciously or more often than in "The Cloud."

Scenic presentation opens the story: "From across the river, one saw a quietly opulent bourgeois glade of light . . ." (251). Who is the "one" who sees this? In the next sentence, a "hidden warbler" sings, and in the second paragraph: " . . . at that very moment a hidden oriole called from the trees behind the mill and gave this particular combination of heat, water and foliage *a voice*" (252, emphasis added). An announcement that the technique of the story will be experimental concludes the paragraph: "So many things . . . were not what one might have expected. If one had been there, of course." But "one" is there, "of course," as the unseen but certainly heard narrator. The "hidden warbler" observes, as the "passing owl" might have done in *The French Lieutenant's Woman*.

The warbler is not alone. The physical landscape of trees and stream provides ample vantage points for the birds that are present throughout "The Cloud" and are mentioned over a dozen times. Some—the oriole, a nightingale, and some high-flying swifts—are heard but never seen. Others—a kingfisher, a wagtail, and a hoopoe—make silent appearances. An owl figures as the magician-author of a fairy tale told within the story. And finally, at the end, the point of view is made explicit once more: "From across the river, if one had been a watching bird in the leaves, one would have seen [the humans] disappear" (312). The subjunctive is appropriate because the point of view is not that of an oriole or an owl, but rather that of an omniscient narrator who reports—without comment and with varying degrees of complexity and completeness—the actions and thoughts of all of his adult characters.

The narrative innovations of "The Cloud" involve more than birds. The subtle, sophisticated narration employs "variations" on previous techniques and also looks forward to aspects of the complexities of narration in *Daniel Martin*, such as shifting between first and second person or past and future tenses. Yet, far more important than these experiments is the landscape of narration that the birds and the characters of the story inhabit.

* * *

Several modern writers have been mentioned as possible influences on the narrative technique of "The Cloud," among them Virginia Woolf, James Joyce, Katherine Mansfield, and Angus Wilson. However, there is an even earlier influence at work. On their way to the picnic, the characters walk through grass containing "the long-stemmed buttercups and the marguerites" (254). Paul will later read aloud from Matthew Arnold's "The Scholar Gypsy," not only providing a link with *Daniel Martin* in its Oxford locale but also allowing the reader to be reminded by the wildflowers of another Arnold poem, "Isolation: To Marguerite," with its themes of loneliness and loss, and its companion poem, "To Marguerite—Continued":

> Yes: in the sea of life enisled,
> With echoing straits between us thrown,
> Dotting the shoreless watery wild,
> We mortal millions live *alone*.
>   The islands feel the enclasping flow,
> And then their endless bounds they know.

This is the opening stanza of the poem that the narrator of *The French Lieutenant's Woman* describes as "perhaps the noblest short poem of the whole Victorian era" (426–27), and which provides the closing words of that novel as Charles Smithson must go" . . . out again, upon the unplumb'd, salt, estranging sea" (467).

At one point in "The Cloud," Catherine muses: "So now everything became little islands, without communication, without farther islands to which this that one was on was a stepping stone, a point with point, a necessary stage. Little islands set in their own limitless sea, one crossed them in a minute, in five at most, then it was a different island but the same: the same voices, the same masks, the same emptiness behind the words" (261). This Arnoldian, island metaphor also describes Catherine's psychological landscape better than she knows, with its isolated sections of consciousness, her occasional near soliloquies, and the cut-off thoughts that sometimes appear like notes for a future fiction.

The metaphor also describes the narrative landscape. Like Arnold's islands, and like the isolated and separate characters, the shifting, separate narrations are not connected with each other and do not communicate. In a later work, *Islands*, Fowles comments on islands as emblematic of both real and fictional worlds:

> In terms of consciousness, and self-consciousness, every individual human *is* an island, in spite of Donne's famous preaching to the contrary. . . . I have always thought of my own novels as islands, or as islanded. I remember being forcibly struck, on my very first visit to the Scillies, by the structural and emotional correspondences between visiting the different islands and any fictional text . . . an insight, the notion of islands in the sea of story, that I could not forsake now even if I tried.[5]

The narrative landscape of "The Cloud" is likewise certainly "islanded," and these islands of narrative—along with the scenic presentations and summary narrative the hidden birds offer from time to time—make up the story.

* * *

The narrative islands are distinct, but they are not identical in their methods of presentation, which vary according to the needs of character and story. Although most of the narrative islands are Catherine's, the thoughts of the minor character Sally, Peter's "bird," are revealed twice. Fragmentary and self-concerned, they reveal Sally's insecurity and youth. The loquacious Paul is presented most often through islands of direct and indirect discourse. The leafy, dreamy yet often intelligent thoughts of Paul's laconic wife, Bel, are in sharp contrast to the selfish, concupiscent consciousness of Peter. He has sexual thoughts about all three of the women. Often these ideas are presented in a fragmentary manner: "Sally best, the rest of her bikini stripped off, behind a bush: a good quick ram . . . the procumbent Bel, collapsed cream dress, two pink-soled feet . . . let's face it, one fancied her, one didn't know why, but always had" (296). This nearly stream-of-consciousness technique is interspersed with a traditional third-person account of Peter's perceptions, abandoning "one" for "Peter" and "he." This approach to Peter's island becomes significant for any discussion of Catherine's later mysterious disappearance.

As for Catherine, the presentation of her consciousness varies even more in technique, beginning with orderly third-person reportage—though with much use of "one," which produces an almost direct-discourse effect—and moving through a fragmentary stream-of-consciousness narrative to culminate in a brief and final burst of first-person point of view. The instability of approach is appropriate, considering Catherine's state of mind: "The erotic sun. Male sun. Apollo, and one is death. His poem once. One lies in one's underclothes, behind dark glasses and fast-closed lids, aware of process, wretched moons; hidden and waiting" (297).

In the story Catherine invents for her young niece, Emma, a naked princess who is lost in the forest is aided by an owl: "'Owls are very clever. And this was the oldest, cleverest owl of all. He was really a magician.'" Like the magic of narrative art, however, the owl's magic has limitations. He can give the princess either new clothes or a palace but not both at once. Emma asks why this limitation must be, and Catherine tells her: "'Because magic is very difficult. And you can only do one piece of magic at a time'" (290). Although simultaneity is not possible, alternative magic can be done, as illustrated by the endings of *The French Lieutenant's Woman*. Of course, a storyteller also has the option of not ending her story at all, making it open-ended like *The Magus*, which is what Catherine does with her princess, leaving her lost in the forest and the question of her rescue unresolved. Emma will not be satisfied with this open-ended fairy tale and will supply what to her will be the more satisfactory closure of a happy ending. But the fate of Catherine, the narrator of the tale, is not so certain. The princess' plight is emblematic of Catherine's own situation. In a variation on a theme of "The Enigma," Catherine even feels at times that she herself is a character in a narrative: "One is given to theories of language, of fiction, of illusion; and also to silly fancies. Like dreaming one is in a book without its last chapters, suddenly: one is left forever on that last incomplete page . . ." (261).

Indeed, "The Cloud" ends as indeterminately as Catherine's fairy tale, but just as Emma will not be satisfied with an open ending, several Fowles readers faced with the last page of the story have projected a future for Catherine, most suggesting that probably she has not only failed to appear, she has disappeared, most likely by taking her own life. Carol Barnum writes: "Catherine . . . having lost love and despairing of ever finding it again, commits suicide." Thomas C. Foster agrees that Catherine "clearly yields to suicidal despair." Simon Loveday writes that the story ends with "almost certainly the death of Catherine," but he adds in a note that this fact is "nowhere definitely stated." James Sollisch says that "we assume Catherine has committed suicide from the sense of emptiness" at the end. Kerry McSweeney refers to her "unnarrated but probable suicide," later calling it "Catherine's surrender to the black hole." Frederick Holmes describes the sexual encounter with Peter as something "perhaps to precipitate her suicide." Barry Olshen refers to Catherine's "possible suicide." Finally, Pamela Cooper finesses the issue with her rather original conclusion, that Fowles "transforms [Catherine] in the direction of literal insubstantiality by replacing her with a cloud."[6]

There are certainly hints of a fatal ending for Catherine throughout the story, particularly the concerns expressed by her sister and her brother-in-law. Catherine even asks, "'Are you and Bel frightened I shall try to kill myself as well?'" (270).

In the final appearance of Catherine's island of consciousness, just before Peter comes across her in the rocks, the narrative switches from Catherine's fragmentary first-person voice to third person in a passage so distanced that it cannot be assigned with certainty to Catherine or even to a hidden bird. The diction is not propitious: "And Catherine lies, composing and composed, writing and written, here and tomorrow, in the deep grass of the other hidden place she has found. Young dark-haired corpse with a bitter mouth . . ."(299). On the previous page, Catherine has considered suicide: "The other side. Peace, black peace . . . the cowardice, waiting, wanting-not-daring. Death" (298). When Peter returns from the boulders, his facetious whisper to Sally is as ominous as the dark cloud that appears on the next page: "'Actually I fancy her like mad. But I'm saving necrophilia for my old age'" (308).

How would Catherine accomplish this suicide—by playing Ophelia in the nearby stream? Seeking out an adder? The answer is not important. However, the more significant question—why Catherine invites the encounter with Peter, or at least allows it—contains a clue to the question of Catherine's future. What happens between them is probably not, as Carol Barnum puts it, a "last meaningless act" (97).

Since the death of her husband, Catherine has lost any "sense of continuity," a loss that has to do with the absence of communication, as she indicates after the passage with the Arnoldian metaphor, quoted above, about how everything becomes islands with "the same voices, the same masks, the same emptiness behind the words" (261). Early in the story, Catherine tells Paul, "'I've lost all sense of the past. Everything is present.'" As for the future: "It's not attainable. You're chained to now. To what you are'" (269). Later, however, just before the encounter with Peter, Catherine realizes: "One had lied . . . it wasn't at all being unable to escape the present; but being all the futures, all the pasts, being yesterday and tomorrow; which left today like a fragile grain between two implacable and immense millstones. Nothing. All was past before it happened; was words, shards, lies, oblivion" (298).

Throughout, Catherine's attitude towards Peter is clear. She is contemptuous of this "worthless, shallow" person, whom she sees as a "wretched little coffin man" of no understanding and someone who abuses language as well, something she abhors. It is all she can do to be civil to this inane television producer who is always looking for an "angle." At one point in the story, when pressed, Catherine provides Peter with a reluctant and reductive explanation of Roland Barthes: his "message" is "'that there are all kinds of category of sign by which we communicate. And that one of the most suspect is language . . . . But the same goes for many other nonverbal sign-systems we communicate by'" (278–79). During her explanation of semiotics, Catherine is aware of Peter's communicating verbally and nonverbally his insincerity, condescension, and lack of understanding. It is then that she comprehends that "it is very simple, she hates him; although he is fortuitous, ignorable as such, he begins to earn his right to be an emblem, a hideous *sign*" (280). It is as such that Peter will appear to Catherine later among the boulders, his function much more semiotic than sexual.

Sunbathing alone, Catherine thinks of her suicide husband and considers her own death. She comes to a critical recognition that if she lacks the will to die, continuing to live will be impossible without ceasing to love the lost lover, without moving out of the past that has trapped her, concluding: "*Il faut philosopher pour vivre*. That is one must not love." A resolution follows, startlingly declared in the first person: "Burn dry and extirpate; ban; annul; annihilate. I will not return. *Not as I am*. . . . To feel so static, without will; inviolable shade; and yet so potent and so poised" (298, emphasis added). The reader is not again allowed access to Catherine's island of consciousness.

The "fortuitous" Peter appears, the "worthless, shallow little *prick*," as she has thought of him earlier (275, emphasis in original). If there is to be extirpation, etymologically an *uprooting*, an annihilation of Catherine's love for the dead poet, what better way than to seduce this symbol, this "sign" of everything the poet was not? To do so wordlessly—without language, in what amounts to a laboratory demonstration of the lecture on semiotics that had gone before—is perfectly appropriate.

The crucial encounter between Peter and Catherine in the boulders is narrated with Peter as the selected consciousness, which deepens the mystery of Catherine's behavior. During the entire five-page scene, she never speaks, and the narration offers no glimpse of her island, only of Peter's. An added effect of limiting the narration to Peter's point of view and moving into what amounts to direct discourse is the forceful demonstration of Peter's crudity and lack of compassion: "She is excited whatever she pretends. . . . It is a pose, of course; just the sick game of a screwed-up little neurotic in heat. Very sick; and very sexy. To have it like this, just once, to have those pale and splintered eyes" (303–4). Although he does not and cannot completely understand, even Peter comes to some realization that Catherine's behavior is more than a "sick game" of hers: "Catherine turns her head and opens her eyes and stares up into Peter's face. It is strange, as if she can't really see him, as if she is looking through his knowing, faintly mocking smile. He has, will always have, the idea that it was something beyond him; not Peter" (304).

The superficial Peter provides the means for annihilating love. And when Catherine returns, she will not return as she was, for the old Catherine will now be a metaphorical "corpse." Living as she had been had become unbearable. Through her silent invitation to Peter, she is no longer "static, without will." The "shade" of her old self and the ghost of her husband are proved not "inviolable" when she invites violation. At the last moment, Catherine demonstrates that what takes place is according to her will by resisting, with "a sudden willfulness, her nails in his shoulders, frantic pushing him away, writhing, struggling, shaking her head violently from left to right" (303–4). At this action, Peter, who may consider himself a great lover but is no rapist, relents. Catherine's resistance is only momentary, but in its violence she establishes that she directs this semiotic ceremony. When she does submit, it is only "as if it is his will" (304). Peter is not Catherine's seducer; he is her instrument. When he returns to the picnic site, the others are waiting to depart. Abandoning Catherine to whatever fate awaits her, they leave the Edenic spot to the forbidding cloud and the watching birds.

Young Emma, who refuses ambiguity, represents the perhaps naive desire of many readers for closure, for something more than what Olshen calls the story's "deliberately inaccessible" conclusion (103). Of course, attempting to extrapolate Catherine's fate through an understanding of her motivation may be as fanciful as "choosing" an ending for *The French Lieutenant's Woman* or writing your own sequel to *The Magus*. But the reader has been invited to do just that. As James Aubrey points out, the open-ended fairy tale within the open-ended story "evidently [is] a cue that the reader has a parallel, creative responsibility to finish 'writing' the characters."[7]

Many readers have accepted this charge of rounding off Catherine's character by refusing to leave her on an incomplete page and postulating or at least positing for her a self-designed physical death, making her a character who submits to despair. Yet, this conclusion is by no means certain. The "composed and composing" Catherine among the boulders, with her realization that love must die in order for her to live, the Catherine of strenuous verbs of resolution not to return *as she is*, may feel "static, without will," but at the same time she is aware of being both "potent and ... poised" (298). She is braced for forceful action that will break the stasis by asserting her will to compose her own fate. From the discussion of Barthes through Catherine's own assertions, Peter has been well-established as a "sign," and she may use him to commit a semiotic and symbolic suicide, enabling her to "return" not as she was but released from her past and from the cloud of depression that had come so close to bringing on her self-destruction. Perhaps she is, indeed, the author of this story. We can never know, for unlike that bird in Ecclesiastes, that "shall carry the voice," the hidden bird of "The Cloud" will never "tell the matter."[8]

The story's major themes of isolation and the absence of communication are emphasized by the metaphor of narrative as island-scape. No one bridges the straits between the islands. Because Catherine and Peter's odd connection among the rocks is seen from the vantage point of Peter's island, the reader is effectively prevented from arriving at any certainties about Catherine's motives or her fate. In fact, the anxious reader, too, is enisled, as if he or she were an isolated character in a similar landscape—a situation that parallels the human condition as Matthew Arnold described it over a century ago.

Notes

1. John Fowles, *The Ebony Tower* (Boston: Little, Brown, 1974), pages 251–52.
2. Barry Olshen, *John Fowles* (New York: Frederick Ungar, 1978), page 103.
3. John Fowles, *The French Lieutenant's Woman* (Boston: Little, Brown, 1969), page 93.
4. John Fowles, *Daniel Martin* (Boston: Little, Brown, 1977), page 11.
5. John Fowles, *Islands* (Boston: Little, Brown, 1978), pages 12, 30.
6. Carol Barnum, *The Fiction of John Fowles: A Myth for Our Time* (Greenwood, Fla.: Penkevill Publishing, 1988), page 98; Thomas C. Foster, *Understanding John Fowles* (Columbia: University of South Carolina Press, 1994), pages 7–8; Simon Loveday, *The Romances of John Fowles* (New York: St. Martin's, 1985), 137, 159; James W. Sollisch, "The Passion of Existence: John Fowles's *The Ebony Tower*," *Critique* 25.1 (1983): 8; Kerry McSweeney, "John Fowles's Variations in *The Ebony Tower*," *Journal of Modern Literature* 8.2 (1980/81): 113, 121; Frederick M. Holmes, "John Fowles's Variation on Angus Wilson's Variation on E. M. Forster: 'The Cloud,' 'Et Dona Ferentes,' and 'The Story of a Panic,'" *Ariel: A Review of International English Literature* 20.3 (1989): 48; Olshen, page 103; Pamela Cooper, *The Fictions of John Fowles: Power, Creativity, Femininity* (Ottawa: University of Ottawa Press, 1991), page 189.
7. James R. Aubrey, *John Fowles: A Reference Companion* (Westport, Conn.: Greenwood Press, 1991), page 116.
8. John Fowles attended the presentation of this paper at the Symposium on 12 July 1996. At the conclusion of the discussion that followed, he demonstrated the power of the novelist over his characters and startled his audience by saying, of Catherine, "Do you want to know the truth? She left that awful place and went to Paris where she had lunch with Roland Barthes and is this moment being deconstructed by Kristeva!"

Dialectical Aesthetics: Interrelations between Image and Text in John Fowles's Nonfiction

Lynne S. Vieth

While conversing on the subject of poetry with a group of students, faculty, and friends at Stanford University in May 1996, John Fowles remarked that the echo of the poet's voice no longer intrigued him quite as much as the arrangement of the words on the page, the texture of fine paper, and the smell of printer's ink. These tactile features of the printed text may have been uppermost in Fowles's mind because of his public appearances on behalf of The Yolla Bolly Press, owned by Carolyn and James Robertson, who had recently published a limited edition containing "The Tree" and Fowles's new essay, "The Nature of Nature," along with eight woodblock prints by Aaron Johnson.[1] Yet this current preoccupation with the graphic qualities of image and text can hardly be called a sudden change of interest on Fowles's part: in fact, it complements a turn from fiction to nonfiction made evident to his readers as early as 1974, the year in which two distinctive works appeared: *The Ebony Tower*, a collection of short stories, and *Shipwreck*, a collection of photos with a book-length essay.

The future direction of Fowles's artistic vision is prefigured in the opening and closing stories of *The Ebony Tower*. In the first tale, bearing the collection's title, Henry Breasley's quest to revitalize the art of painting by recapturing the verbal immediacy of "the spoken word" succeeds only because he cuts himself off from modern society and retreats into his own magical, myth-imbued world.[2] By the end of the final story titled "The Cloud," this retreat into fiction is no longer viable: the heroine's disappearance signals both her failure to communicate with others and, in the narrator's telling words, "the death of fiction."[3] The profusion of references to painting and literature in both stories reveals Fowles's concern with the history of representation, in which the sister arts of painting and poetry have long dominated the Western tradition. Fowles may well have invoked the "death" of the representational arts not only to foreground their reputed decline in the modern age of mechanical reproduction but equally to indicate his turn to nonfictional writing and an alternative aesthetics, whose corresponding media of visual expression would be photography and, ultimately, the wood-block print. Accordingly, in Fowles's oeuvre, photography stands at the crossroads of Western representation and the graphic arts of the East.

Indeed, beginning with *Shipwreck*, photography is Fowles's visual medium of choice. Its affinity for recording death is well expressed in this work, whose images chronicle the destruction of people and their possessions in the countless shipwrecks that have taken place off England's southwest coast on the Isles of Scilly.[4] Similarly, the stark clarity of the classical, black-and-white images not only negates painterly color but also deadens the narrative context out of which the epic voice of seafaring culture still speaks. These photographs, in short, de-romanticize the bodies and objects they depict, thus exposing a gruesome aspect of European imperialism on the high seas. Consequently, what Walter Benjamin has to say about the equally revealing, urban-oriented photographs of Eugène Atget is literally true of those accompanying Fowles's essay in *Shipwreck*: "They pump aura out of reality like water from a sinking ship."[5] That these melancholy photographs of maritime catastrophe were reprinted from the archives of the Gibson family, which has long held the monopoly on documenting shipwrecks in the Scillies, only strengthens their correspondence to Fowles's text, in which he relates the anecdotal histories of similar clans who participated in "the ancient occupation of wrecking" in order to redress their "atrocious economic disregard" by the rest of Britain.[6] Like the photographs themselves, Fowles's narrative is no mainstream cultural history of the British shipping industry, but rather a celebration of a marginalized group whose stories challenge cultural tradition. Already a formal departure from *The Ebony Tower*, *Shipwreck* more explicitly exposes the fictional mythologies and sociopolitical ideologies underpinning European culture.

In *Islands*, published in 1978, Fowles's narrative and Fay Godwin's photography again feature the Scillies. Just as the sea, to quote Fowles in *Shipwreck*, "cuts that green stripling, man, down to size," cleansing him of cultural pretension by submitting him to the mercy of nature, the writer and the photographer continue to do likewise in *Islands*. If Fowles takes storytelling in *Shipwreck* back to its source in the tales told by wreckers' families, he similarly strips epic tradition down to its roots in Greek mythology and Celtic folklore throughout *Islands*. *The Odyssey* provides Fowles with his primary example of the epic voyage homeward, filled with encounters between the hero and the magical denizens of land and sea. Yet from the beginning of this nonfictional work—which is actually all about the origins of Western fiction—Fowles seems less interested in the mythological content of such stories than in the threshold where the name as spoken word becomes philological artifact:

> At Land's End you already stand on territory haunted by much earlier mankind. Their menhirs and quoits and stone lines brood on the moors and the granite-walled fields; and even today the Scillies can in certain lights lose the name we now call them by and re-become the Hesperidean Islands of the Blest; Avalon, Lyonesse, Glasinnis, the Land of the Shades; regain all the labels that countless centuries of Celtic folklore and myth have attached to them. Adam and Eve braved the sea, probably as long as four thousand years ago.[7]

Perhaps it is Fowles's intermixing of archaic words with the proper names so central to Western tradition that gives this flurry of naming its fluid, even fragmentary character—not unlike the fragmentary references to painting and literature so prevalent in *The Ebony Tower* and in *Daniel Martin*, published a year before *Islands*. The ultimate effect of this catalog of names is similar to that which Fowles will attribute to the primal landscape of Wistman's Wood at the end of *The Tree*, where he recalls the poetic insight that nature remains "nameless under an old appellation."[8] Not even Adam's act of naming, Fowles suggests, could adequately articulate the primal essence of nature captured in Godwin's photographs of the Scillies. What might be called their eloquent silence thus exposes and delimits the cultural and aesthetic values associated with naming and the representational power of the spoken word.

Accordingly, Fowles's narrative in *Islands* ends on a different note that reveals the subtle shift from one semiotic sign system to another. Beyond the quasi-human wizards and sea nymphs of oral tradition (104), Fowles asserts, lies the primal gesture of writing itself as indicated in the Greek word *grapho* and the Latin word *scribo* (101). Fowles's philological impulse throughout *Islands* emerges triumphant here to give the ultimate priority to writing itself, an emphasis that also serves to foreground the graphic impulse within the photographic medium. Thus Fowles can say of Godwin's photographs that they reveal the elemental "forms and textures of [the] simplest things" (106). In the essence of the word "textures" lies the subtle resistance of Godwin's images to mythological naming: her aim is not to soften the strangeness of nature by turning it into a humanized pantheon of gods and nymphs but rather to reveal the natural writing already inscribed on the surface of things. Her amazing closeups of trees,

The Old Man of Gugh, the Scilly Isles, by Fay Godwin. Of formations like this one on Gugh, Fowles observes, "Some of the great boulders, naturally carved by Atlantic wind and rain, split and isolated by the Ice Age, that the earliest settlers found there would have profoundly impressed, and baffled, them" (*Islands*, page 5). Photograph courtesy of Collections / Fay Godwin.

buildings, menhirs, and quoits do just this by enlarging the myriad of grooves and lines etched into bark and stone.

Most symbolic of this transition from oral to written word in *Islands* is Godwin's photograph of a menhir dubbed "The Old Man of Gugh," whose name evokes local legend but whose sickle-shaped shadow embodies the cutting gesture linked by Fowles to the origins of writing (86). In the photography analyzed by Benjamin and, more recently, by American critics such as Rosalind E. Krauss, the shadow likewise becomes a prominent sign of linguistic intervention. The outlining and shadowing of objects noted by Benjamin in "A Small History of Photography" are further interpreted by Krauss in "The Photographic

Conditions of Surrealism" as aesthetic signs possessing the semiotic attributes of writing.[9] Photography, consequently, is still delimited by language, but this has become writing rather than speech. Such writing remains committed to representational aesthetics insofar as it reproduces the visible form of the object, yet such shadows and outlines attest to the displacement of color definition by a proto-graphic element. Thus the prominent shadow in Godwin's photograph of "The Old Man of Gugh" has a twofold function: it links the menhir to nature by virtue of its resemblance to the sickle-shaped curve of the island shore—a natural emblem of cutting in *Islands* (48–49)—while its sharpness calls attention to the grooves etched (by nature or by human hand?) on its stone surface. Ultimately, this shadow enacts the Grim Reaper's universal gesture of death, recalling the thematic and aesthetic focus of the photographs in *Shipwreck*.

Even more so in *Land*, Godwin captures this moment when an object's form or texture undercuts and deadens mythological, humanizing narrative to reveal nature's (and second nature's) own tale.[10] Fowles's favorite image is of a lone tree with a cloud, both hovering along the horizon of the methodically furrowed field, though no farm machinery is in sight. In other photographs throughout *Land*, human history objectified into the products of industrialism might also be said to have inserted itself into the larger scheme of natural history—the uncertain results of which give Godwin's images what Fowles rightly calls "an unmistakable undertone of warning melancholy" (xiii). Purged of human presence and artistic intervention to the point where, Fowles notes, "the humanizing is almost forgotten" (xx), Godwin's photographs exemplify what Benjamin called the *dialectical image*, because they illuminate object correspondences between past and present—as if the natural and human-made artifacts of yesterday possessed their own history simultaneously harboring prophecies of the future. It is this intrusion of natural-historical time into the spatial juxtaposition of forms that Fowles admires in Godwin's photographs, especially in *Large white cloud near Bilsington, Kent*, whose formal composition still whispers of balance between nature and humankind. Revealingly, this photograph hangs in the foyer of Fowles's residence in Lyme Regis.

The layout of *Land*, with both Ian Jeffrey's preface and Fowles's essay separated from Godwin's ensuing photographs, improves on the format of *Islands* by dispelling any lingering impression that the images are mere illustrations. This arrangement allows them to express themselves and Fowles's remarks to do the same. Each initially confined to its own domain, text and images are curiously freed to expose genuine intersections between them. They do: just as Godwin's im-

Large white cloud near Bilsington, Kent, by Fay Godwin. At the end of his introductory essay for *Land*, Fowles calls this photograph of a "superbly balanced field, tree, cloud" his "own cherished favourite" and continues: "I have had it beside me all through this writing, and I am convinced it is a very great photograph. Yet I am hard put to analyse why it satisfies and pleases me so much; says things I know I could never write, epitomizes so many unspoken feelings. It is like a certain kind of rare poem, unalterable, perfect in its every syllable" (Little, Brown, 1985, page xx). Photograph courtesy of Collections / Fay Godwin.

ages reveal the mechanization of nature and culture, Fowles's essay similarly implicates the mechanically reproducible image in this cultural-historical process. The interaction between visual image and written text brings out the corresponding element in the other, at the same time transcending the melancholy state of affairs both expose. Fowles overcomes his distrust of most nature photography through Godwin's uncompromising art, while her images benefit from Fowles's patient reading of their subtle messages. It would be difficult to find a work of art that better expresses the dialectical interrelations between classical photography and nonfictional writing.

In the first edition of *The Tree*, published prior to *Land* in 1979, Fowles's essay and Frank Horvat's photographs together move further toward the realm of graphic art.[11] Horvat's images *are* photographs, to be sure, and they share fundamental characteristics with Godwin's, especially the affinity for inanimate objects—though Benjamin would surely have pointed out that Horvat's use of color film betrays a painterly impulse and that certain expressions of nonhuman existence are characteristic of graphic art as well.[12] Yet it is precisely because of their location at this nexus of all three visual arts that Horvat's images support the alternative model of autobiography operating within *The Tree*, in which a third semiotic principle emerges in text and photographs alike.

As Jamie Dopp and Barry Olshen have shown, Fowles's first-person narrative in *The Tree* expresses, on one level, the rebellion of son against father central to classical autobiography.[13] Fowles himself mentions the Oedipus complex while enumerating the early experiences engendering his art (21). In Fowles's recounting of his past throughout *The Tree*, this antithesis is figured in his boyhood experience of the relative wildness of the Devonshire countryside versus that of his father's severely pruned suburban garden. This theme leads (in Fowles's other works as well) to a series of oppositions between the father figure as pseudoscientific collector, categorizer, and namer of nature—that is, the representative of "nature-fearing" cultural values (68)—and the rebellious son, who seeks to escape his naming by the father through immersion in the silence of Mother Nature, only to eventually assume the paternal role and its Adamic imperative to name. Dopp and Olshen speculate that the elimination of Horvat's name, narrative, and photographs from the second edition of *The Tree* could be read, in classical autobiographical terms, as Fowles's assumption of this authority vis à vis Horvat as creative "father" of the project.

Whatever the reason for the elimination of Horvat's preface and images from the Ecco Press edition of *The Tree*, his photographs transcend the documentary, categorizing function to which any identification with paternal authority consigns them. Instead, like Godwin's photographs, Horvat's images resist Adamic naming through the oxymoron of their eloquent silence. Consequently, they not only correspond to Dopp's and Olshen's articulation of a "third" term in the form of "the green man" who evades both conformity and rebellion throughout Fowles's text (40), but they also help define the language of this green man as something more than an oscillation between paternal naming and Mother Nature's muteness. Finally, again like Fowles's text, Horvat's photographs challenge the human-centered paradigm of family history upon which autobiography itself is based.

Fowles goes a long way in *The Tree* toward establishing this alternative language through his reconsideration of naming, the topic with which he had been preoccupied in *Islands*. In the latter text, as Katherine Tarbox has pointed out, names and the narratives they designate are linked to those heroic acts of domination central to the epic tradition in Western literature.[14] In *The Tree,* however, Fowles expands this critique of naming to include any kind of possession enacted through language—including the language of literary critics, who are also acquisitive namers:

> Naming things is always implicitly categorizing and therefore collecting them, attempting to own them; and because man is a highly acquisitive creature, brainwashed by most modern societies into believing that the act of acquisition is more enjoyable than the fact of having acquired, that getting beats having got, mere names and the objects they are tied to soon become stale. There is a constant need, or compulsion, to seek new objects and names—in the context of nature, new species and experiences. Everyday ones grow mute with familiarity, so known they become unknown. And not only in non-human nature: only fools think our attitude to our fellow-men is a thing distinct from our attitude to "lesser" life on this planet. (29–30; see also 47)

Those who have read and studied the first edition of *The Tree* may have encountered the problem of how to cite a passage from it, because there are no page numbers; the only way to locate a quotation, in fact, is to correlate it to the nearest image. Not only does this bind text and photographs tightly together, but it also initiates the defamiliarizing effect by which even critics are prevented from coming to own this work in the usual academic fashion. All readers are forced, instead, to encounter this work (and the unpaginated text of *Shipwreck*) in the same way that Fowles himself encounters Wistman's Wood—that is, by relinquishing the urge to categorize among the visual intricacies of the pictured trees, which insist each time on the freshly felt response. From this point of view, the addition of page numbers in subsequent editions of *The Tree* may not actually be an improvement.

This alternative response is primarily characterized, as Fowles implies in the above quotation, by the willingness to reread that which seems so familiar and known, rather than seeking "new objects and names" in the way of most Western cultures. This response includes "our fellow-men," as Fowles says, thereby suggesting that we need to develop the patience to reread them, too—but in the larger context of natural history that humans share with nonhuman things. Accordingly, the cultivation of this mode of rereading depends on the relaxing of physical and psychological boundaries between inner and outer nature. This does not mean that the "I" disappears. On the contrary, acknowledging the green man's presence within and without oneself can only be accomplished by the individual who has renounced the classical fictions of self-identity apart from nature and of total identity with it: "[Nature] can be known and entered only by each, and in its now; not by you through me, by any you through any me; only by you through yourself, or me through myself" (90). To know nature "in its now" is actually to construct an alternative self, whose individual history has been partially released from family and cultural history in order to be reinserted within the larger paradigm of natural history. Only in this way is it possible for the individual to truly participate in Fowles's version of Richard Jefferies' idea of nature as embodying "the ultra-humanity of all that is not man" (40).

Still, what is the mode of artistic expression that results from this rerooting of the individual in nature? For Fowles in *The Tree*, the answer would seem to be a meandering, improvisational mode of narration that repeatedly circles back to seminal experiences in order to reread them from a slightly different angle—as Horvat implies in his preface the method that he similarly used in taking his photographs of trees, some of which became like "old friends."[15] Even though Horvat and Fowles frequently characterize trees as mute entities resisting all human attempts to understand them, there are at least two instances in *The Tree* in which Fowles comes close to attributing to nature its own language and aesthetic principle of expression. The first is an allusion to the Baudelairean concept of nature's *confuses paroles* (58), whereas the second concerns nature's capacity to perpetually recreate itself :

> But nature is unlike art in terms of its product—what we in general know it by. The difference is that it is not only created, an external object with a history, and so belonging to a past; but also creating in the present,

as we experience it. As we watch, it is so to speak rewriting, reformulating, repainting, rephotographing itself. It refuses to stay fixed and fossilized in the past, as both scientist and artist feel it somehow ought to; and both will generally try to impose this fossilization on it. (49)

His initial claim to the contrary, Fowles appears in *The Tree* to be attempting to do just this: to close the gap between nature and art by repeatedly revisiting themes and events in his narrative. Sometimes this method does result in moments of retrospective understanding indicative of classical autobiography; but more often than not, Fowles's method resists even this much mental closure by perpetually reopening events to interpretation. This is essentially what Fowles means by the "now" in nature, a concept he will further develop in "The Nature of Nature": such epiphanies undermine intellectual and moral certainties more often than they confirm them, perhaps leading to Fowles's current immersion in "the very wildness of novel writing" and the pleasures of endless revision.[16] In this context, Fowles's above reference to nature "rephotographing" itself may initially seem contradictory, because photography is often described as an aesthetic mode of fixing things in the past. Yet if Godwin's black-and-white images can be said to generate that spark of immediacy that Benjamin also designates the "now," then it should not be surprising to find an even stronger sense of the *living* present in Horvat's color photographs of trees.[17]

Trees themselves encourage this creative rereading and revising, because they age from the inside out and thus display their ever-changing histories for all to see. Perhaps that is why ancient Chinese artists chose the juniper tree to symbolize the persistence of youthful vitality within the venerability of old age. In a detail from Wen Zhengming's sixteenth-century handscroll titled *Seven Thuja [Juniper] Trees*, the tree unfurls its complex history across the paper's surface, the gnarled lines and grooves testifying to the accretion of experience through a horizontal intricacy of graphic line, rather than through representational reference to the humanist histories and mythological motifs privileged during the European Renaissance.[18] Horvat's photographs of junipers, oaks, and redwoods do participate in representational mimesis insofar as they reproduce forms in nature; yet like Zhengming's image, their tangled masses of scored trunks and limbs, often combined with a density of foliage, engender an oriental flatness of perspective that dissuades the viewer from seeking further meaning in their depths. "The Form is empty," states a Buddhist aphorism: this articulates the philosophical principle visually expressed in Horvat's and Zhengming's images.

The Seven Thuja [Juniper] Trees (detail), by Wen Zhengming, 1532. Zhengming, or Cheng-ming, used ink on paper. This work in its entirety is about one foot high by twelve feet wide. Photograph courtesy of the Honolulu Academy of Arts, Hawaii.

Oak January Derbyshire, England, **by Frank Horvat. This photograph from the first edition of** ***The Tree*** **is in color, as are the other fifty-seven photographs in the book (Little, Brown, 1979). Later editions of** ***The Tree*** **have not included the photographs. Photograph courtesy of Frank Horvat.**

Fowles's intermittent references throughout his nonfictional oeuvre to the tenets of Zen Buddhism become especially pertinent in this context. At the end of *Islands*, for example, Fowles compares the "austere simplicity" of Godwin's photographs of the Scillies, as well as the "huge Zen garden" composed by the islands themselves, to the Buddhist concept of the mirror that cleanses the viewer's perception by initially reflecting nothing at all (105–6). In *The Tree*, Fowles initially equates this Zen-like perception to immersion in nature's silence, but it soon becomes apparent that this silence or emptiness has incipient semiotic properties—rather like Roland Barthes's blank camera image in his essay on Japanese culture.[19] In fact, the Chinese veneration of this emptiness is evident in Zhengming's respect for the properties of the blank space surrounding his juniper trees. Similarly, Horvat's sparest (and least colorized) images highlight the correlation of line to blank background—for example, his photograph of a lone English oak in the midst of a snowy field. This figuration of an oriental blankness not only deconstructs representational aesthetics but also constructs an empty space in which the artist and nature can mutually create an alternative form of expression.

Wistman's Wood, Dartmoor. This copse of stunted English oaks among boulders on an exposed hillside, higher than oaks normally grow, is an "ecological miracle," according to Fowles. Having used words such as "fairy like," "strange," and "nameless" in his description of this otherworldly environment, Fowles reminds us in *The Tree* that, ultimately, we are alienated from the more familiar-seeming world outside us, and from each other as well (Ecco Press, pages 84–85, 90–91). Photograph by James Aubrey, 1996.

This career-long trajectory toward the aesthetics of graphic art helps to account for Fowles's collaboration with the Robertsons and Aaron Johnson in the creation of the 1995 limited edition of *"The Tree" and "The Nature of Nature,"* which further reveals these concerns to be central to this stage in his artistic development. His complex prose in "The Nature of Nature," for one thing, closely approximates the graphic intricacy of the gnarled Chinese juniper tree or the English oaks in Wistman's Wood, the latter described in "The Tree" as "a natural bonzai nursery" (64). Fowles seems to have had the very form of such trees in mind when he describes his writing as a "tangled nest of memories and thoughts," which he then wryly retitles "The Nature of *My* Nature" to reinforce the insertion of the personal into natural history throughout both essays (73). What is innovative about "The Nature of Nature," which otherwise testifies to Fowles's belief in rereading by revisiting various themes in "The Tree," is the style in which he expresses them: if a certain fluidity in verbal tense infuses "The Tree" with the sense of past informing present, the density of his sentences in the new essay, intensified by frequent parenthetical phrases, coincides with an increased emphasis throughout on his concept of the Now. In fact, the model of the Zen Buddhist garden provides Fowles in "The Nature of Nature" with the exemplary form for perceiving comparable "epiphanies" in nature itself (98).

In more ways than one, the material nature of trees constitutes the subject of this limited edition, which is old and new at once: from the English Waterford paper to the Bembo typeface to the wood-block prints, it embodies more than a nostalgic return to handicraft: more importantly, it actually brings to full expression the graphic tendencies latent in the text and photography of the first edition. Indeed, what is intriguing about the successive editions of *The Tree* is not so much the elimination of the photographs from the Ecco Press edition—though this hiatus may well have provided the impetus for rethinking the correlation between image and text—but rather the aesthetic logic informing the choice of wood-block prints for the limited edition.

One influence must have been Fowles's own fondness for engravings, already evident in the inclusion of Francis Quarles' seventeenth-century etching near the end of *Islands*. Similarly, in the midst of his discussion of Godwin's photography in *Land*, Fowles devotes a lengthy paragraph to the virtues of Thomas Bewick's late eighteenth- and early nineteenth-century woodcuts. Fowles appreciates Bewick's "graphic" renditions of rural life both because of their aesthetic qualities and because Bewick overcame the tendency of his contemporaries to gloss over the brutal realities of nature—the sort of sentimentalizing impulse that Fowles deplores in a great deal of current nature photography (seen in tourist brochures and coffee-table books) which not only prevents viewers from seeing nature whole but also seems bereft of artistic vision.

Fowles's implicit correlations between Godwin's photography and Bewick's woodcuts indeed remind us that the two media share graphic qualities. To take a great photograph, according to Godwin and to Horvat, requires the same passivity before the object that the woodcarver must also display by respecting the natural grain of the wood. Moreover, if photographers like Godwin and Horvat attempt to bring out the natural graphics in the grooved bark of trees or in the lines of their limbs and trunks, the wood-carver does so even more explicitly by cutting shapes and outlines into the wood itself, which has the effect of revealing a form half-inherent in the wood. Perhaps the most compelling correspondence, however, is the concept of reproducibility informing the aesthetics of photograph and woodcut, both of which

Untitled [Trees], by Aaron Johnson. In its original form, this woodcut is printed in gray, green, and black on white and is one of eight illustrations in a limited edition of *The Tree* (The Yolla Bolly Press, 1995). Photograph courtesy of The Yolla Bolly Press and Aaron Johnson.

can be used to produce successive prints. In fact, woodblock printing on paper and silk was invented by the ancient Chinese, who perfected the technique during the Sung dynasty in order to reproduce their own limited editions of Buddhist, Taoist, and Confucian texts.

The increasing commercialization of the mechanically reproducible image and text is of equal concern to Aaron Johnson, printer of Fowles's limited edition and creator of the wood-block prints. Although Johnson occasionally uses photographs as documentary sources for his art, he emphasizes in his commentary "About the Woodcuts" that his primary inspiration comes both from nature and from aesthetic sources far older than the photograph: "When I begin with living trees and then look for ways to express my feelings in human terms, I do not always find the methods close at hand. The images which encourage me, which are complex and resonant, are often ancient ones. In them, the meaning of human life is not set apart from other life."[20] In answer to questions posed in a letter, Johnson elaborated on his "backward pull toward ancient works" that reveal the more intimate interconnections with nature characteristic of earlier cultures.[21] Having studied in Florence during the fall of 1983, Johnson counts the art of "the Etruscans and their earthy vitality" as one such influence, while oriental art constitutes another. Just as important to Johnson, however, are written works such as the Bible, *The Iliad*, and the *Tao te ching* (1). Interestingly, especially for a printer whose craft is intimately involved with the written word, what appeals to him in these ancient texts is the remnant of oral tradition that still infuses them with the aura of the spoken word.

Johnson's formulation illuminates the dialectical aesthetics operating within his wood-block prints for the limited edition. Fundamentally graphic in conception, as befits the art of a printmaker, they simultaneously refer to Johnson's avocation as a painter through the earth-tone colors informing the dynamic between graphic line and blank background. Indeed, as Johnson notes in "About the Woodcuts," a certain blankness pervades his images, starting with the white paper on which they appear: "When ink leaves a woodblock it creates an image on a page which is removed from nature. Between the man-made leaves of the book, a white margin of paper surrounds the image of a tree, the *idea* of a tree. It is the recollection of a tree, a place to sort through concepts and memories of trees" (unpaginated). In this respect, Johnson's aesthetic corresponds to Horvat's discussion in his preface of the Platonic idea of certain trees, precipitated from his memories of them; accordingly, both create images uniquely true to individual experience. Moreover, both set their images off against the whiteness of the blank page. Yet that is where similarities end: blankness permeates the borders surrounding Johnson's images, as well as the images themselves, in a way that explicitly challenges painting and photography by privileging the qualities of the graphic medium and its bringing of the personal and the natural together. Consequently, Johnson's rendition of an oriental relation between line and background could be said to virtually displace the intrusion of language, privileging graphic sign over representational reference to speech or writing. It is surely no accident that Johnson's prints in the Yolla Bolly Press edition are untitled. Indeed, the muted presence of painterly color within these essentially graphic prints suggests that Johnson wanted to preserve only the faintest aura of the word—without invoking the names and narratives imbuing Western representational art.

This, too, is the threshold to which Fowles ultimately takes the reader in "The Tree." Having gradually emptied his narrative of the nature-fearing motifs and myths that haunt Western fiction, the aura of storytelling still hovers about the very end of his essay, infusing his personal experience in the depths of Wistman's Wood with vestiges of oral narrative. In his letter, Johnson has put it best: "One of the things I like about Fowles is his skill as a storyteller, keeping some of this oral quality alive, showing a little resistance to putting it in final, written form" (1–2).

Notes

1. John Fowles and Aaron Johnson, *"The Tree" and "The Nature of Nature"* (Covelo, Calif.: Yolla Bolly Press, 1995). This edition was limited to 185 copies, but the press also has issued 275 copies of *"The Nature of Nature"* bound separately as a "wrappers edition."

2. John Fowles, "The Ebony Tower," in *The Ebony Tower* (New York: Little, Brown, 1974), page 46.

3. John Fowles, "The Cloud," in *The Ebony Tower*, page 278.

4. For photography's association with the representation of death, see Susan Sontag, *On Photography* (New York: Farrar, Straus and Giroux, 1973), and Roland Barthes, *Camera Lucida: Reflections on Photography*, trans. Richard Howard (1980; reprint New York: Hill and Wang, 1981).

5. Walter Benjamin, "A Small History of Photography," in *"One-Way Street" and Other Writings*, trans. Edmund Jephcott and Kingsley Shorter (London: New Left Books, 1979), page 250.

6. John Fowles and the Gibsons of Scilly, *Shipwreck* (Boston: Little, Brown, 1974), unpaged.

7. John Fowles and Fay Godwin, *Islands* (Boston: Little, Brown, 1978), page 5.

8. John Fowles, *The Tree* (1979; reprint New York: Ecco Press), page 90. The first edition is unpaged; and although there have been later reprints of *The Tree*, by the Nature Company and the Yolla Bolly Press, their limited availability has led me generally to cite the text of the Ecco Press edition as a convenience to readers.

9. See Rosalind E. Krauss, "The Photographic Conditions of Surrealism," in *The Originality of the Avant-Garde and Other Modernist Myths* (Cambridge: Mass. Institute of Technology Press, 1985), pages 87–118. See also the essays by Krauss and others in *"L'Amour Fou": Photography and Surrealism* (New York: Abbeville Press, 1985).

10. John Fowles and Fay Godwin, *Land* (Boston: Little, Brown, 1985).

11. John Fowles and Frank Horvat, *The Tree* (Boston: Little, Brown, 1979).

12. See Walter Benjamin, "Painting and the Graphic Arts" and "Painting, or Signs and Marks," trans. Rodney Livingstone, in *Walter Benjamin: Selected Writings*, eds. Marcus Bullock and Michael Jennings (Cambridge: Harvard University Press, 1996), volume 1, pages 82–84.

13. Jamie Dopp and Barry N. Olshen, "Fathers and Sons: Fowles's *The Tree* and Autobiographical Theory," *Mosaic* 22 no. 4 (1989), pages 31–44.

14. In a presentation on *Islands* given at the John Fowles Symposium in Lyme Regis, England, on 11 July 1996, Katherine Tarbox provided support for this point by arguing that *The Odyssey* exemplifies the narrative-psychological grid of the patriarchal quest plot against which Fowles is working throughout this text.

15. Frank Horvat, preface, *The Tree* (Boston: Little, Brown, 1979), unpaged.

16. Patricia Holt, "The Wild Side of John Fowles," *San Francisco Chronicle,* 30 April 1996, page B4.

17. Walter Benjamin, "Theses on the Philosophy of History," in *Illuminations*, ed. Hannah Arendt, trans. Harry Zohn (New York: Shocken Books, 1969), page 261.

18. For a good summation of the humanist art criticism dedicated to the analysis of narrative and mythological motifs in Italian Renaissance art, see Svetlana Alpers, *The Art of Describing: Dutch Art in the Seventeenth Century* (Chicago: University of Chicago Press, 1983), pages xix–xx.

19. Roland Barthes, *Empire of Signs*, trans. Richard Howard (New York: Farrar, Straus and Giroux, 1982), page 83.

20. Aaron Johnson, "About the Woodcuts," prospectus for *"The Tree" and "The Nature of Nature,"* unpaged.

21. Aaron Johnson, letter to the author, 7 August 1996, page 1.

The Nature of John Fowles
Carol M. Barnum

John Fowles has long felt an affinity with nature. He calls natural history his "dominant outside interest," even preferring the company of birds to people.[1] At the same time he recognizes the potential for evil in an overly zealous approach to the cataloging of specimens as a part of the study of natural science. He gives this distorted obsession—one he admits to have once had himself—to two of his earliest protagonists: Clegg in *The Collector* is obsessive in his desire to collect butterflies—and women—and Charles in *The French Lieutenant's Woman* exhibits a narrowness in his fossil collecting.[2]

No longer a collector, Fowles characterizes his relationship to nature as a more deeply personal one of "love" or "need": "My own attitude to nature has changed very considerably during my life, but it has always been important, I would now say vital, to me."[3] His belief in the important role nature can play in one's life is the key to understanding not only Fowles the person but also his fiction. Nature pervades his fiction, as an analogy for the process of choosing, in two important ways: (1) as the process by which the author chooses his characters and events, and (2) as the process by which his protagonists must make choices if they are to succeed in their quests for their natural selves.

In the first case—the author's creative process—Fowles uses the analogy in a 1985 interview with Robert Foulke: "The writer is continually faced with forks, continually sees two possible developments at any given point in his text, very often more than two . . . . Only in the course of writing do you discover a certain habit of choosing among all these possibilities, so that you feel a persistent mystery in the writing process that alone accounts really for your deciding to end something happily or not."[4] In his 1995 essay "The Nature of Nature," Fowles uses the same metaphor to describe the writing process: "All writers make up their own private slang as to what goes on when they write. An important one—at any rate for me in my own practice—is the *fork* (as in a path), by which I mean a fairly continuous awareness of alternatives, both 'learned' (remembered) and 'fortuitous' (wild), in what is done."[5] This view of the writing process explains why Fowles finds writing so compelling: the artist is forced into the same dilemma as his protagonist: free choice, and, once having chosen, learning to live with existential hazard.

Fowles sees a further parallel between writing and the study of nature, as he explains to Foulke: "Natural history seems always something that involves what is happening. In this sense it helps us to feel the presentness of our own socio-cultural arrangements. . . . This is why I read about the nature of matter, because this is where presentness lies. . . . You know, there are extraordinary passages in *The Origin of Species* in which [Darwin] is really writing very much like a novelist in the way he describes what he sees" (378).

This interest in nature and natural history has led Fowles to write nonfiction books with such titles as *The Tree, Islands,* and *Land.* These books help one understand Fowles's interest in nature and the way in which this attitude manifests itself in his fiction. "The key to my fiction," Fowles explains in *The Tree,* "lies in my relationship with nature," which he defines as "an experience whose deepest value lies in the fact that it cannot be directly described by any art . . . including that of words." Later in *The Tree,* he tries to describe the relationship further: "There is something in the nature of nature, in its presentness, its seeming transience, its creative ferment and hidden potential, that corresponds very closely with the wild, or green man, in our psyches."[6]

This green man in the psyche is the "Self," which C. G. Jung describes as the object of the process of individuation, an inward journey that can only progress with the aid of the archetypes. Like Fowles, Jung attributes modern man's "artificial life" to his removal from nature: "Our intellect has created a new world that dominates nature and has populated it with monstrous machines. . . . Our present lives are dominated by the goddess Reason. . . . By the aid of reason, so we assure ourselves, we have 'conquered nature.'"[7] Through the aid of the archetypes, Jung says that man can find the way back to the inner or natural self. He warns, however, that the idea of engaging the archetypes will not be readily accepted by modern man because of the very attitudes we must transcend:

> I am trying to use words to describe something whose very nature makes it incapable of precise definition. But since so many people have chosen to treat archetypes as if they were part of a mechanical system that can be learned by rote, it is essential to insist that they are not mere names, or even philosophical concepts. They are pieces of life itself—images that

are integrally connected to the living individual by the bridge of the emotions. (87)

Fowles speaks of nature's elusiveness in a similar way in *The Tree*, as if he is recognizing nature's correspondence with archetypal tendencies deep in the self: "It, this namelessness, is beyond our science and our arts because its secret is being, not saying.... All experience of it through surrogate and replica, through selected image, gardened word, through other eyes and minds, betrays or banishes its reality" (90). Both the author and the psychiatrist struggle to find words to describe the indescribable journey to the inner self. Although they may choose slightly different words, the journey they describe is the same: the search for the green man in each of our psyches. The sameness is partly a matter of influence; Fowles has admitted his indebtedness to Jung, especially in his early novel *The Magus*, yet Fowles continues to make references to Jung and the archetypes in much of his later fiction. For instance, in one of the many discussions between Breasley and David Williams in "The Ebony Tower," Breasley describes the Celtic tale *Eliduc* in his usual, cryptic way: "'Damn good tale. Read it several times. What's that old Swiss bamboozler's name. Jung, yes? His sort of stuff. Archetypal and all that.'"[8] Not only is Breasley connecting Jung to Celtic myth, but Fowles likewise describes an important parallel in his "Personal Note," which follows the title story. Here Fowles suggests that the idea of quest and discovery is the basis of all fiction extending from Celtic myth to include his own (118–19). In *The Tree*, he is more explicit, writing that we live "in an age that has lost all belief in maidens, dragons and magical castles, but I think we have only superficially abandoned the basic recipe (danger, eroticism, search)..." (60–61).

The quest motif is present in most of Fowles's fiction: a protagonist, usually male, has lost all belief in wonder, yet through some "magical act" finds himself wrenched out of his daily existence and forced to look at the shallowness of his life. The action or event places him on the path of potential discovery—which follows the pattern of the hero's quest of old. To give the basic recipe a modern reality, Fowles provides his quester-hero with the opportunity for archetypal encounters in modern contexts. The quester's acceptance of the energy from the archetypes propels him deeper into his journey of self-discovery. Jung calls this the process of individuation, and Fowles in *The Tree* equates such a journey with artistic creation:

> Some such process of retreat from the normal world—however much the theme and surface is to be of the normal world—is inherent in any act of

artistic creation. . . . And a part of that retreat must always be into a 'wild,' or ordinarily repressed and socially hidden, self: into a place always a complexity beyond daily reality, never fully comprehensible or explicable, always more potential than realized; yet where no one will ever penetrate as far as we have. It is our passage, our mystery alone, however miserable the account that is brought out for the world to see or hear or read at second-hand.

The artist's experience here is only a special—unusually prolonged and self-conscious—case of the universal individual one. The return to the green chaos, the deep forest and refuge of the unconscious is a nightly phenomenon, and one that psychiatrists . . . tell us is essential to the human mind. (75–76; second ellipsis added)

The forest here is interior, but the metaphor reminds us that the internal and the external relate harmoniously in an individuated self. And Fowles reinforces that idea at the beginning of his 1995 essay "The Nature of Nature" when he remarks that perhaps it should have been titled "The Nature of *My* Nature."[9]

In my 1985 interview with Fowles, he makes the same connections among creativity, psychiatry, and nature when he observes, "I am much more interested in how writers work and function, which I have called the ethology of the writer—on the analogy of biology . . . . I take the view that Freud and Jung were both very close to novelists themselves, or myth creators (as was Darwin, by the way)."[10]

Fowles's linking of psychiatrists and writers suggests the common process of exploration of the psyche that each undergoes: the psychiatrist with the patient and the novelist with the characters. It is the parallel between writer and protagonist, each engaged in the search for "freedom, and sheer mystery, of the undiscovered and inexplicable" that I now wish to explore.[11] I will focus particularly on the mandala archetype, or "magic circle," which Jung calls "the archetype of inner order" and "the symbol of wholeness."[12] Fowles's equivalent is the "sacred combe," or "*bonne vaux*"—a phrase borrowed from Restif de la Bretonne and translated by Fowles as a "valley of abundance," a magical place.[13] Such magical places resonate with one's archetypal unconscious and nurture conscious awareness of its forces, for improved psychological health. The mandala archetype usually manifests itself as a circle or a circle in a square, and it often takes the form of a garden. Fowles almost always represents the undiscovered and inexplicable as places of natural beauty or historical significance, or both. Among the many such places in Fowles's novels are the Greek island of Phraxos, and its more secret domain of Bourani, in *The Magus*; the Undercliff in *The French Lieutenant's Woman*; Tsankawi, Kitchener's Island, and Tarquinia in *Daniel Martin*; Exmoor and Stonehenge in *A Maggot*. All such places appeal to our archetypal desire to return to the lost Eden. Such a desire is the force that drives the author to write and that drives the questing character to press on with the journey of self-discovery in pursuit of individuation, what Fowles calls "whole sight."[14]

In his first written and still favorite novel, *The Magus*, Fowles provides a poetic description of this archetypal search for the lost Eden in the lines from T. S. Eliot's "Little Gidding," found on a Phraxos beach by protagonist Nicholas Urfe:

> "We shall not cease from exploration
> And the end of all our exploring
> Will be to arrive where we started
> And know the place for the first time." (quoted in *The Magus*, page 69)

These lines call Nicholas to the quest for knowledge as they call us on ours (for Fowles always engages the reader as a participant in the journey). The Greek island and its secret garden, the villa Bourani, provide the experience of a lost Eden that Nicholas will long to return to in order to reclaim his Eve (or Eurydice), once he has been exiled to London. He is still coming to terms with those desires when the novel leaves him with Alison in Regent's Park, an urban garden—mandala against which Nicholas may or may not be transformed—as the "gods" may or may not be watching from the nearby buildings. At the end, whatever their future, we know that he has matured as a quester and is now capable of love—the psychological equivalent of whole sight.

From this beginning point on his own journey as a novelist, Fowles next takes up the story of a would-be quester who perverts nature by collecting and killing life rather than experiencing life. For Frederick Clegg in *The Collector*, the natural world is to be controlled, as he does with his butterfly collection and with women. When Miranda tries to act "naturally" and proposes that they engage in sex, Clegg is repulsed. He ends up snuffing out her life as she metaphorically flutters against his killing bottle. Because he cannot experience the energy of the archetypes, Clegg fails to grow toward individuation and is destined to repeat his "unnatural" acts.

From this examination of a failed journey, Fowles returns to the journey of a quester on the path of self-knowledge. Like Clegg, Charles Smithson is a collector, but his echinoderms are already dead and fossilized. As his path takes him into the sacred combe of the Undercliff, he discovers his underself by means of encounters with Sarah Woodruff. As he grows, he gives up his "fossilized" psychologi-

Cumberland Terrace, from Regent's Park, London. In the climactic episode in *The Magus* Nicholas and Alison meet in Regent's Park, perhaps under the metatheatrical surveillance of Maurice Conchis, emblematized by the Olympian sculptures on the buildings behind her: "A wall of windows, a row of statues of classical gods. They surveyed the park as if from a dress circle" (page 652). Photograph by James Aubrey, 1994.

cal state to break free into "the unplumb'd salt, estranging sea."[15] Again, as in *The Magus,* Fowles allows the reader to choose the ending as he also leaves himself free to go on choosing paths in search of the right ending. He explains this need to choose paths and its impact on his first three novels: "I wrote and printed two endings to *The French Lieutenant's Woman* entirely because from early in the first draft I was torn intolerably between wishing to reward the male protagonist (my surrogate) with the woman he loved and wishing to deprive him of her—that is, I wanted to pander to both the adult and the child in myself. I had experienced a very similar predicament in my two previous novels."[16]

The unequivocal, happy ending was to come in his next novel, *Daniel Martin,* reflecting not only Fowles's own maturity as a person and a novelist, but also the mature stage of his protagonist, who is struggling with his own desire to write a happy ending against the perceived falseness of such an ending for our age. Fowles admits his own struggle with the notion of a happy ending in his interview with me: "I don't plan books in advance, and it wasn't until *Daniel Martin* was half written that I began to feel clearly that it must end 'happily.' I remember it first seemed an odd, even strange idea—almost an eccentricity, a gratuitous act" (199). As Dan similarly struggles to write the happy ending for his life, which will also be the happy ending of his book in progress, he journeys back to his starting point in search of both the places where he took wrong turns and the special places that have shaped who he is—the sacred combes. Probably speaking for Fowles, Dan describes the meaning of the sacred combe in the chapter of the same name: "a place outside the normal world, intensely private and enclosed, intensely green and fertile, numinous, haunted and haunting, dominated by a sense of magic, that is also a sense of a mysterious yet profound parity in all existence" (273). In particular he recalls the significance of certain lost landscapes: Thorncombe and Tarquinia in the distant past, Tsankawi in the recent past, and Kitchener's Island and Palmyra in the evolving present (future past).[17] In each of these sacred combes, Dan is able to connect with his inner self, to reach out to connect with others, and, eventually, to pull himself out of his isolation and sense of loss to experience moments of whole sight. Jung similarly describes the state of modern human beings in their isolation from the natural landscape of such sacred combes: "Man feels himself isolated in the cosmos, because he is no longer involved in nature and has lost his emotional 'unconscious identity' with natural phenomena . . . . No voices now speak to man from stones, plants, and animals, nor does he speak to them believing they can hear. His contact with nature has gone, and with it has gone the profound emotional energy that this symbolic connection supplied" (85). Daniel Martin regains his contact with nature by means of these sacred places, and in his future past Dan forges a new connection in the desert of Palmyra that restores the desert of his life back to the lost garden of Eden.

Having finally written the previously unattainable happy ending, where was Fowles to go on his novelist's journey? Into fantasy would not seem an unlikely guess, which is, of course, where Fowles has gone in his last two novels. The earlier one, *Mantissa*, is a metafiction that takes a seriocomic look and laugh at the presumed difficulty of writing fiction.[18] The other, *A Maggot,* although appearing to return to the historical form of *The French Lieutenant's Woman*, is rather an exploration of the narrative straitjacket of the deposition as a form for his fiction.[19] Many of the usual archetypal patterns are present: a male character in search of meaning is accompanied on the journey by a woman with special insight. However, the natural world of England's West Country is transformed into the other-worldly, as the devil appears at Stonehenge, Rebecca describes a religious vision of Holy Mother Wisdom, and a maggot-shaped spaceship transports the protagonist to June Eternal, a sacred place of wholeness.

What Fowles may be suggesting with these seemingly incomprehensible events is what Jung calls "the symbols of our dreams. They bring up our original nature—its instincts and peculiar thinking. Unfortunately, they express their contents in the language of nature, which is strange and incomprehensible to us" (95). Fowles ends the novel with just such strange and incomprehensible words, sung as a lullaby by Rebecca to her new daughter, who, we learn in the epilogue, is destined to found the Shaker religious community. The narrative voice intones: "It is very simple, and seems to be of two repeated phrases only. *Vive vi, vive vum* . . . it is clear they are not rational words, and can mean nothing" (448). The language used may seem strange and incomprehensible to us because we are probably out of touch with nature, and a rational explanation of the irrational does not suffice. The story has represented the mysterious, and if we have taken the journey with Rebecca, we at least know that the seemingly meaningless can and does carry a meaning that we, too, seek to understand by reading the novel.

Even as Fowles has evolved in his own exploration of questers who may succeed or who fail to succeed or questers who break free or who escape from the world, his theme has always been presented through the examination of nature, which Fowles says is "above all for me rich in similes and metaphors of man. It is the poetry to the 'prose' of human behaviour, but not just lyrical poetry. I would claim my own experience of nature informs my work in many different ways."[20] In *The Tree,* he explains the most important way as a correlative to himself as writer: "I began this wander through the trees . . . in search of that much looser use of the word 'art' to describe a way of knowing and experiencing and enjoying outside the major modes of science and art proper . . . a way not concerned with scientific discovery and artefacts, a way that is internally rather than externally creative, that leaves little public trace; and yet which for those very reasons is almost wholly concentrated in its own creative process."[21]

The art of John Fowles is primarily, then, about the nature of John Fowles. With its emphasis on internal creativity and its concentration on the creative process, it has the potential not only to inform us but also to engage and challenge us to seek the mystery of our own nature. After his 1989 stroke, Fowles used the language of the lost garden to describe his present dilemma: "I do still 'toy' with the idea of a novel, but I'm afraid real writing still seems to [be] a paradise from which I am barred."[22] His 1996 interview for *Twentieth Century*

Literature indicates that he is, once more, writing fiction. Once again, his novel-in-progress tells two stories—one about the characters and one about the author: "I experience this book (temporarily titled *In Hellugalia*) as I might a living dream."[23] We can only hope that, in his regained paradise, Fowles will—like Rebecca in *A Maggot*—share the vision with us.

Notes

1. Daniel Halpern, "A Sort of Exile in Lyme Regis," *London Magazine*, March 1971, page 37.
2. John Fowles, *The Collector* (Boston: Little, Brown, 1963); *The French Lieutenant's Woman* (Boston: Little, Brown, 1969).
3. Carol M. Barnum, "An Interview with John Fowles," *Modern Fiction Studies* 31, no.1 (1985), page 188.
4. Robert Foulke, "A Conversation with John Fowles," *Salmagundi* 68–69 (1985–86), page 374.
5. John Fowles, "The Nature of Nature," in *"The Tree" and "The Nature of Nature"* (Covelo, Calif.: Yolla Bolly Press, 1995), page 94.
6. John Fowles, *The Tree* (New York: Ecco Press, 1983), pages 31–32 (ellipsis in original), page 51.
7. Carl G. Jung, "Approaching the Unconscious," in *Man and his Symbols*, ed. Carl G. Jung, et al. (1962; reprint New York: Dell Publishing, 1968), page 91.
8. John Fowles, foreword, *The Magus: A Revised Version* (Boston: Little, Brown, 1977), page 6; John Fowles, "The Ebony Tower," in *The Ebony Tower* (Boston: Little, Brown, 1974), page 55.
9. "The Nature of Nature," page 73.
10. Barnum, page 195.
11. Ellen Pifer, introduction, *Critical Essays on John Fowles* (Boston: G. K. Hall, 1986), page 4.
12. Richard I. Evans, *Jung on Elementary Psychology: A Discussion betweeen C. G. Jung and Richard I. Evans* (New York: E. F. Dutton, 1976), page 86.
13. John Fowles, *Daniel Martin* (Boston: Little, Brown, 1977), page 273.
14. *Daniel Martin*, page 3.
15. *The French Lieutenant's Woman*, page 467.
16. John Fowles, "Hardy and the Hag," in *Thomas Hardy After Fifty Years*, ed. Lance St. John Butler (London: Macmillan, 1977), page 35.
17. For an interesting discussion of the further significance of *la bonne vaux* in *Daniel Martin*, see Jeanette Mercer Sabre, "The Sacred Wood in Three Twentieth-Century Narratives," *Christian Scholar's Review* 13, no.1 (1983), page 273.
18. John Fowles, *Mantissa* (Boston: Little, Brown, 1982).
19. John Fowles, *A Maggot* (Boston: Little, Brown, 1985).
20. Christopher Bigsby, "John Fowles," in *The Radical Imagination and the Liberal Tradition: Interviews with English and American Novelists*, ed. Heide Ziegler and Christopher Bigsby (London: Junction Books, 1982), pages 117–18.
21. *The Tree*, pages 48–49. The first ellipsis is added.
22. John Fowles, letter to the author, 7 December 1989.
23. Jan Vipond, "An Unholy Inquisition," *Twentieth Century Literature* 42, no.1 (spring 1996), pages 12–28.

The Archetype of the Green Man in the Writings of John Fowles

Barry N. Olshen

> What would the world be, once bereft
> Of wet and of wildness? Let them be left,
> O let them be left, wildness and wet;
> Long live the weeds and the wilderness yet.
> —Gerard Manley Hopkins, "Inversnaid"

> Ban the green from your life, and what are you left with?
> —John Fowles, *Daniel Martin*[1]

"Green man" is being used today as a generic term for the archetype of our oneness with Nature and for a wide variety of the archetype's cultural manifestations. Evidence of the archetype has been traced back millennia, to a time when human identity was intimately bound up with Nature and the cycle of a living earth. Early Christianity incorporated much of the imagery and ritual of this earlier period, and the Green Man archetype was adapted to the medieval Church, though in complicated and ambivalent ways. Today it seems once again to be at a stage of dynamic adaptation, this time to developments in modern science and technology. Contemporary ecology has fostered in some of us a sense of identity that allows for a concept of self beyond culture, that views the individual as a member of a species within a much more complex ecology.[2] William Anderson concludes his recent book-length survey of the archetype by characterizing it as "the threshold of the imagination between our outer natures and our deepest selves."[3] He expresses the hope that the Green Man in our time will unite what have hitherto been considered antipathetic modes of consciousness, early animism and modern science, and that the union will result in a science and art that are in harmony with wild Nature:

> Our remote ancestors said to their mother Earth: "We are yours."
> Modern humanity has said to Nature: "You are mine."

L'homme et la forêt, by René Magritte, about 1965. One of Magritte's last works was this gouache of a Green Man in a bowler, whose image cleverly erases the boundary between inner and outer nature. Photograph courtesy of SODRAC (Montréal) 1997 and by permission of the Leuwenkroon sisters, Acacialaan 8, 2020 Antwerp, Belgium.

Green Man in Leaf Bower. This print shows "The Chimney-sweeps' Jack o' the Green" in eighteenth century London, reproduced in *English Custom and Usage*, by Christina Hole (2d edition, Batsford, 1943–44, opposite page 67). Photograph courtesy of B. T. Batsford.

The Green Man has returned as the living face of the whole earth so that through his mouth we may say to the universe: "We are one." (164)

These sentiments, as we shall soon see, are very close to those expressed in the works of John Fowles. In fact, to some extent, his writing anticipates them and the green movement currently underway, a movement in which "green" conveys not just the natural world but also the way that the world is perceived and valued. Before turning to the actual texts, however, I want very briefly to outline the traditional manifestations of the archetype in the West, manifestations in such various cultural forms as ritual, dance, drama, and procession; pictorial imagery, carving, and sculpture; and literature and oral tradition. Although such an outline may constitute only a review of what some readers already know, it should also provide a context for Fowles's use of the imagery, which both echoes and reframes the traditional meanings and values of the archetype.

The term Green Man is synonymous in England with Jack-in-the-Green, the walking or dancing leaf bower, covered down to his ankles in thick foliage mounted on a conical frame with a peep hole in its branches for his face.[4] Jack-in-the-Green has been associated with May Day processions and ceremonies since at least the late eighteenth century. He is generally regarded as the English counterpart of the Continental Green George and other figures of European folk drama and ritual, variously referred to as the Garland, the Little Leaf Man, Robin Hood, the May King, the Whitsuntide King, the Queen of the May, and so on. These are the figures of folk tradition treated in Sir James Frazer's *The Golden Bough* as representatives of the tree spirit or spirit of vegetation, central to what Frazer regarded as the death and resurrection rituals of pre-Christian Europe.[5]

The Green Man is best represented in folklore and fiction by such renowned figures as Robin Hood and the Green Knight. Robin's name may have come from a contraction of "Robin of the Wood"; he dwelled, of course, in the Greenwood, and he and his band of men were supposed to have dressed in Lincoln Green. The Green Man pub and inn signs throughout England may reflect this tradition of Robin Hood or may more generally represent the figure of a forester or gamekeeper, who formerly would have worn some kind of green suit.[6] There are said to be more than thirty Green Man pubs in the London area alone. Such pubs are especially popular in East Anglia, where Kingsley Amis sets his novel *The Green Man*, whose title refers to the name of an ancient inn and also to a supernatural hybrid creature called up from the distant past, a kind of cross between Jack-in-the-Green and the Golem. Another literary hybrid may be found in Susan Cooper's *Greenwitch*, a children's novel in which she imaginatively reconstructs the ancient folk ritual of casting the so-called Greenwitch over the cliff and into the sea.[7]

The Green Knight, the mysterious and magical lord of the wild forest in *Sir Gawain and the Green Knight*, is, I believe, the only surviving example of the type in medieval English literature. The poem has been called "a midwinter festival poem," and the magical lord, "no other than a recrudescence in poetry of the Green Man. . . . the descendent of the Vegetation or Nature god . . . whose death and resurrection mythologizes the annual death and re-birth of nature."[8] Fowles makes direct and indirect allusions, in his fiction and nonfiction alike, to both Robin Hood and the mysterious Green Knight.

Their modern counterparts are found in such fictional characters as Rima in W. H. Hudson's *Green Mansions*, Tom Bombadil and his mate Goldberry in Tolkien's *The Lord of the Rings*, and Amleth, a King of the Wood in Henry Treece's *The Green Man*.[9] This last embellishes the same source that Shakespeare's *Hamlet* does, "The Revenge of Amleth," in the *Gesta Danorum* of Saxo Grammaticus. It

Green Man Pub, London. One of many pubs named after the Green Man, this one is on Euston Road. Photograph by James Aubrey, 1994.

attempts an imaginative reconstruction of a society practicing that tree worship and sacrificial system described by Frazer and associated by him originally with Diana's Temple at Nemi (at which her priest was "King of the Wood") and later with the sacred oak groves of the Druids.

If I am not mistaken, Miles Green, the protagonist of Fowles's *Mantissa*, may also have the distinction of belonging to this select group of green figures, though he joins them by the back door, to be sure.[10] If his first name is read in its original Latin form, *miles*, the figure becomes "Soldier Green," a kind of metamorphosed Green Knight, this time, though, stuck in "an unwritable non-text" (183), a bizarre, postmodern parody of a romance (*romance* to be taken in both of its principal senses). The wilderness is here represented by a transmogrified "domed and quilted [hospital room] ceiling," a "forest of little hanging pods, each with its end-button. For all their greyness they were breastlike, line after line of school girls' breasts, a canopy of nippled buds" (14–15). Miles Green's shape-changing mistress is Erato, "the beloved one," muse of erotic poetry and mime, first mentioned in Greek myth as the Oak-queen married to Arcas, who gave his name to Arcadia.[11]

The most mysterious, prolific, and adaptable artistic expressions of the archetype are found sculpted in stone and carved in wood. These remarkably various pieces have been known as Green Men only since 1939, when so christened by the folklorist Lady Raglan, whose discovery of faces peering through gaps in the foliage of carvings on the roof bosses in the Lady Chapel of Ely Cathedral suggested to her a resemblance to the Jack-in-the-Green. They were previously known by such designations as "the foliate head" or "a grotesque" and in French as *la tête de feuilles, le feuillu, le masque feuillu, or le masque herbu*.[12] Though obviously pagan in origin and traceable at least as far back as Roman art, the foliate head was absorbed into the symbolism of the Church as early as the fourth or fifth century, writes Kathleen Basford, and it became a remarkably adaptable motif in Romanesque, Gothic, Renaissance, and even later architecture. She notes further that it is "probably the most common decorative motif of medieval sculpture that has been left to us," at least partly because "it could be manipulated to fit any space or position where ornament was required."[13] The carvings and sculptures can be found nearly everywhere in medieval churches: I have seen them or pictures of them on roof bosses, capitals, corbels, tympana, roundels, fonts, tombs, rood screens, bench ends, poppyheads, armrests, and misericords.

Representatives of the foliate head in the churches of England have been located in at least twenty-three counties, according to Raglan, and in many of these churches it is found to be "the sole decoration" (45, 47). Devon—neighbor to Dorset (where Fowles has lived, in Lyme Regis, for almost three decades) and the county, later celebrated in *Daniel Martin*, in which Fowles spent the idyllic years of his adolescence—turns out to be, according to Basford, "one of the best of all the English counties for studying variations on the Green Man theme."[14] There are at least seventeen Green Men in Exeter Cathedral alone, she observes, "but it is in the country churches that some of the strangest mutants appear" (19). It is surely more than coincidence that evidence of ancient Celtic tree worship has been unearthed in Devon, especially near the village of Bow where remains of a Bronze Age wood-henge, or tree temple, have been discovered. Many of the village names bear the forms Nymet, Nymph, or Nympton, thought by Anderson to derive from the Celtic *nemeton*, meaning sacred place or grove (53).

For so ubiquitous a motif, it is very surprising how little the leaf man has been studied and how little seems to be known about it. Basford notes that there are basically two types of foliate heads: one in which the human and leafy elements are fused into an organic unity (like the leaf masks of antiquity, which are supposed to be its derivation); the other in which the human and vegetative elements remain distinct (15). The face in the leaves, the fused organic unity, seems to suggest the intimacy of humanity and the green world and also at times a mysterious spirit or intelligence underlying the leafy forms. It suggests to Anderson the theme of metamorphosis, and so he connects the imagery with Greek and Roman mythology (44). A great many of these motifs depict the Green Man as disgorger (some say also devourer) of Nature, with vegetation coming variously from his mouth, lips, ears, eyes, nose, forehead, and cheeks. Some depict him as the fruit or flower of vegetation, images that Anderson sees implicating humanity in the mystery of the creative process and the natural cycle of death and rebirth (33, 45).

The celebration of the green world and the deep connection of the human imagination with wild Nature have been central preoccupations of the Fowles corpus from the beginning of his publishing career. The very early essay entitled "On Being English but Not British" contains Fowles's first-published lament, in 1964, on the steady disappearance of modern England's trees and forests—a lament that recurs in his writing, fiction and nonfiction alike.[15] There are two branches of the theme: the conservationist, ecological approach to Nature and the imaginative, metaphorical, archetypal use of the green world. It

Green Man on Bench End, Somerset (1534). This carving in the Holy Ghost Church in Crowcombe shows a Green Man with what seem to be wild mermen coming from his ears and vegetation from his mouth. Photograph by Barry Olshen, 1996.

Green Man on Respond, Wiltshire (early fourteenth century). This carving is in All Saints' Church, Sutton Benger, in the western respond. The Green Man has hawthorn leaves and berries, with birds, growing from his mouth. Photograph by Barry Olshen, 1996.

is the second branch that provides the ideas and images I discuss in the rest of this paper, and it is in this domain that the Green Man hides. This metaphorical green world refers to both external wild Nature and the human interiorization and experience of Nature. Fowles's analogy between external and internal natures is allegorized in the myth and folklore of the Green Man in the trees.

Fowles tends to conflate his Green Man with another figure, the Wild Man, a figure who traditionally inhabits the domain of the Green Man and shares in his wildness, but who has usually been kept quite distinct from him. Unlike the evolution of the Wild Man in our century, in which he has been relegated almost exclusively to a psychological category, Fowles manages to mythologize his Green Man and thus to bridge the modern divide between the natural landscape and the topography of the mind. Hayden White traces the conceptualization of wildness as the repressed content of humanity in the movement of his Wild Man from "out there" to within each of us.[16] He was first conceived of as the representative of an early state of humanity; then as a being unable to participate in any human society, primitive or advanced; and finally as the force within us clamoring for release, a projection of repressed desire and experience, a savage (noble or otherwise), a lost (or inner) child, an iron man, the shadow, the other, the Freudian id, and so on. Fowles's Green (and Wild) Man may be less threatening than some of these, but it still shares with all of them the essential quality of being beyond civilization, indifferent to its advantages, untouched but also undamaged by its institutions.

"What we have done," Fowles asserts in "On Being English but Not British," "is to transfer the England of the trees to our minds. Our life routines, our faces, our social codes and conventions—almost all that is outward in us is hostage now to the eternal enemy, the Sheriff of Nottingham (the power that is); but still our minds look to the forest and keep us . . . at our most English, Just Outlaws" (158). The central English myth of Robin Hood, Fowles claims, epitomizes the English predisposition for seclusion, the pattern of behavior in which the true self is revealed only in private, in the "Greenwood," as it were, and allowed to emerge in broad daylight (under the scrutiny of the Sheriff of Nottingham) only in disguise. "Deep, deep in those trees of the mind the mysteries still take place; the green men dance, hunt and run" (160).

These first references, designed to characterize the split English mentality, contain all the rudiments of the later development of the figure of the Green Man in Fowles's works, especially in the three upon which I focus in this essay: his autobiographical essay *The Tree* and the two fictional works *Daniel Martin* and "The Ebony Tower."[17]

The dichotomies of private and public, sacred and social, intuitive and conventional, spontaneous and practiced, unconscious and conscious, unknowable and known—dichotomies that resonate throughout his fictional corpus as well as *The Tree*—are already present in this early essay. So, too, is the idea of the kinship of wild Nature and human nature, their creative mutuality, and, equally important, their mutual antipathy to society and the powers that be. The idea that the real, the truly significant, is private and hidden has very important consequences for Fowles the man and the novelist. Neither can be understood without it. The conception of the artist who both lives and uncovers the private life, who hints at the psychic and mythic depths, is thus especially privileged in his thinking. As Fowles notes in *The Tree*, places that "hide and isolate"—the woods and the sea, which are "sensorially far too various and immense for anything but surfaces or glimpses to be captured"—are the places of preference in his life and his work (59–60).

In *The Tree*, the Green Man becomes what Fowles calls an "emblem of the close connection" between the nature of Nature and the nature of human consciousness (38). "There is something in the nature of nature, in its presentness, its seeming transcience, its creative ferment and hidden potential, that corresponds very closely with the wild, or green man, in our psyches; it is a something that disappears as soon as it is relegated to . . . a status of merely classifiable *thing*" (51). And again: "As long as nature is seen as in some way outside us, frontiered and foreign, *separate*, it is lost to us and in us. The two natures, private and public, human and non-human, cannot be divorced" (78). The Green Man is resident both without and within, in the "inalienable otherness" of wild Nature and in the slippery, unknowable otherness inside every individual consciousness. He is both ubiquitous and mysteriously elusive—and he must remain so. He is described in *The Tree* as the source of creativity and self-expression, of self-discovery and being in the world, and so he must be respected for what he is and protected, within and without, from those who would seek to tame or explain or destroy him.

Those people are legion, according to Fowles. The "'green' or creating process" of both worlds "is largely private and beyond lucid description and rational analysis" (48). The scientist, the academic, and the professional critic, according to Fowles, wish to articulate the creative process; they wish to make what is unconscious or partly conscious fully conscious, to disclose what is most private and undisclosable, to use the sacred places for profane ends. They would, in his words, "defoliate the wicked green man, hunt him out of his trees" (47), chase him from his "interiority and constant nowness, the green chaos of . . . experience" (49). We—or at least some of us—are cast, so to speak, as the Sheriff of Nottingham's men.

Fowles's argument more generally is directed against the imposition on wild Nature of any utilitarian, ideological, or narcissistic purpose whatsoever. Accordingly, he asserts, we can never fully contact or understand Nature, nor can we ever properly respect it, until we "dissociate the wild from the notion of usability—however innocent and harmless the use" (40). Our culture seems addicted to purpose, "both to looking for purpose in everything external to us and to looking internally for purpose in everything we do—to seek explanation of the outside world by purpose, to justify our seeking by purpose" (52–53). Nature's "only purpose," however, "appears to be being and surviving" (53). This last thought, that Nature's only purpose is to continue being, is connected to the theory of evolution, which is most fully explored in *The French Lieutenant's Woman*.[18] Even what Fowles calls Nature's "only purpose," however, is still attributed to her by us. Nature, after all, remains silent.

Although the ideas and images accruing to the Green Man maintain affinities with aspects of both Freudian and Jungian psychology, the most pointed and revealing parallels, to my mind, are with the metaphors and the mind-set of Fowles's fellow Englishman D. W. Winnicott, pediatrician and psychoanalyst for half a century before his death in 1971. Whereas Freud took us back to the triangular family relationships of the child incorporated in the so-called Oedipus complex, and Melanie Klein provided a glimpse into the pre-Oedipal mother-child relationship, and Jacques Lacan imagined for us the preverbal six-month-old infant (but, alas, left the little fellow alone in front of his mirror far too long); it fell to Winnicott to transport us empathically all the way back to the days and weeks following birth, to the earliest feeding experiences within the infant-mother dyad. Here we get to the core issues of human relations (at least from a psychoanalytic perspective), to the heart of Winnicott's contribution to psychoanalytic thought, and to some of the mysteries of human life, which Winnicott's theories always manage to consider and which make him so valuable a resource for a discussion like this.[19]

Both Winnicott and Fowles take experiential and process-oriented approaches to their subjects. Both eschew broad theoretical structures and the naming, systematizing, generalizing, and categorizing of the modern scientific method. What Fowles in *The Tree* calls a "wander through the trees" (48)—a metaphor for his life writing and for his way of being in Nature—finds its most illuminating psychological correspondence in what Winnicott in *Playing and Reality* calls "playing." Both insist that the creative process springs from the necessarily private, undisclosable experience of apparently aimless but nonetheless profoundly significant "wandering." Creativity for Winnicott *is* "play" and the playing of a child the very model for human creativity—and for vital spontaneous living more generally. As with Fowles's experience of wild Nature, it is of the utmost importance for Winnicott's playing that it remain entirely nonutilitarian, without conscious goal or direction, without conscious use or purpose beyond itself.

The Robin Hood myth and Fowles's notion of the hidden and undisclosable creative process find their truest psychological correspondence in Winnicott's famous theory of the True and False Self.[20] Very briefly, the False Self is an elaborate structure of defense linked in Winnicott's theory to compliance and submission, as the True Self is to freedom, spontaneity, and play. Human personality can range from a very low to a very high degree of False Self defense, ranging, that is, from relatively healthy, polite, mannered social attitudes to a genuinely split-off, or psychotic, compliant False Self that is usually mistaken for the whole child in early development or the real person in adulthood. The Green Man (and the Wild Man), like the True Self, must remain well hidden to remain themselves; the green process must remain the cherished, private process that it is and always has been. In its less severe manifestations, when it does not usurp the personality, the False Self may be seen to have the positive and healthy protective function of allowing the True Self its secret growth and social adaptations. So Winnicott's theory can provide another fruitful perspective on the complexities of the English mentality captured in the myth of Robin Hood.

The repeated connections in *The Tree* between the green worlds of the imagination and the forest give rise to subordinate analogies between the act of creative writing and the isolated exploration of wild Nature and between prose fiction and trees (75). A "retreat from the normal world ... is inherent in any act of artistic creation, let alone that specific kind of writing that deals in imaginary situations and characters. And a part of that retreat must always be into a 'wild,' or ordinarily repressed and socially hidden, self: into a place always a complexity beyond daily reality, never fully comprehensible or explicable, always more potential than realized; yet where no one will ever penetrate as far as we have. It is our passage, our mystery alone ..." (75–76). Fowles's writerly self image in *The Tree*, in fact, turns out to be a metamorphosed Green Man writing his "endless combe in leaves of paper" (57) and his idea of the artist a "'green man' hidden in the leaves of his or her unique and once-only being" (43).

This complex of images, which helps to create the rich and layered textures of *The Tree*, also contributes in a host of ways to the meaning and effect of Fowles's novels—especially, I think, to *The Magus*, *The French Lieutenant's Woman*, *Daniel Martin*, *A Maggot*, and "The Ebony Tower," in which, to my mind, the Green Man imagery is most evident and affecting.[21] In these works Fowles has devoted a great deal of creative energy to the evocation of wilderness, isolated green landscapes, and sacred spaces. There is more than enough material here for a book-length study, much too much even to contemplate in this essay. Just think, for example, of the importance of the wilderness setting of Seidevarre for Conchis's epiphany, or the evocation of the sea, mountains, and pine forests in *The Magus*; the importance of the Undercliff and the space devoted to its description and to green imagery in *The French Lieutenant's Woman*; Thorncombe, Tsankawi, Tarquinia, Palmyra, and Kitchener's Island in *Daniel Martin*; the Forest of Paimpont and the Manoir of Coëtminais in "The Ebony Tower"; and the Exmoor of *A Maggot*. These are the settings that evoke the majesty, mystery, and power of Nature; that provoke epiphany and whole vision in his characters and readers; that challenge conventional notions of language and time and enable profound transformations of feeling and perception.

If I were writing that book I suggested, I would begin by establishing the parallels between the quest of the autobiographical "I" of *The Tree* and the quests of the fictional characters, and between the function of the meditation on Wistman's Wood that concludes *The Tree* and the roles of wilderness and wildness in the novels.[22] I am not writing that book, however, and must return to what remains of the much shorter work at hand, specifically to a brief account of parts of *Daniel Martin* and "The Ebony Tower," Fowles's two narratives in which the Green Man themes and images seem to me most prominent.

Daniel Martin was published two years before *The Tree* and, as the second epigraph to this paper suggests, shares many of the same preoccupations. It also revisits the material on Englishness and Nature found in "On Being English but Not British." *Daniel Martin* is an autobiographical novel in both life pattern and detail. It returns again and again to the spirit of the "green" world, to *la bonne vaux* or "the sacred combe," and to the power, beauty, and therapeutic value of both wild and bucolic settings. The metaphors of fiction as forest and the novelist in retreat help to shape its principal ideas concerning the novel and novel writing; allusions to Robin Hood hiding in the trees of the Greenwood elucidate the previously discussed English mentality. Dan's retreat to Thorncombe in the novel is analogous to the metaphorical retreat of the writer into the green world of his imagination. It is there that Dan decides finally to abandon the craft of the screenwriter for the art of the novelist, Hollywood for the sacred space.

The short chapter entitled "The Sacred Combe" contributes most to the Robin Hood myth, here the "archetypal national myth—perhaps the only one, outside the Christ story—that literally every English person carries in his mind all through his life" (287–88). Like Fowles himself and like the author-narrator of *The French Lieutenant's Woman*, Dan has the "desire to create imaginary worlds other than the world that is the case," and this desire is linked with "the notion of retreat, in both the religious and the military sense; of the secret place that is also a redoubt." It is because of this, Dan says, that the Robin Hood myth becomes more than folk aspiration; it "enshrin[es] a dominant mental characteristic, an essential behavior, an archetypal *movement* . . . of the English imagination" (288–89).

Even a brief study of "The Ebony Tower" should suffice to indicate how thoroughly infused it is with Fowles's green images and ideas. The thematic focus of this novella is not on nature but art, and on the great but aged artist, Henry Breasley. He maintains an old-fashioned, rearguard, but nonetheless vital and admirable stand against the trend towards abstraction in twentieth-century art and all that that trend is made to entail: the turning away from nature and the physical world on the one hand; and the fear of the body, desire, and appetite on the other. Breasley is currently at work on what is likely to be his great final project, a series of large canvases characterized as "mysterious," "archetypal," "Celtic," "with the recurrence of the forest motif" (12). Breasley is the artist who has devoted himself uncompromisingly to his art, the rugged individualist who has always managed to go his own way, the thoroughly English eccentric now living abroad in near-total seclusion, in his "uncontemporary," "timeless," "mythic," "Celtic," "green" world. He is, to my mind, Fowles's clearest fictional embodiment of the archetypal Green Man. His portrayal is also in perfect consonance with the principal ideas of Winnicott discussed above.

Breasley is initially introduced and repeatedly referred to as "the old man" (4). His other epithets include "old devil" (4), "old demon" (40), "wicked old faun" (6), "great man" (10), "frightful old bastard" (10), and "wild old outlaw"(81). The reiteration of "old" in connection with his figure refers of course to his age, but also to his agelessness. He is old and *of old*. "Naïve as a child in some ways" (10), Breasley still retains "an umbilical cord to the past . . . . That [is] the real kernel of his wildness. . . . the old green freedom" (110).

The setting of "The Ebony Tower" is the Forest of Paimpont, "one of the last large remnants of the old wooded Brittany" (3). This sheltered Celtic space provides the perfect nourishment for the green and "pagan" (59) imagination that gives rise to Breasley's mythic art:

"Perhaps it constituted the old man's real stroke of genius, to take an old need to escape from the city, for a mysterious remoteness, and to see its ancient solution, the Celtic green source, was still viable; fortunate old man, to stay both percipient and profoundly amoral" (74).

Situated within a "clearing among the sea of huge oaks and beeches" is the Manoir de Coëtminais—*coët* meaning "wood or forest," *minais* meaning "of the monks" (39). The narrator tells us, however, that Henry "did not really live at the *manoir*, but in the forest outside" (80). Henry calls it "my forest" (51), and the narrator acknowledges it as "his" (54). Henry identifies and is identified with it: both the man and the wood have their "antique mysteries" (56); both are wild, savage, ancient, out of place in the contemporary world; both are under attack and need, for their vitality, even for their very existence, to remain remote from their enemies at large.

The final pages of "The Ebony Tower" shift their focus from the old man to his foil, David Williams, who has entered Henry's domain to interview him. David is everything that Henry is not. He is an abstract artist and an art critic, a family man half Henry's age. He is associated with the qualities of the enemy discussed above in connection with *The Tree*: "encapsulated in book knowledge, art as social institution, science, subject, matter for grants and committee discussion" (110); "crippled by common sense, he had no ultimate belief in chance and its exploitation" (112). He is made to represent the new generation that is on the verge of losing contact with the green world. His short encounter with the Green Man is shattering because, at least for the moment, he sees clearly and unmistakably what he has missed. He "and his generation, and all those to come, could only look back, through bars, like caged animals, born in captivity, at the old green freedom. That described exactly the experience of those last two days: the laboratory monkey allowed a glimpse of his lost true self" (110).

Just before this narrative shift, however, Fowles provides a final paragraph on Breasley, epitomizing much of the Green Man imagery and sentiment discussed above. The passage is quoted here in full so that the extent of the Green Man connection will be evident and the echoes from the earliest nonfiction may be heard:

> What [David] would finally remember about the old man was his wildness, in the natural history sense. The surface wildness, in language and behavior, was ultimately misleading—like the aggressive display of some animals, its deeper motive was really peace and space, territory, not a gratuitous show of virility. The grotesque faces the old fellow displayed

were simply to allow his real self to run free. He did not really live at the *manoir,* but in the forest outside. All his life he must have had this craving for a place to hide; a profound shyness, a timidity; and forced himself to behave in an exactly contrary fashion. It would have driven him out of England in the beginning; but once in France he would have used his Englishness—for it was remarkable, when one thought, how much of a native persona he had retained through his long exile—to hide from whatever in French culture threatened to encroach. The fundamental Englishness of the Coëtminais series was already argued in a paragraph of the draft introduction [of David's book], but David made a mental resolution to expand and strengthen it. It began to seem almost the essential clue; the wild old outlaw, hiding behind the flamboyant screen of his outrageous behavior and his cosmopolitan influences, was perhaps as simply and inalienably native as Robin Hood. (80–81)

Notes

1. Gerard Manley Hopkins, "Inversnaid," in *Gerard Manley Hopkins,* ed. Catherine Phillips (Oxford: Oxford University Press, 1986), page 153, lines 13–16; John Fowles, *Daniel Martin* (Boston: Little, Brown, 1977), page 381.

2. Peter Bishop, *The Greening of Psychology: The Vegetable World in Myth, Dream, and Healing* (Dallas, Texas: Spring, 1990), page 1.

3. William Anderson, *Green Man: The Archetype of Our Oneness with the Earth* (London: HarperCollins, 1990), page 164.

4. Roy Judge, *The Jack-in-the-Green: A May Day Custom* (Totowa, N.J.: Rowman and Littlefield, 1978).

5. James George Frazer, *The New Golden Bough,* ed. Theodor H. Gaster (1890; reprint New York: New American Library, 1959), pages 120–24.

6. That at least some of the Green Man signs are representations of the gamekeeper, especially in late eighteenth-and early nineteenth-century England, there is convincing evidence in the following lines from "Letter XI" of George Crabbe's *The Borough* (1810):

> But the Green Man shall I pass by unsung,
> Which mine own James upon his sign-post hung?
> His sign, his image, for he once was seen,
> A squire's attendant, clad in keeper's green.
>   (*The Poetical Works of George Crabbe,* ed. A. J. Carlyle and R. M.
>   Carlyle [London: Oxford University Press, 1914], page 155)

On the other hand, there is Lady Raglan's speculation that the signs derive from an earlier time, when the May Day Procession led by the Green Man (the Jack-in-the-Green, that is) used to stop to allow dancers to perform before every inn on the route (Lady Raglan, "The 'Green Man' in Church Architecture," *Folklore* 50 (1939), page 53). She also asserts that, in England and Scotland, at least in the fifteenth and sixteenth centuries, "the most popular name for this figure [the Jack] . . . was Robin Hood. There are reasons for thinking that Robin Hood is really Robin of the Wood. Skeat suggests that 'wood' originally meant a twig, and then a mass of twigs or bush, so that Robin Hood would be Robin of the twigs or bush, and this would very well describe the headdress worn by the Green Man to this day" (50). Graves traces "Hood" (or "Hod" or "Hud") to "log": "the log put at the back of the fire—and it was in this log, cut from the sacred oak, that Robin had once been believed to reside" (Robert Graves, *The White Goddess: A Historical Grammar of Poetic Myth*, 2d ed. [New York: Farrar, Straus and Giroux, 1966], page 397).

The issue is a thorny one. When dealing with these and other similar speculations, I think it best to keep in mind Withington's early opinion that "the relation between wild-men, green-men, foresters, [and] Robin Hood . . . is very difficult to clear up. A great many cross-influences must exist; and it seems obvious that all these figures are connected" (Robert Withington, *English Pageantry: An Historical Outline*, 2 vols. [1918; reprint New York: Blom, 1963], vol. 1, page 74). Judge is also circumspect in his more recent monograph, where his history of the Jack concludes as follows: "Certainly [the framework of *The Golden Bough*] has given the Jack-in-the-Green a range of interesting and romantic associations which its English historical setting could hardly justify. One may conclude quite simply, that this name and this leafy structure appeared together at the end of the eighteenth century in a context of May Day begging. They make adequate sense within that context and there is no evidence for any earlier history or other interpretation" (76–77). Concerning the mythic, legendary, and historical character of Robin Hood, the following are of particular value: R.B. Dobson and J. Taylor, *Rymes of Robin Hood: An Introduction to the English Outlaw* (London: Heinemann, 1976), pages 1–64; Maurice Keen, *The Outlaws of Medieval Legend*, 2d ed. (London: Routledge, 1977), chaps. 8–14; and Stephen Knight, *Robin Hood: A Complete Study of the English Outlaw* (Oxford: Basil Blackwell, 1994), appendix 1.

7. The estimate about London is from Anderson, page 20; the comment about East Anglia is from Lady Raglan, "The 'Green Man' in Church Architecture," *Folklore* 50 (1939), page 53; Kingsley Amis, *The Green Man* (London: Jonathan Cape, 1960); Susan Cooper, *Greenwitch* (New York: Collier / Macmillan, 1974).

8. John Speirs, "Sir Gawain and the Green Knight," *Scrutiny* 16 (1949), pages 274–300.

9. W. H. Hudson, *Green Mansions: A Romance of the Tropical Forest* (1916; reprint New York: Random House, 1944); J. R. R. Tolkien, *The Lord of the Rings* (1954; reprint Toronto: Methuen, 1971); Henry Treece, *The Green Man* (New York: G. P. Putnam's Sons, 1966).

10. John Fowles, *Mantissa* (Boston: Little, Brown, 1982).

11. Robert Graves, *The White Goddess: A Historical Grammar of Poetic Myth*, 2d ed. (New York: Farrar, Straus and Giroux, 1966), page 391.

12. Raglan, page 45; Kathleen Basford, *The Green Man* (Ipswich: Brewer, 1978), page 15; Anderson, page 20.

13. Basford, pages 18, 7.

14. As part of the evacuation of civilians from the London area, the Fowles family moved to Ipplepen, Devon, in June 1940, when John was fourteen years old, according to James R. Aubrey, *John Fowles: A Reference Companion* (Westport, Conn.: Greenwood Press, 1991), pages 8–11; Fowles's adolescent experience of nature was later epitomized in *Daniel Martin* as "the whole buried continent that nature had been for me in my adolescence" (Boston: Little, Brown, 1977), page 68.

15. John Fowles, "On Being English but Not British," *Texas Quarterly* 7 (Autumn 1964), pages 154–62.

16. Hayden White, "The Forms of Wildness: Archaeology of an Idea," in *The Wild Man Within: An Image in Western Thought from the Renaissance to Romanticism*, ed.

Edward Dudley and Maximillian E. Novak (Pittsburgh: University of Pittsburgh Press, 1972), pages 3–38.

17. John Fowles, *The Tree* (New York: Ecco Press, 1983); "The Ebony Tower," in *The Ebony Tower* (Boston: Little, Brown, 1974).

18. John Fowles, *The French Lieutenant's Woman* (New York: Little, Brown, 1969).

19. D. W. Winnicott, *The Maturational Processes and the Facilitating Environment: Studies in the Theory of Emotional Development* (Madison, Wisc.: International University Press, 1965); *Playing and Reality* (London: Tavistock / Routledge, 1971).

20. See especially *Maturational Processes*, chapters 3 and 12; *Playing and Reality*, chapters 4 and 9.

21. John Fowles, *A Maggot* (Boston: Little, Brown, 1985). Incidentally, the hanged servant with the violets in his mouth in *A Maggot* "was a deliberate Green Man image," Fowles acknowledged at the Lyme Regis Symposium on the Writings of John Fowles, 11 July 1996. To me it combines images of both Green Man and Hanged Man, a combination suggested also by several of the more grotesque foliate heads with open mouths and protruding tongues. For a different interpretation of the hanged servant image, see James R. Aubrey, "Uncrucifying the Self; John Fowles and the Motif of the Hanged Man," *Journal of Evolutionary Psychology* 13–14 (August 1992 and March 1993), part 2, page 112.

22. See Jamie Dopp and Barry N. Olshen, "Fathers and Sons: Fowles's *The Tree* and Autobiographical Theory," *Mosaic* 22 (Fall 1989), pages 31–44.

The Corpse in the Combe: The Vision of the Dead Woman in the Landscape of John Fowles

Eileen Warburton

In an early scene in *The French Lieutenant's Woman*, Charles Smithson, protagonist of the novel, explores the landscape of the Undercliff looking for fossils, specifically for sea urchin "tests."[1] He is the embodiment of Victorian order, "overdressed and overequipped" in all the recommended, "methodical" equipment of his science: "stout nailed boots and canvas gaiters . . . Norfolk breeches of heavy flannel . . . long coat . . . hat . . . massive ashplant . . . voluminous rucksack . . . hammers, wrappings, notebooks, pillboxes, adzes and heaven knows what else" (46–47). Looking at the blue lias rock, "he saw in the strata an immensely reassuring orderliness in existence," although the narrator tells *us* to observe that this same stone is "treacherous, since its strata are brittle and have a tendency to slide" (45, 49). Charles's life is also "stratified," and his expectations of its future also have, to his way of thinking, "an immensely reassuring orderliness." In fact, his superficial analysis of the landscape he is exploring and his comprehension of the perceived surface of his own life are virtually identical. In all ways, Charles is betrothed to what he believes is a safe, knowable future—to financial and domestic security with Ernestina, to intellectual respect as a scientist, to social position and well-defined traditional values as a baronet. Charles finds his fossils, then is surprised to discover that he is behind schedule and that the tide has cut off the easy shore path. He takes another path and comes across Sarah Woodruff, asleep on the cliff's edge. That moment, of course, is the beginning of Charles's "slide" into uncharted territory.

Startlingly, when Charles stumbles across the sleeping Sarah, his first reaction is to believe that he has stumbled upon a corpse. His second perception is to realize, with relief, that she is not dead, merely asleep. At that moment, when he recognizes that she is alive, Sarah wakes and they look into one another's eyes. In this moment of shared vision, says the narrator, "the whole Victorian age was lost" (72).

This narrative motif—the male protagonist who sees, or expects to see, or is afraid he will see a dead woman—is repeated several times in *The French Lieutenant's Woman*. Over and over again, seemingly without cause, Charles expects to see Sarah as a dead woman and then is astonished to find that she is alive. The pattern is repeated in Fowles's other fiction as well—so often that we may generalize and say that the trouble with the protagonist in a Fowles novel is that he has a vision of a dead woman. She is loved and longed for, we will find, because she is the door through which is recovered a pre-lapsarian landscape consistently associated with a time of personal optimism and imaginative possibility.

Let us look at this scene once more: Charles has been wandering in the Undercliff, "an English Garden of Eden"(67). Ostensibly, serious amateur scientist that he is, he is collecting fossils. However, what he is really experiencing is a division between his sensuous and immediate emotional perceptions and his cultural-intellectual rational expectations. "At least he tried to look seriously around him," the narrator qualifies, "but the little slope on which he found himself, the prospect before him, the sounds, the scents, the unalloyed wildness of growth and burgeoning fertility, forced him into anti-science"(68). Charles is caught between a world the narrator calls "the Renaissance," which represents "an end to chains, bounds, frontiers," where "what is, is good," and his own, more confining Victorian world, where "he was too pampered, too spoiled by civilization ever to inhabit nature again." Charles has an "obscure feeling of malaise, of inappropriateness, of limitation." He remembers "his duty to Ernestina" (68–69). In this weary moment of resigned acceptance, this static expectation that the world is too much with us and too knowable, Charles takes an unexpected fork in the path. "And there, below him, he saw a figure. For one terrible moment he thought he had stumbled on a corpse. But it was a woman asleep" (70). In the midst of an Edenic landscape, in which Charles feels himself an intruder, he finds a "corpse," a compelling woman who wakes to his gaze and, sharing her vision with him, will allow him access to the lost landscape.

In another dramatic example, later in the novel, Charles goes to his rendezvous with Sarah at Carslake's Barn. We are again presented with a sensibility divided. Charles's great expectations have just been dashed by his uncle's upcoming marriage, which has effectively disinherited him. Only the night before, he had confessed: "'Oh my dear Grogan, if you knew the mess my life was in . . . the waste of it . . . the uselessness of it. I have no moral purpose, no real sense of duty to anything. It seems only a few months ago that I was twenty-one— full of hopes . . . all disappointed. And now to get entangled in this miserable business . . . '" (225, ellipses in original). Rationally, Charles perceives his life as mutilated, as past resuscitation, and the emotional landscape he projects is one of desolation. He sets out the following morning to keep his appointment with Sarah in "a dangerous despair." Charles marches grimly out of town, thinking that "he would rather have seen a few symbolic corpses littering the street than those bright faces" [of early risers]; marches with expectations trimmed to match those of Dr. Grogan, the vicar, and the other residents of Lyme who search the cliffs and countryside for a suicidal madwoman (238–39).

Charles's way takes him through the Undercliff as dawn is breaking, and he finds himself trespassing in a sensuous natural landscape of primeval intensity: "It seemed strangely distinct, this undefiled dawn sun. It had almost a smell, as of warm stone, a sharp dust of photons streaming down through space. Each grass-blade was pearled with vapor. On the slopes above his path the trunks of the ashes and sycamores, a honey gold in the oblique sunlight, erected their dewy green vaults of young leaves; there was something mysteriously religious about them, but of a religion before religion; a druid balm, a green sweetness over all . . . and such an infinity of greens, some almost black in the further recesses of the foliage; from the most intense emerald to the palest pomona. A fox crossed his path and strangely for a moment stared, as if Charles was the intruder" (239, ellipsis in original).

Charles *is* the intruder, of course, but he experiences a moment of epiphany. Confronted by this vision of "Eden," Charles is likened to Antonio Pisanello's Saint Hubert, shaken with astonishment by the appearance of a stag with a crucifix in its antlers. Charles, however, is astonished by the song of a wren who "trills its violent song . . . a midget ball of feathers that yet managed to make itself the Announcing Angel of evolution," of "a perfect world . . . in which each was appointed, each unique" (239–40). But Charles, in despair and in the expectation of a failed future, is "bitter," "lost," "shut out," "excommunicated." He extends these perceptions of the world and of his own life to his understanding of Sarah, believing her desperate enough to seek the end of her life, rather than a new beginning.

Metaphorically, and with a small, deft touch of comic melodrama, as Charles arrives at Carslake's Barn, the narrator expresses Charles's vision as the anticipation of a corpse: "Perhaps because of his reading the previous night he had an icy premonition that some ghastly sight lay below the partition of worm-eaten planks beyond the bonnet, which hung like an ominously slaked vampire over what he could not yet see. I do not know what he expected: some atrocious mutilation,

Vision of St. Eustace (?) [or St. Hubert], by Antonio Pisanello (1436). In *The French Lieutenant's Woman* Fowles describes this painting of the conversion of St. Hubert while hunting in the woods, where he encounters a stag with a crucifix in its antlers. "The saint is shocked, almost as if the victim of a practical joke, all his arrogance dowsed by a sudden drench of Nature's profoundest secret: the universal parity of existence" (page 239). Photograph courtesy of the National Gallery, London.

a corpse . . . he nearly turned and ran out of the barn and back to Lyme. But the ghost of a sound drew him forward. He craned fearfully over the partition" (242, ellipsis in original). Instead of the expected corpse, however, Charles again sees a peacefully sleeping woman who arouses in him a confused flood of tenderness and desire. Waking, she conveys a shocking "wildness of innocence, almost an eagerness" (247–48). "There was a wildness about her," the narrator observes, "that same wildness Charles had sensed in the wren's singing " (247), which announces, "I am what I am, thou shalt not pass my being now" (240). Sarah is thus linked with the radiant immediacy of the natural world, magically described during Charles's dawn walk. Sarah's look (which sees him "whole") not only belies all Charles's gloomy sense of the ending of the possibilities of his life, but also electrifies him with erotic desire (258). Within minutes of expecting to see a corpse, he is passionately kissing the living woman.

Charles's repeated expectation that he will see a dead woman, and his surprise and arousal at finding a living woman, corresponds to his dualistic vision of himself and the world at large. When Charles expects to see a dead woman, the motif consistently connotes a mode of perception that expects to see the world inside and outside himself as definable, static, knowable, predictable, measurable—indeed, metaphorically "dead." Charles resignedly accepts this perception, though sad or even in despair over it. In both of these cases, furthermore, he is surrounded by a landscape universe of "unalloyed wildness of growth and burgeoning fertility," "an exquisitely particular universe, in which each was appointed, each unique," yet he might as well be blind to it for he feels himself "an intruder," "a victim," where this wild universe is actively "hostile" to him. When the dead woman rises, alive, out of this projected landscape of static expectation, Charles ceases to be the "outsider." For a brief moment, he is embraced, enfolded, and sees clearly and "whole."[2]

Space limitations do not permit me to consider all the variations on this motif that incite the action in so many of Fowles's narratives, including displaced variations, such as those in the stories of *The Ebony Tower*.[3] I must consider, however, the motif variation that shapes Fowles's first published novel, *The Collector*. The pathetic Clegg with his narrow, soured soul is the man whose mode of perception, his vision, leads to the death of a young woman, the vital Miranda. Imprisoning her in his cellar, Clegg metaphorically buries her alive, just as he literally buries her corpse after his selfish behavior has caused her death.[4] All of Clegg's selfishness and possessiveness, his impotent mechanized mode of vision, his substitution of money for relationship, his need to "fix" reality (as he affixes his butterflies), his determination to name, finalize, and dehumanize—all are contained in this powerful metaphor. Although this novel might seem to contradict my argument that the dead woman is reborn in Fowles's narratives, Fowles has confessed to having "had the very greatest difficulty in killing off my own heroine" in *The Collector* and has accepted that Clegg's preparation for a new "guest" represents the writer's own need to resurrect the dead girl."[5]

In *The Magus*, the masque or "godgame" played out by Nicholas, the exasperating yet endearing protagonist, is also very much informed by this pattern of double vision. Nicholas, who like Charles Smithson, so needs to define, explain, analyze, categorize, and fix the events of his life and how the world works, is presented with a script in which he is twice given his heart's desire—a dead woman. Like Charles Smithson, Nicholas thinks that he has made a complete mess of his life: he is an orphan, an isolate, and virtually friendless. He is grudgingly aware of his massive selfishness in relationships with women and of how badly he has used the one semi-successful, intimate relationship of his life. He is a failed poet, he thinks he has syphilis, and he botches suicide. This is the static, miserable surface he projects, the emotional landscape of his life. It is future hopeless, "down and down and down," as he is surrounded by, but not part of, the magnificently perfect, seductive landscape of Greece.[6] "When that ultimate Mediterranean light fell on the world around me, I could see it was supremely beautiful, but when it touched me, I felt it was hostile. It seemed to corrode, not cleanse" (49). For Nicholas, although deep "in the heart of the divine landscape, . . . this unflawed natural world became intimidating. I seemed to have no place in it" (51, 56). Like Charles Smithson, Nicholas walks through a primeval, natural landscape—"the world before the machine, almost before man" (51)—but is an excommunicate from it. When spring arrived, "the earth was covered with anemones, orchids, asphodels, wild gladioli . . . birds everywhere, on migration. Undulating lines of storks croaked overhead, the sky was blue, pure, the boys sang, and even the sternest masters smiled. The world around me took wing, and I was stuck to the ground; a Catullus without talent forced to inhabit a land that was Lesbia without mercy. I had hideous nights . . ."(60). Then, as the masque begins, Conchis presents Nicholas with "Lily," a reincarnation of the ghost-girl in Conchis' own fictional life story, his beloved and idealized fiancée who died of typhoid in February 1916. When Lily comes to life, first as a "ghost" (168), then as an impersonator, then in all her polymorphic modes and personalities, Nicholas feels the projected surface of his expectations shatter. The wild, Greek landscape now receives him: "I enjoyed the cool air, the delicate pink sky that turned primrose, then blue, the still-sleeping grey and incorporeal sea, the long slopes of silent pines." As he walks, Nicholas has the "the strangest feeling . . . of having entered a myth . . . . As if the world had suddenly . . . been re-invented, and for me alone" (157). In a manner similar to Charles Smithson's experience, Nicholas projects a surface of what appear to be hopeless but rational explanations, which are then shattered and cast off by his vision of the emerging dead woman. When he is able to see her as a living woman, the mysterious landscape of the masque welcomes him, and there is the constant, growing feeling of hope for some better future.

At the halfway mark in *The Magus*, the role of the dead woman is transferred to Alison Kelly, Nicholas's working-class lover from the "real" world of England who has, he is made to believe, committed suicide in the aftermath of their aborted reconciliation in Athens. For the rest of the novel it is Alison who plays the role of the buried maiden—the abducted Kore of the Greek Eleusinian mysteries of Demeter, the Eurydice to Nicholas's seeking Orpheus, Arethusa, and so forth—all those roles so appropriate to the mystical religious initiations of the ancient world.[7] Alison, of course, is the living woman who will emerge from her "underground" by the end of the novel. Nicholas is a great seeker after the experience, but it is not easy to teach him to let go of his need to control the experience himself. Strictly from a realistic narrative perspective, what I have always found particularly disturbing about Alison's fictional death is how much Nicholas comes to rely on its terrible finality to give meaning to his world, to make events comprehensible. "Suddenly her honesty, her untreachery—her true death—was the last anchor left," he claims. "I strained back through time to seize Alison, to be absolutely sure of her. . . . And the tears that for a brief moment formed in my own eyes were a kind of bitter guarantee that she was indeed dead" (492–93).

Alison herself, of course, has accurately forecast this appalling attitude: "'If I killed myself, you'd be pleased,'" she accuses Nicholas in boozy hysteria. "'You'd be able to go round saying, she killed herself because of me. I think that would always keep me from suicide. Not letting some lousy shit like you get the credit'" (42).

Nicholas's acceptance of Alison's fabricated death brings up another parallel aspect of the experience of projected surface of expectations and the woman who wakes or emerges through it. His initial adjustment to Alison's death is figured in aesthetic terms. He edges the fact of her death "out of the moral world into the aesthetic, where it was easier to live with." It is a "sinister elision, this slipping from true remorse . . . to disguised self-forgiveness . . . so that . . . by this characteristically twentieth-century retreat from content into form, from meaning into appearance, from ethics into aesthetics . . . , I dulled the pain of that accusing death" (401–2).

Surely there is a relationship between these buried women and the ill-fated wife of the mason of Arta in "A Greek Legend." In this poem Fowles dramatizes both the artistic experience and the cost of creating a solid structure capable of spanning the gulf over fluid reality from here-where-we-are to there-where-we-need-to-go:

> That mason of Arta
> Who built a bridge
> And the bridge fell down;

> Who built it again
> And the bridge fell down;
> Again and again
> And the bridge fell down.
>
> Until he was told
> The price to pay
> To have it stand;
> So buried his wife
>
> Alive below, with
> His own hard hand.
>
> Amid the dust,
> I understand.[8]

To the maker—whether mason or novelist—there comes a point where the shifting possibilities and alternative choices must end. The story must be told, the presses must roll, the form must be fixed, the bridge must stand. Yet the moment of formal fixing—wherein the surface ceases to be fluid—is a death in which the beloved, textual "woman" is actually buried alive. "Most novelists feel a death as soon as a text is in print," Fowles once said. Another time he added, "As soon as a book leaves this room, this house, there's always a diminution."[9] For a novelist, the projected surface, not surprisingly, is as much a textual surface as a described landscape surface. The dead woman is a function of publishing, but the dead woman who lives is a phenomenon of the writing.

In his fiction, what Fowles has always celebrated is the astonishing refusal of this buried woman to stay dead. To the contrary, like Lily Montgomery in *The Magus*, she is polymorphic—shifting identities, names, roles, as easily as she changes her costume. She is erotic, rude, funny, cruel, independent, occasionally tender, empathic, completely unpredictable and alive, alive, alive. In *Mantissa*, years later in 1982, she will appear as Erato, a character in constant metamorphosis, in that deliciously odd book that Fowles has explained as "about the muse. She's a joker, That's the point of it—endlessly luring and denying."[10] Fowles's heroines, like the narrative surface of so much of his work, are forever breaking the rules. Sarah was, he has said, a "rebellious" character, going and doing what she pleased against Fowles's plans.[11] Jane Mallory in *Daniel Martin* was "troublesome"; "the role I had planned for her," Fowles once explained, "was very different. . . . Characters do grow with you and very often that will change stories."[12] These headstrong women characters act independently and with vitality to alter the aesthetic landscape of the shifting, fluid textual surface that the author is exploring through the writing of his narrative.

"What really interests me," Fowles once emphasized in an interview, "is what goes on inside myself when fiction is taking place."[13] He has always been interested more in the ongoing process rather than in the product. So psychological or academic theories offering some useful explanation of the interior process have occasionally caught his attention. In correspondence with American psychiatrist Gilbert Rose, in particular, Fowles tried to describe the actual process of novel writing and its irrational mysteries. It was Dr. Rose who wrote the now-famous 1972 Freudian analysis of *The French Lieutenant's Woman,* in which he described what he thought was the author's need to recapture the past and a unity with a lost original mother through novel writing. What Fowles argues in an important 1974 letter to the psychiatrist is that Rose fails to see that the fluid, changeable, multiple experience of the actual process of writing is far more important than the fixed, published book. The processus is alive, the book dead.[14]

> Almost all literary accounts of novel-writing omit, or grossly under-rate, the acute pleasure of the writing or 'pre-natal'* stage (*or pre-separation, with the published book equalling the awareness of separate identity *[handwritten in ink at the bottom of the page]*). I write far more than I publish simply because my being centres in the processus (increasingly, as I grow older) and its delights and has only a peripheral attachment to the born' (also dead') book. . . . Though I am sure you are right to trace the source of this back to an infant stage, it seems (at least to this conscious writer) less of a recessive—irredentist, as you put it—experience than a kind of sideways one. I think very much of novels in process as parallel and contemporaneous worlds . . . and even when story and narrative method require a "capturing" of the past, the dominant time sense is actually of a kind of futureness. This has perhaps to do with the impermanence of drafts, the knowing one will rarely get a passage right first time—or even the hundredth, alas—and the absolute need to believe in a future time when all will come good. I am trying to say that seeing one's book as a backward thing, a failure to capture an unconscious past, as a remote and now irremediable conspiracy of infantile biography, is a phenomenon of the finished, published book. The experiences of the fluid, incomplete stage are a great deal more mysterious, and I'm not convinced your account fully explains them. . . . Another very bizarre part of the writing (as opposed to the written) experience is the relationship between author and characters . . . the experience seems to me much more like hide-and-seek, and this again is a component of futureness: one knows, or hopes, one will finally track them down. I can't believe all these shadowy figures in

the dark house are fragments of the primal mother . . . Some more present "ghost" is needed? (letter to G. Rose, 1974)

Although Fowles was prepared to argue over the details with Rose, the theory of recovering an infant polymorphic world through memories of a primal mother did intrigue him. Given the repeated pattern in his novels of a dead and resurrected woman in an Edenic, primeval landscape, his fascination is not too surprising. Four years after their first correspondence, he was writing again to Gilbert Rose: "I suspect a lot more than one page in *Daniel Martin* is owed to that paper of yours," he says, "It has continued to echo very fruitfully in my mind"(letter to G. Rose, 1978).

Through the 1970s, Fowles referred to this theory in a number of interviews—for example, Tom Zito's for *The Washington Post*—but his most complete and self-revealing analysis appears in the essay "Hardy and the Hag," Fowles's own brilliant assessment of Thomas Hardy's *The Well-Beloved*, which appeared in 1977 in the collection *Thomas Hardy after Fifty Years*.[15] Here Fowles explains the process whereby the adult novelist reaches "back to an indulged primal self" by transmogrifying "that eternal other woman, the mother . . . the vanished young mother of infancy . . . ." He adds, "Both transmogrifications, into the idolised love-object or the unforgiven whore,' may very often be seen side-by-side in the same novel" (33). Characteristically, after warmly crediting Rose's article for introducing him to these concepts, Fowles sidetracks the primary thesis of it—that the artist desires a unity with the lost mother—in favor of the paper's secondary thesis—D. W. Winnicott's suggestion that the artistic experience has its origins in the period when the "I" of the little child first begins to be organized (during the first two years, particularly around the age of 18 months). During this time, the world is new, the sense of self is insecure but wonderful, the growth of sensual perception changes at such a rapid pace that the world is perpetually being recreated, reorganized, and renewed. This is not the period of total unity with the mother, but the period of early separation and return, where the categories of "self" and "other" ("I" and "thou") begin to be distinguished. This time of life, Fowles says in "Hardy and the Hag," is "deeply marked by the passage from a unified magical world to a discrete realist' one": "What seemingly stamps itself indelibly on this kind of infant psyche is a pleasure in the fluid, polymorphic nature of the sensuous impressions, visual tactile, auditory and the rest, that he receives; and so profoundly that he cannot, even when the detail of this intensely auto-erotic experience has retreated into the unconscious, refrain from tampering with reality—from trying to recover, in other words, the early oneness with the mother that granted this ability to make the world mysteriously and deliciously change meaning and appearance . . ." (31). Fowles goes on to describe how the transmogrifications of this "original lost woman" become "a prime source of fantasy and of guidance, like Ariadne with her thread, in the labyrinth of his other worlds" (40). Ironically, it is her repeated loss that is "so fertile and onward" (34) for the novelist, the reason why the beloved woman is so often translated into a corpse in the works of so many novelists—"why we can, as we grow older, kill them off with so little real pain" (34, 38).

During Fowles's very fertile period of the 1970s, the vision of the dead woman who emerges through the textual landscape became an even more complicated metaphor—one that I believe was more consciously crafted, manipulated, and informed at least in part by these very psychological theories that Fowles found so interesting. Masterful, powerful uses of the motif in several variations occur, for example, in *Daniel Martin*. Here, as in the earlier fiction, the fragmented or divided perception of the male protagonist is dramatized by his vision of a dead woman. Here, too, the task of the hero—set for him by his dying friend, Anthony—is not only to bring this woman back to life by his vision, but to make that vision "see whole" (181). "Whole sight"—the opening words of the novel—is related, among other things, to Fowles's remark in the letter to Gilbert Rose that "even when story and narrative method require a 'capturing' of the past, the dominant time sense is actually of a kind of futureness." Capturing the past makes the future possible for Daniel Martin, giving both him and Jane Mallory a genuine present time. Not seeing whole is the divided vision dramatized by Dan's memory of the day when, as university students punting along the river, Dan and Anthony's girlfriend, Jane, discover a female corpse, strangled and floating among the reeds along one of the side canals.[16] On the same day, later called "the day of the woman in the reeds" (624), in the "false paradise" of Oxford, Dan and Jane go to bed together (47). The body of the murdered, decomposing whore—"the grey buttocks like uncooked tripe, the reported maggots seething in the hair"—who floats up from beneath, breaking the surface of the water balances the encounter with Jane, the virginal, formally composed, young "bride" in the smooth, unbroken reflective surface of Dan's mirror-lined room (53). Dreamlike, the women are two aspects of the same ontological experience, of original being that Fowles describes in "Hardy and the Hag" (33). Jane and the corpse are "the idolised love-object and the unforgiven whore' . . . seen side-by-side in the same novel," the transmogrified lost mother. Again, the task of the

Punting on the River Cherwell, Oxford. In *Daniel Martin*, while Dan and Jane are attending Oxford University, they discover a corpse as they are poling their punt along a side canal: "A sedge-warbler chatters ahead in the reeds, he swings the punt round a first projecting screen. Beyond, a much denser curtain of reeds and bulrushes stretches across the water. . . . He sinks the pole and thrusts with all his weight at where there seems most water between the barring stems. The girl gives a little scream as they crash into the first green barrier, bows her head protectively in her hands. The flat prow pushes, some three yards in, then hits a soft obstruction, rises slightly, stops" (23). The corpse in the lush vegetation—and the death-haunted sexual intercourse of Dan and Jane later that day—seem to represent the mixture of life and violent death that constitute wild nature. Photograph by James Aubrey, 1988.

hero is, by the end of the novel, to transform the landscape of failure and desolation by reunifying these divided aspects of the mother and making the dead woman live in his vision.

Dan's renewed relationship with Jane twenty years after these events is frequently figured in terms of an Oedipal search for the lost mother. Dan, as narrator, is even conscious of the connection, mentally exploring the association for the reader's benefit: "Dan was very slowly realizing something: that he was looking or seeking for her old self as if it were a reality she was deliberately hiding from him; which was not only, of course, to dismiss the much greater reality of all that had happened since, but betrayed a retardation in himself, a quasi-Freudian searching for the eternally lost, his vanished mother" (482–83).

So in many ways, Dan's possession of Jane on that fatal day is even more than the conscious betrayal of his best friend, Anthony; it is an Oedipal possession, an act fraught with primal guilt. However, the real guilt that poisons all their lives is not the love, not the desire, and not even the act committed. It is their failure to acknowledge the act and to assume responsibility for it. In the years to come the pretense that it never happened, that this act fraught with Oedipal significance is not the foundation of all their relationship with one another and with their work, distorts and divides all of them. They all refuse to know and refuse to remember. Anthony becomes icily intellectual and arrogantly religious. Jane is increasingly shut in upon herself, "buried alive" we might say. Her sister Nell, who becomes Dan's wife, is largely shut out. Dan's art, writing film scripts when he is capable of writing serious plays and novels, Fowles represents as false, as Dan's denial of his own gifts. In his erotic life, Dan flees perpetually from woman to woman to always younger woman. As though constantly seeking the virginal bride, he retreats from the corpse in the reeds. This retreat, this refusal to put the fragments of his life together—to see whole—is a refusal to know the nature of the original relationship that models the structure of all human love and desire, all separation and eventual death. It is, by terrible irony, a retreat that obliterates everything most desired, the reality one most wishes to remember.

Denial, the failure to remember, in *Daniel Martin* is expressed as being exiled from a primal landscape of innocence and abundance. First and foremost, it is the rural Devon landscape of the protagonist's childhood, the paradisiacal, green, pastoral world of the novel's opening chapter, "The Harvest." All time is gathered into this perpetual present moment in which young Dan is enfolded: "And the day will endure like this, under the perfect azure sky, stooking and stooking the wheat ... without past or future, purged of tenses; collecting this day, pregnant with being" (5,11). The older Dan loses access to this world by editing it in his memory, by trying to remember only the glory and serenity of the day and shutting out certain grisly and fearful incidents. Just as he tries to distance himself from the drowned corpse at Oxford and the betrayal of his friend with Jane, so he censors the memory of the paradisiacal childhood landscape and, thereby, loses it all. Dan and Jane at Oxford, shuddering after they have left the cleanup of the drowned woman to others, touch upon this. By analogy, Dan recalls this emblematic harvest day, described in the first chapter, and remembers the "rabbit caught in the mower blades of the reaper." Then, terribly, he says to Jane, "That's all I can remember about that whole day now. The whole summer." By trying to forget the "agony in the mower's blades, the red stumps" and the terror of "dying, dying before the other wheat was ripe" (11), Dan has shut himself out of the green, pastoral, Edenic landscape of his childhood.

The repugnant image of the dead woman decomposing in the reeds looks back to Catherine in "The Cloud": "Young dark-haired corpse with a bitter mouth ... composing and decomposed, writing and written, here and tomorrow, in the deep grass of the other hidden place she has found."[17] The corpse is also associated in *Daniel Martin* with the long-dead mother lying "protective, quietly watching" under the long grass and carefully tended flowers in the churchyard (83). However, all of these are present in a much different way in the warm reality of Nancy Reed, that other girl "at the Reeds" who is cast in the role that the narrator will call "the original girl" until she is metaphorically buried alive by a refusal to fully acknowledge the past (597). Nancy lives in and embodies Thorncombe, the farm that the older Dan will buy in an attempt to reroot himself and recover lost values. Pastoral in spirit, ancient rural English in architecture, it is inhabited by the sort of affectionate, deeply rooted family that the boy Dan envies for its "mysterious warmth, some inner life, some grace that we lacked" (347). Lying "isolated, orcharded in a little valley of its own," Thorncombe, with its surrounding landscape, is an example of "*la bonne vaux*: the valley of abundance, the sacred combe ... a place outside the normal world, intensely private and enclosed, intensely green and fertile, numinous, haunted and haunting, dominated by a sense of magic that is also a sense of a mysterious yet profound parity in all existence" (273).

In the chapter "Phillida," Fowles presents Dan's adolescent first love for Nancy. As awkward and comic as it is innocent and sensual, these two half-grown children come together in a first erotic experi-

Dornafield Farm, Two Mile Oak, Newton Abbot, Devon. Dornafield provided useful physical and emotional material for Fowles's imagination as he wrote *Daniel Martin*: "I've taken the literary license every novelist is allowed. I don't fully reflect the real place, although it does have the old doorway I described in the book. Obviously, it's romanticized, but I lived in that village [Ipplepen] described in my book, as a boy" (James R. Baker, "An Interview with John Fowles," *Michigan Quarterly Review*, 25 [1986], page 681). Fowles may have used similar imaginative license with Dornafield in *The Collector*, where Clegg's country house in Sussex has a doorway with a date over it (page 155). Photograph by James Aubrey, 1988.

ence that initiates an extraordinarily sweet and special perception of the world. The familiar landscape is the primeval paradise of Fowles's private mythology, and Nancy is the lost dead mother, erotically resurrected. Dan and Nancy find their way to a private, wooded place, "up through the trees to where the rocks rose vertically for twenty feet from the earth (355). Nervous and incredulous, young Dan thinks himself in "the Garden of Eden," with strawberries, centaury and eyebright, caraway, thyme, and rabbits running on the greensward they had won from the bracken (356–58). When Nancy allows Dan to kiss her, "her body was his lost mother's, her giving forgave in a few seconds all he had thought he could never forgive" (358). Their embrace is an eruption through the entire surface of perception, both of the wild natural world around them and of the textual surface: "He had a strange sensation: the stable wood around them abruptly changed into an explosion, a hurtling apart of each leaf, branch, bough, smell and sound that constituted it. It disappeared, in fact. There was only Nancy, Nancy, Nancy, Nancy; her mouth, her breasts, her arms round his back, clinging as well, until she pulled her head away without warning and *buried it* against his shirt" (359, italics added). It is an erotic apprehension of a totally polymorphous world, the original maternal world . . . "the fluid, polymorphic nature of the sensuous impressions, visual tactile, auditory and the rest," which Fowles discusses in "Hardy and the Hag." As this natural landscape of the "sacred combe" explodes into the uniqueness of its components and vanishes into fluid space, we must recall that, in the chapter entitled "The Sacred Combe," Fowles finally identifies this "intensely private and enclosed, intensely green and fertile, numinous" place with "the 'private' form of the read text . . . the printed text (as) an escape for its perpetrator." It is language itself that is "the forest" (273–74). It is, therefore, the writer's reviving embrace of this beloved woman buried in the landscape that sets that textual landscape surface into sensuous, fluid motion and that makes it come *alive*.

In *Daniel Martin* the guilt is not in the desire nor in the act, it is in the forgetting. As Dan grows older, he grows ashamed of the "agony of Nancy" and puts it from him (347). Yet, it is this failure to acknowledge the shared experience that is the shame, the rotting corpse. Years later when Dan owns Thorncombe, the house of Nancy's birth, she returns briefly, faintly searching for her own past. Stout and middle-aged, her attempts at attractiveness are pathetic and conventional. The encounter is all "frightened gentility" on her part, all "odious urbanity" on Dan's. There is only pretense, silence about the past. In not acknowledging the relationship, they fail the world they once held in common. "I could have asked what happened that terrible day: what did you feel, how long long did you go on missing me? Even if I'd only evoked a remembered bitterness, recriminations, it would have been better than that *total burial*, that vile, stupid and inhuman pretense that our pasts are not also our presents; that what we did and felt was in some way evil and and absurd . . . immature. Ban the green from your life, and what are you left with?" (381, italics added, ellipsis in original).

The variation on the dead woman metaphor most important to the novel, of course, is the resurrection of Dan's relationship with Jane Mallory. She represents a unity, a "whole sightedness": "I knew something in Jane's presence satisfied some deep need in me of recurrent structure in both real and imagined events; indeed, married the real and imagined; justified both" (396). We might say, in fact, that she is symbolically like the mason of Arta's bridge, spanning past and future, real and imagined, composed and decomposed. In terms of realistic narrative, Jane is not really 'dead,' of course, but her marriage to Anthony has kept her metaphorically buried alive for over twenty years. When she and Dan meet again, she is full of dry sadness and hopelessness, explaining: "It's partly Anthony . . . . I don't mean the death. The living with him. All the failures there" (591).

On Dan's journey back through his personal past, coincidental with the journey through a significant landscape of our collective social past (the trip to Egypt, up the Nile, and into Palmyra), Jane is his companion. Her body is the human correlative of Dan's attempt to bring his lost, forgotten world to life again. When he first sees her in Oxford before Anthony dies, Jane is tired, worn, middle-aged: "her face seemed much, much older . . . In close-up she looked her age. There were lines of tiredness as well as of natural age" (150–51). As they journey back, the years seem to fall away; she becomes more attractive, more interested in the world; and there are flashes of the young woman Dan once loved. When he finally sleeps with her, he rediscovers in her "no time, no lost years, marriage, motherhood, but the original girl's body" (597).

Significantly, the rediscovery of the original girl—one who looks at him "maternally"—is not enough (600). Jane and Dan must find their final unity, their joining of past and future, in a landscape so totally desolate that Fowles calls it "The End of the World" in his chapter title. Only in the ruins of Palmyra, in that "unique landscape, so chilling, so hopeless, so static, so vast, so without forewarning" is Jane finally able to emerge into hope and a new beginning (603). It is, I believe, important that this renewal occurs against reason, after all rational arguments have been exhausted and both Dan and Jane are in a despair as desolate as the landscape itself. The scene is "like a supremely bizarre cinema still," "an extraordinary, almost surrealist sight" that "transfixed . . . the hills behind with their grim watchtowers, the silent back, her sitting as if before an invisible picnic lunch" (611–12). Jane is presented as though floating upon the surface. Symbolically, she has been both corpse and original girl. Now, as she removes her wedding ring (symbol of her underground marriage) and leaves it on the surface of that bleak, hopeless place, she reveals a band of pink new flesh around her ring finger, a circle of bright infant flesh about the bone—both mother and child, life and death, writing and written, past and future. The circle of rebirth emblazoned in the flesh of the beloved woman is also, we have seen, the language of the novel brought full circle. Embracing her with the vision of "whole sight" empowers the writer (Daniel Martin or John Fowles) to turn his "impossible last" unwritten sentence into "his own impossible

Palmyra, Syria. In *Daniel Martin*, one of the last episodes takes place at the ruins of Palmyra, where Dan and Jane come to terms with their own emotional histories. In the chapter "The End of the World" this symbolic landscape, emptied of wild nature, provides them a starting point for building on their pasts: "To the north the sky remained faintly lighter, but around them brooded darkness and the scattered, veiled debris of a lost civilization: crumbled walls, a colonnade, a bank littered with shards. It was the weather, they decided; it took all the serene aura out of classical antiquity, reduced it to its constituent parts, its lostness, goneness, true death . . . and the contrast of the reality with the promise of the name: Palmyra, with all its connotations of shaded pools, gleaming marble, sunlit gardens, the place where sybaritic Rome married the languorous Orient" (page 595). Photograph courtesy of Boxer Publishing and Anthony King.

first,"the opening sentence of the novel itself (629). As he magically and silently recalls the words, "Whole sight; or all the rest is desolation," Fowles *re*-turns to the beginning, to the rich green world of "The Harvest," to the sacred combe of his childhood, to the perpetual present of the written word (3).

Even from this limited treatment of only one of the fictions of the period, it is evident that the psychological theories that fascinated Fowles so in the 1970s and beyond do indeed inform his work, particularly this important metaphor of the protagonist who has a vision of a dead woman. How then do we reconcile Fowles's more recent recantations? In a 1996 interview, Dianne Vipond specifically asks him about Gilbert Rose, psychoanalytic theory, Oedipal separation and loss of the original mother / child bond, and "Hardy and the Hag." Fowles answers: "I found Rose's use of separation-and-loss theory useful, but to say that it has deeply influenced me is not really true." He explains this casual discarding of a profoundly motivating narrative pattern by continuing: "As always I am driven back to a natural history image. A common small fly of trout streams over here, the caddis (*Trichoptera*), builds a case for its chrysalis out of the grit on stream-beds. I've been the same over countless theories and views of existence and literature. I have made them a part of me, but never the whole of me. . . . Fragments of Freud and Jung have long helped me make my chrysalis-case, especially the latter."[18]

The great explanatory hypothesis of the lost mother, then, like the Oedipal psychoanalysis, and even the symbolic dead woman are mere bits of scaffolding. Used, and used up, they are consigned to the dustbin of "countless theories and views" of existence and literature." They and all the rest of it are there to help build a case, a cocoon, a shell, a protecting shape, around a chrysalis. Fowles has always been trying to express or indicate the chrysalis itself, something that is pretty much inexpressible. Meanwhile, most of us pay attention to the case, the shell.

Fowles's most recent attempt to describe the chrysalis itself occurs in the personal essay "The Nature of Nature."[19] Here he indicates the chrysalis in the case he has constructed of so many metaphors as simply, "being, being, being . . . a perpetual miracle, so vivid and vital that ordinarily we cannot bear it; always rare enough to be a shock, no similes or metaphors convey it; like a sudden nakedness, a knowing oneself laid bare before a different reality. There looks to be nothing; then, as with the thunderbolt, all." This "acutely rich sensation of beingness" he describes as impervious to the summons of reason. It is, he says, "as transient, as fugitive, as some particle in atomic physics [that] refuses all attempts at willed or conscious evocation, it is deaf to pure intelligence alone" (92, ellipsis in original).

In the absence of the beloved fictional woman who wakes to offer the writer / protagonist recovery of the Edenic landscape of possibilities, what else, then, can deliver Fowles into the presence of this "acutely rich sensation of beingness?" In "The Nature of Nature" he describes the dynamic of a pattern identical to the kind of event so frequently figured in his fiction as expecting to see a dead woman but being surprised back into hope and wholeness by her aliveness. Fowles describes how sorrow and desolation in the landscape of the human heart are *suddenly* transformed into hope by the agency of natural landscape, by means of a wry confession about his life after he left Oxford: "I later went to live in France and plunged even deeper into sin, having a passionate, life-changing affair with a shatteringly beautiful and rich young woman. I found her only in the remoter countrysides. I had glimpsed her in England, though never quite declared my fascination, already sensing that her true home was further south, in the Mediterranean. I called this lovely creature *la sauvage*, the wild. . . . She is that aspect of wild nature beyond all we normally attach to culture and civilization, the naked reality of the *rus* far beyond all *urbs*" (81). In his descriptions of encounters with the "savage old mistress," there are echoes of the resurrected woman and her perpetual gift of irrational optimism. For example, we began our exploration in this paper with Charles Smithson collecting fossils, pondering extinction, and sadly making his rational assessment of life's limitations when, against all reason, by chance or hazard, he suddenly takes an unexpected forking path and finds Sarah, emphatically not a corpse, sleeping, waiting for him. In this moment, as "the whole Victorian age was lost," Charles experiences this sense of pure being and moves into the narrative landscape of the future possible. In "The Nature of Nature" the dynamic pattern is the same. The observer, John Fowles, projects an emotional landscape of rational despair but is redeemed, swiftly and suddenly, by the intervening, mysterious vision of wild nature. He begins, "Nature in England, if still more in danger of dying than dead, is in a parlous state; we slowly slide into the zero of extinction." He continues: " . . . unless some great change in mankind occurs (unblinds, converts, transmogrifies), our gross stupidity and apathy will one day doom the Earth. "Yet here my savage old mistress pulls me back from total gloom. My study in Lyme Regis looks out on a green May garden over the English Channel and evokes both present and past. . . . My reason tells me that so much . . . must seem to consign not just ours, but all species to extinction. I have no belief at all in any divine power that might save us from this threatened nostricide . . . . Yet something in wild nature, though often dumb, masked or hooded has touched my individual soul. It is a perhaps foolish optimism . . . but I will not believe that all sentient, intelligent being must end" (90–91).

In another incident, he tells the tale of seeing Los Alamos for the first time and "loathing" it, "knowing its history" (82). The New Mexico development site for the atomic bomb is arid physically as well as historically, and analogous emotionally and symbolically with the landscape of Palmyra in *Daniel Martin*, a metaphor of the desolation we have wreaked on the world and on ourselves. When we encounter this static, forbidding landscape in that novel, Fowles makes it as much the objective correlative of the pessimism and emotional despair of the failed past lives of his middle-aged heroes as it is the symbolic landscape of our ruined civilization. Yet, it is in the midst of this landscape of the desolate past that the woman given up for lost, suddenly, without warning, and against all reason, chooses to end her death-in-life and transform everything into future possibility. The identical pattern prevails in Fowles's experience of Los Alamos. This time, however, it is not a Jane Mallory figure delivering the observer into "a future time when all will come good."[20] The agent is Fowles's declared totem bird, the "august, quasi-mythical" raven: "But as I stared grimly past [Los Alamos'] boundary warnings there was a *kwark*, a call from the very soul of freedom, high in the blue sky over it. I might perhaps have taken that as darkly, sickly, and 'symbolically' as Poe did, implying that all was death and desolation in this world. In that black speck two or three miles away I saw life, and 'evermore'" (82).

For Fowles, wild nature is the *vessel* of being, the savage mistress who comes to life in the landscape of our rational human foolishness and sad mortality—-against all reason—to give us hope and a common future.

Notes

1. John Fowles, *The French Lieutenant's Woman* (Boston: Little, Brown, 1969), pages 45–50, 66–72.
2. There are numerous other occasions when Charles expects to see a dead woman or when Sarah is presented as a corpse. I have briefly discussed two more of these (Sarah's "confession" in Chapter 20 and the "double ending" of the novel) in my article "Ashes, Ashes, We All Fall Down: *Ourika, Cinderella*, and *The French Lieutenant's Woman*," *Twentieth Century Literature* 42, no.1 (summer 1996), pages 165–86. In the novel there is also a truly uncanny presentation of Sarah as avatar of Elizabeth Siddal Rossetti, a Victorian woman whose corpse is of historical interest. Briefly, Lizzy Siddal was the wife of artist Dante Gabriel Rossetti and was his inspiration and the model for many of his "blessed damozel" paintings. She died tragically in 1862, and, guilt-ridden, Dante Gabriel Rossetti buried in the coffin with her beautiful, red-haired corpse the only manuscript of his poetry. In 1869, the very year in which the fictional Sarah Woodruff and Charles Smithson are reunited in Rossetti's house, the agonized poet had his wife's body exhumed and his poetry retrieved. The dramatic nighttime scene in Highgate Cemetery became legendary: how in the leaping light of the bonfire the beautiful corpse was "wonderfully preserved" (unchanged by seven years in the grave), and how rich and splendid was the red-gold of the dead woman's hair, having grown after her death to fill the coffin to overflowing. Sarah, who frequently appears as a Pre-Raphaelite woman, was partly modeled on Elizabeth Siddal—as Fowles himself remarked at the John Fowles Symposium on 12 July 1996. In view of this close association, how eerily reminiscent becomes the scene where Charles lies with Sarah in Exeter, overwhelmed by his unconquerable need for her: "Again his eyes were fixed on her. The nightgown buttoned high at the neck

and at her wrists. Its whiteness shimmered rose in the firelight, for the lamp on the table beside him was not turned up very high. And her hair, already enhanced by the green shawl, was ravishingly alive where the firelight touched it; as if all her mystery, this most intimate self, was exposed before him: proud and submissive, bound and unbound, his slave and his equal. He knew why he had come: it was to see her again. Seeing her was the need; like an intolerable thirst that had to be assuaged" (272). I have interpreted this particular corpse and a number of other such references to dead women in *John Fowles and the Vision of the Dead Woman: The Theme of Carnal Knowledge and the Technique of Source Inversion in John Fowles's Fiction*, my doctoral dissertation at the University of Pennsylvania, 1980.

3. John Fowles, *The Ebony Tower* (Boston: Little, Brown, 1974).

4. The motif of the woman imprisoned underground was the inspiration of *The Collector*, as Fowles recalls for Roy Newquist: "Some time during the 1950s, I went to see the first performance in London of Bartók's opera *Bluebeard's Castle*. It wasn't a very good performance, but the thing that struck me was the symbolism of the man imprisoning women underground.... With *The Collector* I knew I had the story I wanted. I felt sure of the novel from the start." *Counterpoint* (New York: Rand, McNally, and Company, 1964), pages 219–20.

5. John Fowles, *The Collector* (Boston: Little, Brown, 1963); "Hardy and the Hag," in *Thomas Hardy After Fifty Years*, ed. Lance St. John Butler (Totowa, N. J.: Rowman and Littlefield, 1977), page 38.

6. John Fowles, *The Magus: A Revised Version* (Boston: Little, Brown, 1978), page 63. Kirke Kefalea discussed the idea of Greek landscape as female at the John Fowles Symposium, Lyme Regis, 10 July 1996.

7. For an expanded discussion of these mythic patterns, see James R. Aubrey, "Eleusinian Mysteries in the Trial Scene of John Fowles's *The Magus*," *Journal of Evolutionary Psychology* 15, no. 2 (March 1994): 129–33.

8. John Fowles, *Poems* (New York: Ecco Press, 1973), page 31.

9. John Fowles, "Why I Rewrote *The Magus*," *Saturday Review*, 18 February 1978, page 25; Richard Boston, "John Fowles, Alone but not Lonely," *New York Times Book Review*, 9 November 1969, page 53.

10. John Fowles, *Mantissa* (Boston: Little, Brown, 1982); Eileen Warburton, "Fowles Takes a Risk for 'Minor' Work: An Interview on *Mantissa*," *Los Angeles Times*, "Books," page 18.

11. John Fowles, "On Writing a Novel," *Cornhill* 1060 (summer 1969), page 292.

12. Bob Cromie, "*Daniel Martin* by John Fowles," interview for *Book Beat*, produced by Pat Enney for PBS-WTTW Chicago, broadcast by WHYY Philadelphia-Wilmington, 4 January 1978.

13. Warburton, "Fowles Takes a Risk," page 18.

14. The important article that stimulated Fowles's interest in object relations psychology is by Gilbert J. Rose, "*The French Lieutenant's Woman*: The Unconscious Significance of a Novel to its Author," *American Imago* 29 (1972), pages 165–75. The two letters from Fowles to Rose, both of whom have kindly granted permission to quote from them, are dated 13 July 1974 and 15 May 1978. Fowles makes similar arguments about the "fluid polymorphic livingness of the process" as opposed to the "dead imperfection of the being in print" in "Lettre-Postface de John Fowles," in *Études sur "The French Lieutenant's Woman" de John Fowles*, ed. Jean-Louis Chevalier (Caen: Centre Régional de Documentation Pedagogique, 1977), pages 51–52.

15. Tom Zito, "The Mysterious Magus of Lyme Regis," *Washington Post*, 21 March 1978, page B11; John Fowles, "Hardy and the Hag."

16. The incident of the drowned woman discovered by a couple punting at Oxford and the lovemaking of the same couple on the same day was first explored by John Fowles as a short story, "The Woman in the Reeds," *Michigan Quarterly Review* 4 (1965), pages 131–45. Focusing on themes of postwar English class consciousness, it is a very different tale from the chapter in *Daniel Martin*, although many narrative elements are alike. Clearly missing are the emphasis on the lost mother and the betrayal of a close friend. What the reader may miss the most, however, is the powerful, tenderly ironic, middle-aged voice of the narrator of *Daniel Martin*. In an unpublished interview with the author on 12 January 1981, Fowles said of the earlier story, "the central image of the woman in the reeds" was where the novel began. "Really, it embarrasses me to read it now .... It's awful ... [a] very amateurish effort."

17. John Fowles, "The Cloud," in *The Ebony Tower*, page 299.

18. Dianne Vipond, "An Unholy Inquisition," *Twentieth Century Literature* 42, no.1 (spring 1996), page 16.

19. John Fowles, "The Nature of Nature," in *"The Tree" and "The Nature of Nature"* (Covelo, Calif.: Yolla Bolly Press, 1995), pages 73–99.

20. John Fowles, unpublished letter to Gilbert Rose 13 July 1974.

The Undercliff of John Fowles's *The French Lieutenant's Woman*: A Note on Geology and Geography

Liz-Anne Bawden, Kevin Padian, and Hugh S. Torrens

The undercliff of Lyme Regis functions in *the french lieutenant's Woman* much as Egdon Heath does in the Wessex novels of Thomas Hardy. Sarah Woodruff roams its hollows, secret places, and green glades much as Eustacia Vye slips among the furze and pathways of Egdon Heath in *The Return of the Native*.[1] Yet, neither woman is of the landscape, and neither frequents it to admire its natural beauty. Rather, each woman borrows the landscape for her own purposes and ultimately leaves it (Sarah by choice, Eustacia by death), without having made any impression on its face, and without having been impressed by it.

The extent of heath in Dorset has shrunk to one-fourth of what it was in Hardy's time, but even when he was writing its area was much diminished from the earlier times in which some of his novels are set.[2] This effect was mostly a result of fuel cutting, grazing, and (latterly) development. By contrast, the Undercliff has always been dramatically different from the austere heath, and since the nineteenth century its foliage has proliferated. The Undercliff today, as seen in the film version of *The French Lieutenant's Woman*, is lush, wooded, and secluded, and many of the novel's events depend on it as a refuge for hiding, solitude, or clandestine meetings. However, in 1867, when the novel is set, the vegetation was different and the landscape was not so uniformly covered. Such matters affect the characters of this novel, so the evolutionary history of the Undercliff is important for readers of the novel to understand as well.

* * *

The term *Undercliff* is perhaps misleading, because the Undercliff is actually above the cliffs that directly meet the sea—the ones that Charles climbs from Pinhay Bay the first time that he encounters

Warmwell Heath, Dorset, May 1912. In *Thomas Hardy's England*, Jo Draper explains that Egdon Heath was Hardy's general name for the various heaths east of Dorchester when, in practice, heathland was customarily identified by appending the name of the nearest village (edited by John Fowles for Little, Brown, 1984, page 183). The first chapter of *The Return of the Native* opens with a description of Egdon Heath at twilight: "The sombre stretch of rounds and hollows seemed to rise and meet the evening gloom in pure sympathy, the heath exhaling darkness as rapidly as the heavens precipitated it. . . . Haggard Egdon appealed to a subtler and scarcer instinct, to a more recently learnt emotion, than that which responds to the sort of beauty called charming and fair." In its wildness, the heath was for Hardy something like what the Undercliff is for Fowles. Photograph courtesy of the Dorset County Museum, Dorchester.

Sarah, asleep on a grassy ledge overlooking the water to the south (50, 56). There are more cliffs behind them, however, continuous with the lower cliffs to the sea but made of entirely different geological material. The Undercliff refers more directly to these cliffs further inland, which are "under" the farmland to the north on the Devon-Dorset plateau.

There is also an important difference between current and historical understandings of the extent and topography of the Undercliff. The present image of the Undercliff is evoked by the wild and thickly wooded area now comprising a National Nature Reserve. The Under-

View along the Cliff at Lyme Regis, by George Cumberland, 1820. Cumberland's ink-and-watercolor depiction of the Undercliff as viewed from beside Whitlands Cliffs, above Pinhay Bay, shows how much less overgrown the area was in the early nineteenth century than it has become in the twentieth. The toothlike projection on the horizon is Fowles's esteemed White Chapel Rock. Photograph by Don Larsen, courtesy of the Stanford University Museum of Art 1976.308, Committee for Art Acquisitions Fund.

Undercliff from the Cobb, Lyme Regis, Dorset. In the opening chapter of *The French Lieutenant's Woman* Fowles calls the Cobb "the most beautiful sea rampart on the south coast of England" and "a superb fragment of folk art" (pages 3–4). The slope of the Undercliff is discernible in the background, as it tumbles toward the sea—and tilts toward the sun, making it a semitropical oasis. Photograph by James Aubrey, 1993.

Pinhay Bay, Devon. In *The French Lieutenant's Woman* Charles Smithson is looking for fossils along the cliffs when rising tide forces him to climb up from the beach in order to return to Lyme Regis—via the Undercliff, "an English garden of Eden" (67). Photograph by James Aubrey, 1996.

cliff used to begin about two miles west of the town, at Whitlands Cliffs, and has always been wild, though parts have at times been cultivated for orchards or used for grazing. The Undercliff National Nature Reserve now incorporates the additional area east of Whitlands, which includes Whitechapel Rocks, Pinhay Cliffs, Ware Cliffs, and, below them, the former Ware Common. The secluded rendezvous called "Donkey's-Green" is thought to have been nearby, but its exact location is a matter of conjecture. Southeast of Ware Cliffs is Underhill Farm, known as "The Dairy" during the action of the novel and until the early twentieth century. East of Underhill Farm, to the edge of Lyme Regis, are Ware Fields, now a National Trust property.

Although Ware Common, where the Undercliff scenes of the novel almost entirely take place, was more open and domesticated, and considerably less wild than the Undercliff proper to the west, the two areas are topographically and geologically continuous. Today they are indistinguishable parts of the Undercliff National Nature Reserve, but even nineteenth-century descriptions of the two areas, in their similar emphasis on diverse vegetation, make them sound alike. In 1840 geologist W. D. Conybeare and surveyor William Dawson described the landslip of the Undercliff:

> In the central point of this district at Whitlands Cliff, this upper range is mantled over by luxuriant screens of ash and elm growing wherever the less precipitous slope of the escarpment will allow a root to attach itself, and often where nothing but a veil of ivy could have been expected. . . . Between this upper range of cliffs and the beach, a space intervenes . . . from 200 to 300 feet above the sea occupied by a series of broken terraces formed by successive subsidences. These terraces are very generally divided from each other by deep dingles, commonly shrouded with underwood, but occasionally cleared and planted as apple orchards.[3]

Some of these plantations, now overgrown, can still be found. H. Rowland Brown, writing in 1857, reinforced these historical differences in the views in *The Beauties of Lyme Regis* . . . .[4] Describing the prospect west of Holmbush, on the edge of Lyme Regis, Brown wrote:

> Before us, we see a number of hills, which after a succession of Landslips, are broken in various directions, into almost every imaginable shape, these enshrine numberless little dells, carpeted by the softest turf, covered with luxuriant copse-wood, and festooned with the blossoms of the wild rose, white clematis, and wild convolvulus.

Looking inland from the "entrance-gate to the Cliffs," which, from his description, must have been approaching Ware Cliffs from the end of the lane to the Underhill Farm house, Brown continued:

> The hills above rise to a height of about 500 feet, whose rugged sides are partially concealed and beautified by the luxuriant vegetation—the dark

Underhill Farm, Devon. This photograph, taken around 1900, shows the farm that John and Elizabeth Fowles purchased in 1966 and lived in for two years. In *The French Lieutenant's Woman* "The Dairy" is a historical version of Underhill Farm, so when the narrator says in Chapter Thirteen, "perhaps I now live in one of the houses I have brought into the fiction," he is being teasingly authorlike—as he will continue to be in the novel's later metafictional moments. Photograph courtesy of the Lyme Regis Philpot Museum.

Underhill Farm house, Devon. Fowles composed *The French Lieutenant's Woman* in this room, working at the window on the left, according to Neil Reid, Fowles's gardener and the occupant in 1996. The view is southward, across the landscape that descends to the English Channel. Photograph by James Aubrey, 1996.

foliage of the black thorn, relieved by the variegated petals of the foxglove; and brighter green of the graceful ferns, and long grasses, even the profusion of thistles, nettles and gorse, crowding the green slopes and wooded acclivities, produced a beautiful effect in the charming landscape.

Having climbed to Chimney Rock, looking over "an extensive view of the Undercliff," he then described "a chaotic mass of hills, steep banks and knolls, here and there separated by fertile surfaces of pasturage, where flocks of sheep are quietly browsing, surrounded by little clumps of trees and luxuriant thickets." These passages provide a vivid sense of the landscape ten years before the time in which the novel is set. Much of the land on Ware Fields east of Underhill Farm was enclosed during the early nineteenth century, and it was cultivated as well as used for grazing until well into this century. Orchard cultivation and grazing in the area west of Underhill were common in the eighteenth and nineteenth centuries, and these uses kept the land clear of most woodland and shrub until equally recent times. Today, however, the whole area appears as one thick wood, and any distinction between the old Undercliff and the former Ware Common has been further blurred by the designation of both areas as the Undercliff National Nature Reserve. Apart from some apple trees, the Undercliff shows few traces of former cultivation.

In Chapter 10 of *The French Lieutenant's Woman*, Fowles discusses the extraordinary geography of the Undercliff, how its southern exposure and tilt toward the sun, combined with abundant springs, have lent the area "botanical strangeness" (67). Its unusual flora owes its preservation to the mild coastal climate, the protection of the surrounding cliffs, and the sun's direct light, which have allowed plants to flourish there that were otherwise extirpated over the rest of England after the milder climates of several thousand years ago deteriorated. Just as the Undercliff's geological topography is responsible for its flora, its inherent instability is also responsible for its relative seclusion and persistent wildness. An important event in the recent history of the Undercliff was the sudden monumental exfoliation and slumping of some 15 million tons of land over Christmas 1839, about four miles west of the Ware Cliffs area. George Roberts, historian of Lyme, wrote in an 1840 pamphlet on "The Mighty Landslip of Dowlands and Bindon, December 15, 1839":

> A great distinction must be made between the *land in tillage* and the *Undercliff*. Bindon estate [the site of the Great Landslip] has perhaps only lost twenty acres of tillage land, and this has become Undercliff and will be of some little value though the fissures render it dangerous to send cattle there as usual. Dowlands farm has only lost five or six acres of tillage

The 1839 landslip in the Undercliff. The original title of this illustration is "A View of the Landslip from Great Bindon, Looking Westward to the Sidmouth Hills and the Estuary of the Exe," in *Ten Plates Comprising a Plan, Sections and Views Representing the Changes Produced on the Coast of East Devon, between Axminster and Lyme Regis* . . . (W. Dawson, W. D. Conybeare, Mrs. Buckland & Professor Buckland [John Murray, 1840]). Of this plate, John Fowles has noted, "The wheat on the slipped part was successfully harvested the next summer. The central plateau of the slip is known as Goat Island, and the ravine to the right, now heavily overgrown with trees, as the Chasm," in *A Short History of Lyme Regis* (Little, Brown, 1982), page 41. Photograph courtesy of the Lyme Regis Philpot Museum.

land. Little Bindon estate . . . has had twenty acres of top tillage land go down.

After the slippage, when the nearby farmers deemed the land more or less stable, the wheat that remained on the unsubmerged surface of the erstwhile fields was harvested, though not without trepidation and difficulty. Lyme historian Cyril Wanklyn transmitted to *Pulman's Weekly News* (Lyme, August 27, 1929) a copy of a letter from Dawson to Buckland (see note 3), dated 20th August 1840. Wanklyn noted that the land just discussed,

when severed from the mainland in December, 1839, had had a crop of wheat sown on it. This crop in due course grew up and ripened. Certain ladies and gentlemen of Lyme and neighbourhood then thought that this would be a splendid occasion for a festivity and picnic. They went forth from Lyme, attired in fantastic costumes, to reap the crop—with the results described by Dawson, in spelling that is not immaculate.

Dawson himself testified of the proceedings and attendance:

> ... from the best calculation I could make I think Six thousand about the number. They got up a procession which was in my humble opinion not quite in good taste—a *Committee* with Blue Ribbands round the neck— 6 Lady Reapers in white kid gloves and wreaths of artificial flowers, the sickles tied with Blue, and 6 Gentlemen to match in Blue vests and white trousers. They had however a good Band of Music, the effect as they wou[n]d down the Zig Zag Path into the Valley of the Chasm with the Banners, and the assembled thousands lining the cliffs on both sides was picturesque and fine. Sir W. Pole was there and furnished a Battery of Four guns from Shute. . . . [5]

It is obvious from the foregoing that this section of land, four miles from Lyme in the heart of the Undercliff, was not as wild as it is today. This extraordinarily large and intact piece of subsidence was eventually named Goat Island. Because it was not planted thereafter, the area of the Undercliff atop Goat Island is today preserved as a valuable piece of "Victorian" landscape, with wildflowers as they grew in the 1840s.[6] However, slippage remains a major threat to life and property in this area.

Around the time of the Great Landslip, largely for economic reasons, crop farming in the area was supplanted by grazing, which had long been practiced over much of the Underhill-Ware Cliffs area and continued at least until the turn of the century.[7] Eventually this livelihood also proved unprofitable, and the land became more overgrown, as it is today. The eastern half of the former Ware Commons, east of Underhill Farm, is the only part today that remains strikingly different from the rest of the Undercliff as we know it, precisely because it was enclosed and farmed until the 1950s. Geologists Rowe and Sherborn remarked in 1903 on the area west of Bindon Cliffs that "the great landslip alone would stamp any coast with a distinctive individuality, and the contrasts afforded by the juxtaposition of red Trias marl, yellow Greensand, and white Chalk realise a field of rare geological interest and a picture of surpassing beauty." By 1970, however, W. A. MacFadyen observed that "this picture is now largely masked by vegetation," and that situation is true for the rest of the Undercliff as well.[8]

It is of some historical importance that seclusion could readily be sought in the Undercliff. Two centuries before 1867, the persecuted dissenters who used to assemble there for worship in secret gave Whitechapel Rocks the name by which they are still known. Both before and since then, the Undercliff has concealed the contraband of an active smuggling trade, as well as the plunder from shipwrecked boats.[9] As Undercliff warden and local historian Norman Barns notes about the novel, its action takes place during the early spring, before the leaves would have unfolded and the grasses grown high, so concealment for Charles and Sarah would have been more difficult than in high summer.[10] The area seems never to have been completely free of wood and shrub, however, and the natural topography of the broken hillocks allows many depressions that can offer concealment from passersby. Barns also remarks that the sycamores that now dominate much of the Ware Cliffs woods were not there in the mid-1800s, a point supported by Conybeare and Dawson (cited above). Clearly the topography was heterogeneous, and it was more overgrown and wild farther west from town. Ashes and beeches were the largest trees, and more open areas were shaded by hawthorns and bracken ferns. The latter are remarked in the novel to grow commonly to a height of seven feet. The vegetation is beautifully described in the opening paragraphs of the tenth chapter of *The French Lieutenant's Woman*. Of course, as Sarah reminds Mrs. Poulteney, privacy does not depend only on the density of the vegetation: one can be alone in the Undercliff because so few people go there (91).

Some geological peculiarities about the Undercliff also figure importantly in the novel. The rocks that make up the Undercliff area belong to two sharply divided geologic ages and compositions. From the base of the cliffs to a level that ends along the coastal path just above the traditional precincts of the town, the bedrock is Early Jurassic ("Lias") limestone about 206–8 million years old. The part of this limestone often referred to as the "Blue Lias," near the base of the cliffs, has yielded a great many fossils formed on what was once an ancient muddy sea bottom. Most of them are invertebrates, principally ammonites, but there are also the ichthyosaurs, plesiosaurs, and pterosaurs (marine and flying reptiles) that brought fame to the town and to its principal collector of the early 1800s, Mary Anning.[11] These are the strata from which Charles Smithson collects ammonites, such as the one he brings home to Ernestina, following his first paleontological excursion along the beach (50).

On his second outing, however, Charles climbs the path from Pinhay Bay to the higher reaches above the Blue Lias. This path is called in the novel the "flint," and the path through Ware Commons exposes many beds of flint, a white, grey, or reddish rock that, like chert, is a siliceous replacement of limestone. These flints outcrop in irregular

Monmouth Beach, Dorset. Named after the ill-fated Duke of Monmouth, whose history is mentioned in the first chapter of *The French Lieutenant's Woman*, this beach later will lead Charles Smithson west from Lyme Regis to these fossil-bearing cliffs of blue lias. Photograph by James Aubrey, 1996.

Lyme Bay, English Channel. Across the bay is Golden Cap and the village of Charmouth, where Sarah Woodruff formerly worked as governess for the Talbot children and as nurse to the French Lieutenant Varguennes (31–33). In the foreground are rock pools such as the one where Charles experiences "a thoroughly human moment," in which he "looked cautiously round, assured his complete solitude and then carefully removed his stout boots, gaiters and stockings," and watched a crab scuttling (48). The moment is also thoroughly un-Victorian, as Charles symbolically divests himself of culture to enjoy just being in nature. Photograph by James Aubrey, 1996.

The Aristos, with ammonite. John Fowles selected this photo of a fossilized ammonite for the cover of a recent edition of his book of philosophy. This common fossil is used in *The French Lieutenant's Woman* as a symbol of Charles and of doomed English aristocracy, and even of the human condition, subject to powerful but indifferent forces and, ultimately, to extinction as a species if it fails to evolve. Photograph courtesy of Picador / Macmillan Publishers.

nodules and lenses amid the softer yellowish sandstone that comprises much of the upper bedrock of the Lyme region. These rocks are mid-Cretaceous in age, separated by a vast gap of about 100 million years from the underlying Lias. On the cliffs to the east of Lyme, past Charmouth, the same distinction between the steel-blue Early Jurassic and blond Cretaceous strata is very clear (see figure 49). The Cretaceous beds begin with a dark siltstone layer about 25 feet thick (the "Gault"), above which lies about 150 feet of the "Upper Greensand," a yellowish sand with lenses of chert, and topped by up to 225 feet of "Chalk," a fine-grained siliceous stone with flints. A layer of loose sandstone near the base of the Greensand, called the Foxmould, is known to become semifluid in periods of heavy rain, and it is apparently this layer that slips and causes the great exfoliations responsible for Goat Island and other shifting features of the Undercliff. Chasms in this area are concealed by overgrown vegetation, and the area is considered dangerous for surveyors as well as for the public. Ammonites come from these rocks as from those of the Lias below (though they are of different lineages), but this higher, more open area is where Charles also must go to look for his echinoderm tests, or sea urchin fossils, which do not come from the Lias.[12]

* * *

Wishing not to constrain literary interpretations but to enrich them, we suggest two points of potential interest that emerge from these geologic and geographic considerations. One is that the upper reaches of the cliffs, formed of the Cretaceous rocks from which the echinoderm tests come, must have been considerably more open than they are at present, or only someone with infinite patience (unlike Charles) would have explored them for fossils, especially rare ones. Charles, who is not especially observant, notices more outcrops and slumps than would be obvious amid the overgrowth today. So for the characters in the novel, concealment in this area, past the outlying houses along Ware Common and the dairy at Underhill, would have entailed slightly different strategies than the present landscape suggests.

A second consideration stems from Charles's fateful visit to the redoubtable Mrs. Poulteney's house with Tina and her Aunt Tranter, during which he mentions in Sarah's presence the importance to paleontology of the echinoderm tests. On the same day, Sarah crosses Charles's path during his third venture on the outcrops, and she presents him with two of the uncommon fossils.[13] Sarah and Charles met there inadvertently once before, and it may be presumed that she generally knows what he is looking for, though she has had no previ-

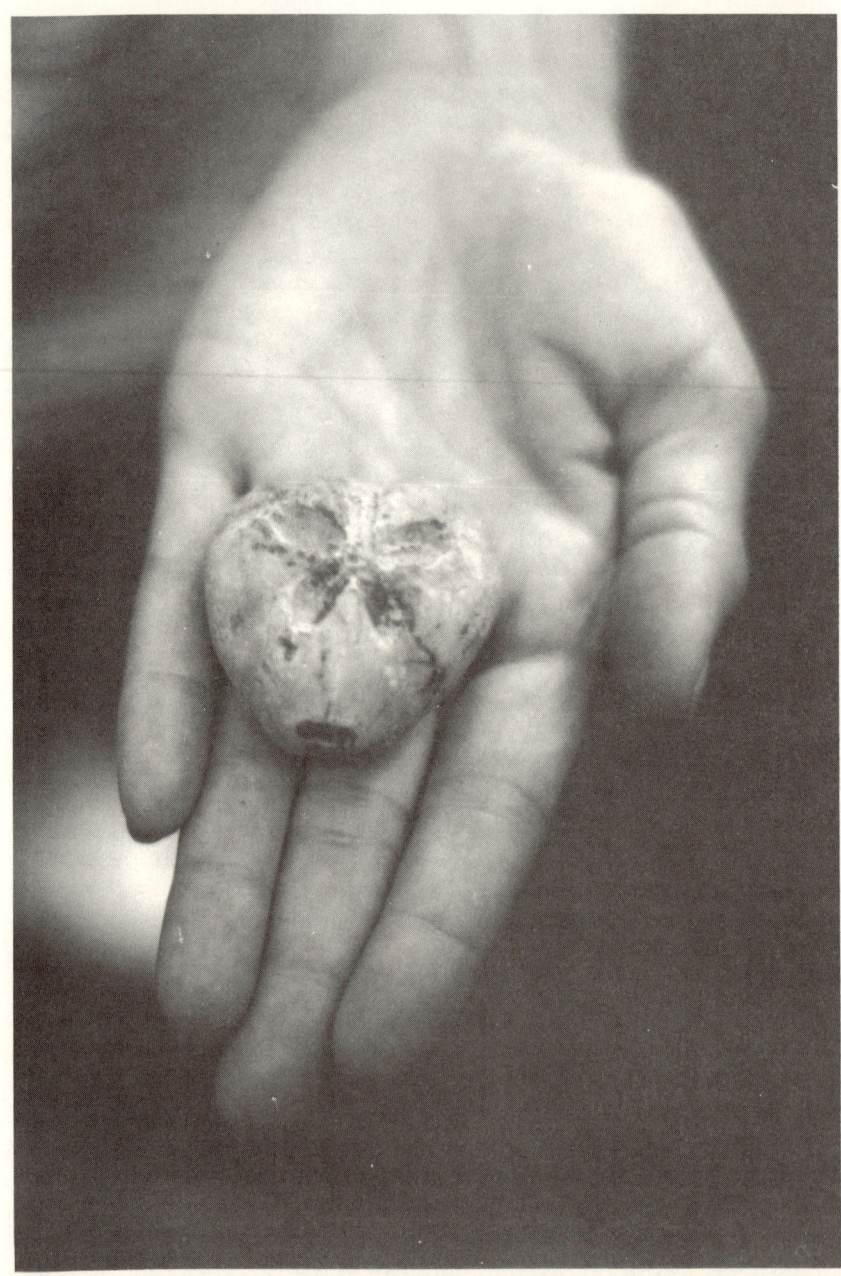

Petrified sea urchin. Fossils like this one are also referred to in *The French Lieutenant's Woman* as "*Micraster* tests," two specimens of which Sarah gives to Charles during one of their meetings in the Undercliff. Charles points out "the mouth, the ambulacra, the anus"—and then puts them in his pocket (138–39). Photograph by James Aubrey, 1996.

ous experience with the fossils. Sarah is a keen observer, with "instinctual profundity of insight" that the narrator compares to a computer's, so she may realize that she has seen fossils like those he described that morning (52–53). Could she also have realized that his search would necessarily take him through the upper reaches of Ware Cliffs, where she was in the habit of walking?

* * *

An acute sensitivity to nature is a central characteristic of John Fowles's writing. Ancient history, as well as the human history of a region, is a recurring motif in the novels, from *The Magus* and *The French Lieutenant's Woman* onward, and "natural history," in the best sense of the term, is a principal focus of much of his later work. He uses Nature for many literary purposes: the great age of the rocks of the Undercliff, with the gigantic hiatus in time between their upper and lower reaches; the harbinger of the past as well as the future, represented by the extinct fossil species littering the cliff's flanks; and the peculiar wildness of the Undercliff, with its promise of freedom in contrast to the iron-bound constraints of Mrs. Poulteney's drawing room. The erotic effects of its beauty and its seclusion lend an almost palpable excitement to Charles's meetings there with Sarah.

Fowles is not only an accomplished observer of nature, but also a synthesizer of its grander dimensions of time, space, and life. He weaves the great history of the many layers of the Undercliff's geology into the uses that humans make of it—whether scientific, agricultural, or amorous. He allows fossils to stand as symbols of human interaction as well as providing mute testimony to a long-dead past unwitnessed by human eyes. He educates his audience about the depths of time and the imponderables of existence that presented themselves to Victorian scientists, while treating the exercise as a mere pastime for a bored gentleman. The narrative's seemingly anachronistic jumps from 1867 to 1967 are jarring, initially, but to Fowles they are part of the same flow in which the scales of time converge, to express a continuity of history between the ancient past of the ammonites and before, down to the present day. Many literary critics have remarked on Fowles's didactic tendency in *The French Lieutenant's Woman*, structured as if he were teaching the novel as he went along. Fewer have noted that this device also conveys a great deal about the science that helps to set up the action of the plot.

To Fowles, it matters that the science is a natural extension of narrative. As Henry David Thoreau has written, "In wildness is the preservation of the world," and preservation is to Fowles a deeply personal matter. In order to preserve nature—to become more than mere collectors—we as its human superintendents have to understand it, and one means to this understanding is to read such writers as Hardy and Fowles, who weave scientific understanding seamlessly into the fabrics of their novels. The comings and goings of Charles and Sarah are minor events, but the wild Undercliff with its secret hollows, its ancient *Micrasters,* and its blooming milkworts is to Fowles's inner eye a major dimension of the novel, a landscape that is both evolving and timeless—the nature he once described, by virtue of its existing, as "*the poetry of survival.*"[14] In his fiction no other landscape figures Nature more scientifically yet poetically than does the Undercliff of *The French Lieutenant's Woman.*[15]

Notes

1. John Fowles, *The French Lieutenant's Woman* (Boston: Little, Brown, 1969); Thomas Hardy, *The Return of the Native* (London, 1912; reprint New York: W.W. Norton, 1969).

2. Jo Draper, *Thomas Hardy's England* (Boston: Little, Brown, 1984), page 179.

3. W. D. Conybeare, W. Dawson, Mrs. [William] Buckland, and Professor [William] Buckland, *Ten Plates comprising a plan, sections and views representing the changes produced on the coast of East Devon, between Axminster and Lyme Regis* . . . (London, John Murray, 1840). William Buckland was a geologist and paleontologist at Oxford; his wife prepared the plates for the volume. A contemporary map of the coast "used in court at Exeter Assize, March 15th, 16th, 17th, 18th, 1841 . . . enlarged from the Ordnance Map by means of a Pentagraph," a copy of which is in the Lyme Regis Philpot Museum, is our source for the local geographic nomenclature. Apple orchards are shown planted above Pinney (Pinhay) Bay at that time.

4. H. Rowland Brown, *The Beauties of Lyme Regis, Charmouth, the Land-slip, and their vicinities* . . . (Lyme Regis: Daniel Dunster, n. d. [1857]).

5. Letter with enclosure from C[yril] Wanklyn to the Editor, *Pulman's Weekly News,* Lyme Regis, August 27, 1929.

6. James Aubrey, unpublished interview with Norman Barns, 11 July 1991. Barns notes that, ironically, the growing dominance of holm oaks is tending to open up the foliage of the Undercliff once again, by reducing the growth of other plants in their shade. Accounts and illustrations of the formation of Goat Island are displayed in the Lyme Regis archives and at the Lyme Regis Philpot Museum.

7. Photographs illustrating the contrast between cultivated and wild areas can be seen in John Fowles's *Lyme Regis Camera* (Stanbridge, Dorset: Dovecote Press, 1990), especially numbers 7, 90, 91, 122, and 124 (background).

8. A. W. Rowe and C. D. Sherborn, "The Zones of the White Chalk of the English Coast. 3. Devon." *Proceedings of the Geological Association* 18 (1903): 1–51; W. A. MacFadyen, *Geological Highlights of the West Country* (London: Butterworths, 1970), pages 41–46, 90–107.

9. John Fowles, in L.-A. Bawden, *Lyme Regis Museum Curator's Report 1995/ 96* (Lyme Regis Philpot Museum, 1996), notes the recent reprint of Sabine Baring-Gould's (1900) *Winefred* (Praxis Books, Sussex, 1994), an historical novel about the Victorian smuggling trade at the Axmouth end of the Undercliff. Thomas Hardy's

short stories "The Distracted Preacher" and "A Tradition of Eighteen Hundred and Four" (*Wessex Tales*, 1888/1912; reprinted 1991, Oxford University Press) are two of many other works concerned with this tradition along the Dorset coast, where the absence of an Undercliff forced the local inhabitants to develop many ingenious means to hide and transport their loot.

10. Kevin Padian, unpublished interview with Norman Barns, 12 July 1996. See Chapter 10 for Fowles's description of the Undercliff as "the nearest this country can offer to a tropical jungle" (67).

11. Crispin Tickell, *Mary Anning of Lyme Regis* (Lyme Regis: Philpot Museum, 1996); H. S. Torrens, "Mary Anning (1799–1847)," *British Journal for the History of Science* 28, (1995), pages 257–84. The blue-grey limestones are distinct from those of many other Jurassic regions; the term *lias* appears to come from a Saxon word for "bed."

12. These tests of the genus *Micraster*, said to be uncommon, tend to be found more often in open geologic exposures, and even today they can often be found in the fields above the cliffs after heavy rains, according to Norman Barns (see note 10). A. W. Rowe's (see note 8) famous descriptive work on these fossil sea urchins was one of the early documentations of gradual evolution in the fossil record.

13. Echinoderms are a group (phylum) of invertebrates that includes starfish, sea lilies (crinoids), sea urchins, sand dollars, and about twenty other groups, most built on a pattern of five radial canals or arms, and most extinct. The term *test*, as applied to the sea urchins that Charles covets, is a quaint one: coming from the Latin *testa*, a round pot or shell (the same word from which the French *téte*, or "head," evolved), it is used to describe any round, oval, or ellipsoid shells, usually of microscopic foraminifera, one-celled marine organisms. The word *testicle* is a diminutive form of *testis*, which is suggested by the *Oxford English Dictionary* to have a possible common origin with *testa*, though Roland W. Brown derives the words from two different sources, with *testis* coming from *testificor*, or "bear witness," as in the English *testator* (*Composition of Scientific Words*, Smithsonian Institution Press, 1956, page 788). As to the former derivation, the etymological irony in Sarah's presentation to Charles of a pair of these small, testicular shells has not escaped the notice of literary commentators. The latter derivation suggests that these ancient shells bear witness to the course of evolutionary history, a central theme of the novel, as well as to much of the intrigue surrounding its characters.

14. Henry David Thoreau, "Walking," *Excursions and Poems*, vol. 5 of *The Writings of Henry David Thoreau* (New York: AMS Press, 1968), page 224. John Fowles, "The Blinded Eye," *Animals* 13.9 (January 1971): 392 [Italics in original].

15. We are indebted to James Aubrey for his great interest and attentive help in preparing this contribution, to Norman Barns for his insights into local natural history, to John Fowles for clarifying some literary and historical particulars, and to the Lyme Regis Philpot Museum for permission to reproduce some of the illustrations.

Deep Time, Evolutionary Legacy, and the Darwinian Landscape in John Fowles's *The French Lieutenant's Woman*

KEVIN PADIAN

> Time is the great mystery of life.
>
> —John Fowles[1]

LANDSCAPE HAS OFTEN BEEN NOTED AS A MAJOR THEME OF THE NOVELS and poetry of John Fowles. Love of landscape and its identification with the Earth, with what is natural, powerful, mysterious, and even unknowable are commonly encountered in his work, and perhaps nowhere more dramatically than in his novel *The French Lieutenant's Woman*.[2] An interest in both the natural and the temporal landscapes of Fowles's work has led me, as an evolutionary biologist and paleontologist far afield from my discipline, to comment on this text, but I do not propose any imprimatur of scientific correctness to constrain literary interpretations. Doing so would ultimately violate the spirit of John Fowles's attitude to nature, which includes a wariness toward scientific classification. The narrator's occasional disdain of Charles Smithson, protagonist of *The French Lieutenant's Woman*, is not because he is an amateur, but because he is little more than a collector, as the pun on his name and the eponymous national museum of the United States signals. For Fowles, nature is there not to be labeled but to be cherished and conserved, and most of all to be appreciated.

I would like to bring an evolutionary perspective to *The French Lieutenant's Woman* by showing how two often overlooked arguments of Charles Darwin's works—deep time and evolutionary legacy—resonate in this novel, and how they enrich its naturalistic themes by deepening the focus on the Darwinian landscape. For Fowles, as well as for other writers sensitive to nature, landscapes are not only geographic or topographic, but also historical: they are shaped by what has happened to them through time. Because the duration of a landscape is so much longer than that of any human life, or indeed of human consciousness, its history is far slower to evolve but also far richer and more deeply layered. In short, the temporal landscape describes how a natural surrounding has changed through time, and change through time is the simplest descriptor of the process of evolution—a key theme in the novel.

Charles Smithson is a devotee of another Charles—Darwin, of course—whose theory of evolution is a matter for discussion on various occasions in the novel.[3] Darwin in turn had a substantial influence on Thomas Hardy. Hardy, as Fowles himself points out, is "the great novelist who towers over this part of England of which I write." Darwin's influence on both Hardy and Fowles is deeper than the simplistic version of Darwin that is often presented in biological as well as literary circles. In order to discuss Fowles's use of Darwin, I must also discuss Hardy as an intervening presence, both as a user of Darwin and as a shaper of Fowles's Victorian landscape.

I would like to make four points. First, evolution was a central paradox in the intellectual life of the Victorian era, itself an age of contradictions, and this tension of contradiction informs much of Fowles's novel. Second, we commonly think of natural selection, one of Darwin's main contributions to evolutionary thought, as the simple bromide "survival of the fittest," but this phrase both misrepresents Darwin's view and colors how we perceive Darwinian themes in literature. Third, a full understanding and acceptance of what John MacPhee has called "deep time"—the recognition that the Universe is impossibly ancient, that the processes of the Earth and its life have been going on for an enormous span of time—were necessary for Darwin's theory to work.[4] Fourth, because evolution is a Markovian process—that is, where you can next go in time depends on where you have been—everything in the Universe, animate and inanimate alike, bears the marks of its evolutionary history.[5] Deciphering these marks, unraveling their history, seeing the influence that the past has had on the present—this is the business of evolutionary biology. Darwin was well aware of all these points (in fact, they were central to his thinking), and both Hardy and Fowles, reading Darwin, internalized them and made them intrinsic elements of their fiction.

Evolution as Paradox

In *The French Lieutenant's Woman*, Fowles makes a central theme of the idea that the Victorian Era was an age of contradictions—among them personal hypocrisy, unrepentant social injustice, and the legislation of a morality that was privately flouted by all classes and types of Victorians. There were philosophical paradoxes, too. The novel's repeated allusions to Darwin, Karl Marx, and Sigmund Freud underscore the intellectual evolution that was emerging. Such new ideas raised the awareness of contradictions through the reexamination of every facet of social existence. Charles Dickens wrote of France in the 1780s, "It was the best of times; it was the worst of times," but he might well have been describing the Victorian era, which is similarly characterized by Fowles as one that tried to balance apparent differences—particularly between two ideas that were difficult, but necessary, to understand at once.[6] Evolution presented the ultimate paradox for Victorians: humans are uniquely possessed of divine souls and consciousness, yet they also are part of the "Great Chain of Being" that includes other animals, indeed all life.

To accept a contradiction, one has to maintain a balance in thinking about it, as an artist must balance disparate elements of nearly any aesthetic work. *The French Lieutenant's Woman* explores the concept of dual identity, which is itself a contradiction, a paradox. Charles, for example, is a liberal-minded scientist and a meliorist, but at the same time a member of the ruling class with interest in preservation of the social order. Ernestina is a clever young woman, but constrained by inferior opportunities and social oppression. Sarah is of poor gentility, but educated and bred for appetites beyond her social station. These conflicting elements resonate in the theory of evolution: each species, indeed each individual, is part of a continuum of genealogy that stretches back through the divergences of all species to the beginning of life; yet each is also an individual, unique. This central idea of evolution becomes an essential paradox of Victorian life, and by extension for the intellectual landscape of *The French Lieutenant's Woman*.

The epigraph to the first chapter of Fowles's novel, from Hardy, introduces such a contradiction:

> Stretching eyes west
> Over the sea,
> Wind foul or fair,
> Always stood she
> Prospect-impressed;
> Solely out there
> Did her gaze rest,
> Never elsewhere
> Seemed charm to be. (3)

There is a rhythm of sound and silence in these lines, from one of Hardy's loveliest lyrics, "The Riddle." The sibilance of the *s*'s and *f*'s, the balance of "foul" and "fair" and of "never" and "always," recall in the short lines the tightly regulated Celtic poetry that Graves describes in the first pages of *The White Goddess*.[7] Fowles seems to have found in this verse partial inspiration for the novel; however, he omits the poem's second verse, in which Hardy completes the rhythm of contradiction and symmetry:

> Always eyes east
> Ponders she now—
> As in devotion—
> Hills of blank brow
> Where no waves plough.
> Never the least
> Room for emotion
> Drawn from the ocean
> Does she allow.[8]

The two verses are united in theme, parallel in structure, yet different even in their rhyming patterns. There is balance here, but the balance is of contradiction. The hinted narrative of this poem parallels the eventual end of Sarah's obsession with the sea, as she finds a different life at the end of the novel. For Hardy's character, these "hills of blank brow" form a psychologically barren landscape with "never the least room for emotion drawn from the ocean."

The first chapter of *The French Lieutenant's Woman* proceeds to introduce a litany of internal contradictions. The Cobb "invites what familiarity breeds," a mild paradox (3). There are many kinds of contradictory word plays in the conversation of Charles and Tina, as convention seems to prevent them from discussing anything sincerely, even when they most need to. Paradoxically, they are in "mutual solitude," these London sophisticates transplanted to the comparative outback of Lyme Regis (4). The bright colors of Tina's clothes contrast with the expected meekness of Victorian women (5). Despite her nearsightedness, it is she who notices the fossils that pave the Cobb; Charles, who is supposed to be a scientist, seldom notices much of anything (8). The Cobb itself is both culture and landscape, a sort of ancient earthwork of "folk art" (a phrase that some would consider an oxymoron), "primitive yet complex, elephantine but delicate" (4). Sarah Woodruff, whose behavior is even more contradictory than Tina's, is described as a "living memorial to the drowned" (5).

Perhaps the most interesting contradiction is set up in the confrontation of social evolution between Charles and his prospective father-in-law. As the events of the book unfold, Charles comes to see himself more and more as a living fossil, evolution's ultimate oxymoron.[9] He is unwilling and unfit to make his way in the economic society that his family investments have spawned. It is, of course, ironic that he would embrace the ideas of a man like Darwin; Charles does not at first realize that the implications of transmutation and natural selection spell death for stratified society and his social class. Tina's father, the aptly named Ernest Freeman, is Charles's polar opposite. He has worked, sweated, saved, and conformed in order to build a mercantile empire and gain entrance into an exclusive society. He represents a product of natural selection, adapting successfully to changing environmental conditions over time. Yet, ironically, he argues with Charles against Darwin. He does not want his daughter to marry a man who considers his grandfather to be an ape—even a titled one, in Charles's case. Charles may lose that title, and his economic prospects are risky. As the novel develops, Charles begins to see the degeneracy of a lineage doomed to extinction. Evolution is bypassing his social class. The lesson of inevitable change and natural selection seems clear, but Victorian society prefers not to learn it, rather to maintain the cognitive dissonance of its own contradictions.

The point of the foregoing is to demonstrate that, in an age of contradictions, the concept of evolution was central to disestablishing the notion that humans had a fixed, finite existence and purpose, despite the evidence of one's senses and the cultural edifices that surrounded the Victorians. Evolution brought a clear contradiction between the apparent permanence of everyday existence and the postulate, not directly sensible, that the human lineage, like all life, has changed through time to become what we are today: animals as well as sentient beings. Fowles is not the first author to face this contradiction. As Gillian Beer writes, "The two major emotional and creative problems which evolutionary theory forced on Hardy were to find a scale for the human, and a place for the human within the natural order."[10] This scientific understanding had well-known consequences for philosophy and theology, but in *The French Lieutenant's Woman* these considerations, while recognized, take second place to their importance for societal structure, played as they are as a backdrop for the stories of the involvement of Charles and Sarah, the rise of Mr. Freeman in society, and the economic success of Sam and Mary.

The Varied Components of Evolution: Population Processes, Deep Time, and Legacy

What did Darwin say in *The Origin of Species* that had such a profound effect on novelists, and particularly on novels by Hardy and

Fowles, centered in the landscape of southwestern England? Most scholars—biologists as well as scholars in the humanities—concentrate on the idea of natural selection, and this idea is certainly important in Hardy's novels and in *The French Lieutenant's Woman*. Natural selection incorporates the processes of what we might call "immediate time"—that is, the phenomena of biological interactions that are perceptible in natural populations today. These phenomena are evolution in action, though on a short timescale of birth, death, fertility, fecundity, emigration, and local extirpation. Prominent as these processes are in, for example, many of Hardy's novels, they do not by themselves account for his Darwinian landscape. Two other components of Darwin's "long argument," as he put it, are also crucial, and they figure in both Hardy's and Fowles's work. One is the fact that vast stretches of time—deep time, which Darwin figured in the hundreds of millions of years—were both available and necessary for his theory to work. The second is that, given this time, and given the fact that everything in the universe has a history, it follows that everything bears the marks of its history—the organisms of the landscape and all the human modifications to it, as well as the landscape itself. Nothing escapes unchanged, and history can be read literally in the features of both the animate and the inanimate.

Darwin's natural selection has been reduced in the minds of many to the phrase "survival of the fittest." This development is unfortunate because Darwin meant so much more by natural selection. He did not see Nature just as an endless competitive struggle but also as a harmonious whole. He explicitly saw no moral turmoil in the capture of prey by a predator, the destruction of eggs, or the waste of seed, and he saw no *Angst* of suffering. Many passages in *The Origin of Species* attest to this fact.[11] But even more importantly, as Hardy realized, Darwin showed the limitless continuity and relatedness of all life. He established how important deep time was, as time without measure, time beyond human conception, numbers with exponents, ten to the ninth or tenth or eleventh years. What does it matter to most of us when, after ten to the third, after thousands of years, we cannot possibly conceive of it anyway?[12] Yet, to Darwin deep time was not only real, but absolutely instrumental if his theories were going to work. His last book was on the action of worms in soil. As Stephen Jay Gould has pointed out, this study was no indulgence of a great man in his dotage; it was an essential component of his thought. If worms, slow and humble as they are, could change a landscape as British worms have been observed to do within the course of human memory, what could Nature have accomplished in the hundreds of millions of years at its disposal?[13]

This part about deep time is very difficult to comprehend. The concept is not intuitive; it requires all the analogies one can devise, but it is still only a parade of numbers (see note 12). However, Darwin realized in the 1840s that it was absolutely essential as a temporal backdrop for his theory of selection.

In the first chapter of *The French Lieutenant's Woman,* we are taught to experience time itself as a set of contradictions. The narrator often intrudes to jar us anachronistically with what has since become of people, their descendants, and places that he describes in 1867—for example, with the remark that Ernestina would live until the day Hitler invaded Poland (27), or that Mary's great-great granddaughter would be a film star, "twenty-two years old this month I write in" (75). Hardy occasionally did the same, but more often he would reach farther back in time to describe the history or original purpose of a structure that figured in his narrative, usually ironically. Fowles appears casual in his use of such anachronisms, but they are not there only for irony. Like Hardy's, these tropes underscore the inevitability of time and change—in short, evolution. Their use in *The French Lieutenant's Woman* also relates to Fowles's conviction of the importance of chance and randomness in evolution, the sense that all things must pass, regardless of temporary success. The anachronistic passages in the novel, therefore, remind us of a deeper temporal scale that, though often hidden, is just below the surface. In another sense, they also provide a situational perspective that reminds us of the relative insignificance of the lives of individuals against the sweep of time and history.

The Origin of Species appeared when Hardy was 19, and there is a substantial literature about Darwin's influence on him. Much of what has been published, however, is not fully Darwinian: it tends to be limited to a Spencerian view of natural selection, and the apparent remorseless effects of circumstance, fate, and both natural and human laws on the characters of the novels. These facets have been thought to reflect Hardy's own life—his marriage, his family history, and so on. Yet, these often pessimistic themes were not really aspects of Hardy's thought, nor are they of Fowles's. What sets apart Hardy and Fowles from many other authors in whose works evolutionary themes can be read is that they incorporated not just the Spenserian populational aspects of evolution, but also those of deep time and evolutionary legacy.

Darwin understood deep time as few biologists did then or have since, because he was trained in geology and paleontology. Darwin credited his own sense of time to his senior colleague and mentor Charles Lyell, whose *Principles of Geology* (1830–33) became the standard 19th-century reference. The understanding of deep time was in the first place a direct result of the study of landscape—that is, of geology. Fossils were found in rock layers, and they came to be correlated across wide distances, allowing geologists to recognize the superposition of strata that brought home just how long it must have taken to make the earth's crust. Hardy also understood the ramifications of deep time, because he was so attached to nature and to the Earth, particularly to the landscape of Dorset. Most important, however, Hardy understood the Darwinian idea that everything in the Universe bears the marks of its own evolutionary legacy—the stamp of its ancestry. This idea is most clearly focused in *Tess of the d'Urbervilles,* Hardy's strongest exploration of evolutionary themes, and the novel closest in many respects to *The French Lieutenant's Woman.*[14] Most obvious in *Tess of the d'Urbervilles,* as its title suggests, is the contradiction between her family's ancient status and its present one, and her family's pretensions to nobility that eventually ruin her. Tess shares with Sarah Woodruff this slide in status, the result of vain aspirations of parents who make their daughters fit for neither world.[15]

In the language of evolutionary biology, the term *historical legacy* (or *evolutionary legacy,* as I will call it here to reduce confusion with events confined to the scale of human history) is often used to describe characteristics that are possessed simply because they are inherited, as opposed to being ideally adapted for some functional solution. In biological terms, for example, land vertebrates (tetrapods) have a body plan in which both forelimbs and hind limbs have a single bone attached to the girdle, two bones attached to that, and then a series of small bones connecting to five digits (instead of six or seven or ten), all because their most recent common ancestors in the Pennsylvanian Period had that formula when they crawled out onto land.[16] *Evolutionary legacy* can also refer to the apparent limits or constraints on evolutionary potential in a given lineage. For example, though wheels would no doubt be very useful in locomotion, no vertebrate has evolved them, and this seems to be because the genetic and developmental constraints on their form prevent it: that is, there are no morphogenetic resources from which to design or make a wheel.

Still other examples of evolutionary legacy may apply not just to animate beings, but to the characteristics of a landscape. The composition of rocks in an area determine to a large extent its water and soil potentials, and hence what plants will grow there. How long hills and mountains have been standing, whether they have been raked and stripped by glaciers, and many other historical factors also determine the topography and character of a region. Events in the Pleistocene, such as glaciation, may have been as important to the history of a range of hills as the Permian lagoon that first laid down a series of shallow limestone beds, or the tectonic upheavals of the Triassic that made mountains out of them.

Evolutionary legacy is a continuous process, a becoming, that has many different temporal scales and modifications on its eventual products. This concept is crucial to understanding the Darwinian landscape in the novels of Hardy and Fowles. The epigraph to Chapter 3 of *The French Lieutenant's Woman*, taken from the first edition of *The Origin of Species*, illustrates this perfectly by showing that some features, once useful, are no longer adaptive:

> But a still more important consideration is that the chief part of the organization of every living creature is due to inheritance; and consequently, though each being assuredly is well fitted for its place in nature, many structures have now no very close and direct relations to present habits of life. (11)

Tess of the d'Urbervilles, like *The French Lieutenant's Woman,* is a novel in which evolutionary history is inseparable from the plot. Some of the first words spoken in *Tess* ("Good night, Sir John"), which set in motion the entire ineluctable, tragic mechanism of the narrative, are tied to genealogical legacy. Parson Tringham, the speaker, is a genealogist interested in the histories and evolutionary fortunes of the people of his parish. The events of history mark those who bear their legacy: Parson Tringham notes that John Durbeyfield retains the nose and chin of his noble ancestors—as the parson says, "a little debased" (14). This legacy both enables and haunts Tess, and it eventually brings her to her doom in a way that is not possible for her rural companions.

The scales at which Hardy explores evolutionary legacy in *Tess of the d'Urbervilles* vary from the cultural and genealogical to the geological and even astronomical. Again, it is perhaps strange to think of all these scales as "historical," when they might so clearly be divided into historic and prehistoric, but they are all a function of time. Hardy constantly moves among these scales, here pointing out a church from Gothic times, there reminding us of the ancient age of the stones used to build it. In *The French Lieutenant's Woman*, the ammonite that Tina notices in the paving of the Cobb is one that Charles knows from the Mesozoic oolite quarries of nearby Portland (8). Hardy also shows that, in the course of evolution, much can be ephemeral. Laws change, people move, families die out, noble titles are purchased and perverted. In *The French Lieutenant's Woman*, too, Fowles sometimes appears to deny the long-term effects of evolutionary history (or legacy), at least as they regard the present and future in 1867. Rightly so, because natural selection can reverse the past fortunes of evolutionary history. Sam and Mary, the servants, are among the first of what will be a rising middle class, and a humble Victorian cottage will be the weekend retreat of a famous London architect a century later (158). On the other hand, the great bustard that Charles shoots (to his uncle's delight) is "one of the last . . . on Salisbury Plain" (14), a harbinger of extinction for both the bird and the squire; and Charles is called a "victim of evolution" not so different from the ammonite. These are the results of natural selection. Change is inevitable, but there is legacy.

In Hardy's novels, the descriptions of landscapes are not there only to show the splendor and peace of bucolic life, the economy of nature, or the oneness of country people with their surroundings. Hardy constantly makes us aware of the *history* of these forms of pastoral life: they are ancient, they are traditional, they are beyond human memory. Fowles seems to take his cue from Hardy's descriptions of landscapes. In *The French Lieutenant's Woman*, the Undercliff looms as an island of prehistoric independence from human concern and control, much as Egdon Heath does in Hardy's novels. The context in which Fowles uses deep time is subtle and often rather different from Hardy's. Deep time, for Charles Smithson, is an escape, as the Undercliff is for Sarah. Emotionally, for Charles as a scholar, time is a *situating*, a feeling of belonging. Fowles provides Charles a strong identification with evolutionary views, through which both can muse about Charles's uncle's quaint way of life and Mr. Freeman's social pretensions. Fowles shows us how deep time can become an intellectual panacea for men like Charles, to whom leisure was life (and vice versa) and the problem was not how to find the time to do all the things one wanted, but "spinning out what one did to occupy *the vast colonnades of leisure available*" (12, emphasis added). Charles cannot communicate his fascination with deep time to Ernestina, nor does Sarah pretend to understand it. Tina has decided early on that she will interest Charles not by flattering his love of the past but by ignoring it. In turn, he decides to make her a present of the ammonite he finds, not to share his interest, but because it is pretty enough to placate her for his tardiness that afternoon: ironically, his pursuit of the relics of deep time has made him late.

The scale of the human in both Hardy's novels and *The French Lieutenant's Woman* is constantly shifting from the central to the ephemeral. H. B. Grimsditch notes that "Hardy is fond of beginning his stories with a road, along which a pedestrian makes his way."[17] These people, at first mere flyspecks in the distance, become humanized characters through the course of the narrative. We similarly first see Charles and Tina at a distance on the Cobb, through a telescope (4). Before Hardy's people can be explored, his road typically acquires deeper significance: it becomes a Roman road, or (like many around Egdon Heath) a more ancient path or track, or it passes a pre-Christian burial mound, or it cuts through Paleozoic strata that regard the progress of the traveler impassively. Hardy constantly reminds us that we are as ephemeral against the landscape as are the birds, insects, leaves, and flowers that Darwin described in *The Origin of Species*. Historical scales operate, emerge, and converge: humans modify the landscape by constructing farms, fields, towns, cultures, laws, history itself; yet, time bypasses each individual human and each culture, against the nearly immutable face of Nature. All things and actions become in time equally significant and small.

In a similar way, many passages in *The French Lieutenant's Woman* insist that the characters are beyond the author's control, once started on their destinies; societal and animal forces take over and direct the action relentlessly. This idea again stems from Fowles's conviction of the importance of chance and randomness in evolution: their actions can upset eons of stasis, whether evolutionary or cultural. Here is a great contradiction of evolution: it tells us that the fates and actions of *individuals* are not important, but those of *groups* of individuals are the motor of change.[18] Again, the actions of individuals can do virtually nothing; in populations, where individual identities are lost, there are effects of lasting significance. For Hardy, on a human scale, the picture is even bleaker. Fate directs the affairs of humans, usually with awful consequence. The individual has no chance against cosmic forces. Is this concept so radically different from Darwin's view? After all, what matters in evolutionary biology today is not the success of the individual—we are all doomed to die some day—but the continued propagation of the species, the passing on of shared traits, modified to adapt to ever-changing surroundings through geologic time. If we pass on our traits—our genes, in modern parlance—that is our best hope. Yet, there is a gruesome kind of hope at the end of Hardy's *Tess of the d'Urbervilles*, when Angel walks off with Tess's sister, who of course carries more genetic similarity to Tess than anyone else in the world. In at least one ending of *The French Lieutenant's Woman*, homage is paid to the same idea when Charles examines the child Lalage, "intent on her face, her hands, her every inch," in search of genetic clues (457).

However, this is the difference between fiction and science. To an evolutionary biologist observing literature from a distance, it appears that the tragedy of novels is possible only because we allow ourselves the luxury of ruminating on the scale of individual lives. There is a famous and often-analyzed passage in Hardy's *A Pair of Blue Eyes*, where Knight tumbles over a cliff and is left grasping roots to save himself from falling to his death. He comes face to face with a trilobite fossil, embedded in the rock, and he contemplates this low creature, which once had a body like his own to save. Meanwhile, the world of prehistory (cribbed from Mantell's *Wonders of Geology*, which Knight would have been expected to know) rushes through his desperate mind. Hardy is pointing out that we are all like Knight's trilobite, frozen in an eternal anonymity, while at the same time capable through the individuation of circumstance of a real human poignancy that transcends time: "They were grand times, but they were mean times too, and mean were their relics. He was to be with the small in his death."[19] In *The French Lieutenant's Woman*, the drama of Charles, Sarah, and Tina is played out against a constant background of social, technological, and intellectual change, carrying some characters along and leaving others behind, like ammonites in the mud. Grand and mean times become simultaneous in the rush of Victorian time toward the future. It may be significant that, to appease the tiny Lalage, as he had done long ago with the prostitute's child, Charles again takes out his timepiece and dangles it (457). The fact that the child's name is inspired by a name in an aptly titled Hardy poem, "Timing Her," is an additional cue to the reader to read this episode symbolically (438).

Evolutionary Contingency and the Riddle of Time

In paleobiological circles, there is renewed interest in talking about "evolutionary contingency," the "what if?" component of history writ (very) large. If the dinosaurs had not died out, for example, what would mammalian life be like, and would humans ever have evolved? This sort of intellectual exercise, which is really a way of testing how certain we are of the importance of imputed paleontological events, has been called by David Raup "replaying the evolutionary tape," and it has been examined at some length by Stephen Jay Gould in his book on the Burgess Shale, *Wonderful Life*. Gould, like others, marvels at the great diversity of soft-bodied life preserved in this Canadian outcrop, some 500 million years old, close to the dawn of known metazoan life. Many of the Burgess Shale animals cannot be fitted into living groups and (like most long-deceased humans) have no descendants today, a condition that gives pause. Yet, this fact is overshadowed in an anthropomorphic sense by the presence of *Pikaia*, the single representative of the Chordata, the group that includes vertebrates. The Burgess Shale may not encompass all the diversity of its time, but Gould raises the possibility that had *Pikaia* become extinct before giving rise to another species, vertebrates never would have evolved at all.

Contingency plays its role in the novels of Hardy and Fowles. Hardy's narrator, reacting in distress to fateful events that could have been avoided with foreknowledge, sometimes remarks, "Had someone told her . . ." or asks, "Why did no one . . . ?"[20] This device functions as a pointed reminder of what might have been, and a helpless plea for the mercy of the alternate contingencies of fate. Fowles's narrator in *The French Lieutenant's Woman* is more intrusive, even emerging as a silent character at several junctures in the novel. More to the point, in three chapters in the novel (45, 55, and 61) the narrator deliberately "changes" the plot. He is playing with contingency, replaying the tape of time. In one ending, Charles returns to Tina and never sees Sarah again; in another, he finally locates her in London and is united with her and their infant daughter; in the third, their reunion is not successful and he walks out on her. Is any one ending more satisfactory or natural than any other? Fowles's narrator tells us to disregard the first ending (339) but to take the last two equally seriously (406). To ask which ending is more natural is like asking whether unextincted dinosaurs would be a more fitting evolutionary culmination than the hairless apes that fancy themselves the dominators of the planet today. In paleobiology, one can examine rates of evolution and extinction to reveal that dinosaurs declined not because of a sudden mass extinction, but because for many years before their ultimate demise they simply failed to produce new species to replace those that were naturally continuing to become extinct. The structure of the novel, however, ultimately does not provide internal logic to help decide what ending is satisfactory or natural: that prerogative belongs to the reader.

* * *

I hope to have demonstrated here some reasons why evolution is one of the central paradoxes of the Victorian Age of Contradictions, and by extension is a resonant theme in many novels that reflect the *Zeitgeist* of the age. Evolution simultaneously affirmed the unity of life and took away much of the special status of humans, a development that terrified some people (and still does). To understand evolutionary themes in Darwin, Hardy, and Fowles, we need to understand not only (1) natural selection but also (2) deep time for evolution to do its work, and (3) the concept of evolutionary legacy, the stamp of history on everything. These concepts taken together explain why, in the long run, the events in the novels are not random. Natural selection is morally neutral, and the struggle for existence (as Darwin saw it) is inevitable, blameless, and relatively painless. In Hardy and Fowles, characters are caught in this struggle, but the human scale of novels allows us to see those characters as individuals, not simply as particles in the Brownian motion of evolution.[21]

Notes

1. Fernando Galván, "The Writer as Shaman: A Talk by John Fowles, and an Interview," *Atlantis* (journal of the AEDEAN [Asociación Española De Estudios Anglo-Norteamericanos]) 14, nos.1–2, page 264.
2. John Fowles, *The French Lieutenant's Woman* (Boston: Little, Brown, 1969).
3. See especially pages 48–49, 160–62.
4. John MacPhee, *Basin and Range* (New York: Farrar, Straus and Giroux, 1980). See also Stephen Jay Gould, *Time's Arrow, Time's Cycle* (Cambridge: Harvard University Press, 1987).
5. If you chart a series of rolls of dice, it will soon be apparent statistically that the numbers that have already come up have no effect on the result of each subsequent throw; in other words, each throw is causally independent. A Markovian series is more like a board game: you can throw a die and advance a variable (but finite) number of steps, but where you wind up will always depend largely on where you have just been. The path of evolution is Markovian, though we often describe the incidence of mutations and some other evolutionary features as random. The point is that heredity, in its genetic and environmental senses, constrains evolutionary history and potential.
6. Charles Dickens, *A Tale of Two Cities* (London: J. M. Dent, 1994), page 3; *The French Lieutenant's Woman*, pages 266–67. Note also that Fowles refers to Robert Louis Stevenson's novel of dual and contradictory identity, *Dr. Jekyll and Mr. Hyde*, as "the best guidebook to the age" (369).
7. Robert Graves, *The White Goddess: A Historical Grammar of Poetic Myth* (New York: Farrar, Straus and Giroux, 1948).
8. Thomas Hardy, "The Riddle," *The Complete Poetical Works of Thomas Hardy*, 2 vols., ed. Samuel Hynes (Oxford: Clarendon Press, 1984), vol. 2, page 183.
9. *The French Lieutenant's Woman*, page 333; see also pages 49–50, 209, 296.
10. Gillian Beer, *Darwin's Plots* (London: Routledge and Kegan Paul, 1983), page 252.
11. Charles Darwin, *The Origin of Species*, ed. Ernest Mayr (1st edition facsimile; Cambridge: Harvard University Press, 1964). See especially Chapter 3: "We behold the face of nature bright with gladness, we often see superabundance of food; we do not see or we forget, that the birds which are idly singing round us mostly live on insects or seeds, and are thus constantly destroying life; or we forget how largely these songsters, or their eggs, or their nestlings, are destroyed by birds and beasts of prey; we do not always bear in mind, that, though food may be now superabundant, it is not so at all seasons of each recurring year. . . . When we reflect on this struggle, we may console ourselves with the full belief, that the war of nature is not incessant, that no fear is felt, that death is generally prompt, and that the vigorous, the healthy, and the happy survive and multiply" (62, 79).

12. Paleontologists tend to use such temporal descriptors with a certain glibness. We speak, for example, of the first dinosaurs as having appeared 225 million years ago, as if it were yesterday. It is likely that even those of us who deal constantly with geologic time can understand the "225" part, but not the "million years" part: we only evaluate it in comparison with another like figure, such as the extinction of dinosaurs 65 million years ago. We perceive that the origin was over three times as remote from today as the extinction was, but we cannot conceive of these as multiplicands of millions. If you counted one number per second, eight hours a day Monday through Friday, it would take just two hours short of seven weeks to reach a million. And it would take thirty years to count back to the origin of the dinosaurs.

13. Darwin's last book was *The Formation of Vegetable Mould, through the Action of Worms, with Observations on their Habits* (London: John Murray, 1881). See also Gould, "Worm for a Century, and all Seasons," *Natural History,* April 1982; reprint *Hen's Teeth and Horses' Toes* (New York: Norton, 1983), pages 120–33.

14. Thomas Hardy, *Tess of the d'Urbervilles,* ed. Juliet Grindle and Simon Gatrell, World Classics (1983; reprint New York: Oxford University Press, 1988).

15. See K. Padian, "'A Daughter of the Soil': Themes of Deep Time and Evolution in Thomas Hardy's *Tess of the d'Urbervilles,*" *Thomas Hardy Journal* 13, no.3, October 1997.

16. Living amphibians have only four fingers on the hand, the bird hand is reduced to three fused digits, and snakes have no digits at all. However, the ancestors of all these taxa, as the fossil record shows, ultimately had five-fingered appendages. Even more ancient creatures, such as *Ichthyostega* and *Acanthostega,* had seven, eight, or more digits; though these Devonian animals are close to the ancestry of tetrapods, they are not the most recent common ancestors of the living groups, and there is now considerable doubt whether they had terrestrial habits at all.

17. H. B. Grimsditch, *Character and Environment in the Novels of Thomas Hardy* (London: Witherby, 1925), especially chapters 2 and 4.

18. It is important to stress that the populational concept of evolutionary change is a modern (neo-Darwinian) one; Darwin himself does not seem to have thought in populational terms, but to have been concerned with the individual animal as its fate influenced the hereditary potential of the lineage (for example, the species).

19. Thomas Hardy, *A Pair of Blue Eyes,* ed. Alan Manford, World's Classics (New York: Oxford University Press, 1985), page 209.

20. Beer, page 240.

21. I would like to acknowledge the help, support, and comments of Jim Aubrey, Liz-Anne Bawden, Cathy Gallagher, Tony Jackson, John Lynch, Jennifer Miller, Susan Posner, Suzanne Ross, Eileen Warburton, and this book's anonymous peer reviewer. I am grateful to John Fowles for insights into his creative process. This essay is offered as part of a long-standing debt to Norris Birnbaum, Bob Sabol, and Fred Busch. This work was supported by the University of California Museum of Paleontology.

The Undercliff as Inverted Pastoral: The Fowlesian *Felix Culpa* in *The French Lieutenant's Woman*

PATRICIA V. BEATTY

IT IS NOT SURPRISING THAT MANY COMMENTATORS HAVE NOTED THE PASTOral elements in John Fowles's works, and some have examined them at length. Few, however, have captured the ambiguity with which these elements appear. Indeed, it might be argued that Fowles establishes an antipastoral pattern in his novels. Ironically juxtaposing idyllic Arcadian landscapes with realistic natural or urban sites, Fowles typically gives us a protagonist who must extricate himself from a pastoral mode of existence into the fluid freedom of a constantly changing world. In *The French Lieutenant's Woman,* Fowles delineates this pastoral mode by focusing on gardens—real or metaphoric, natural or human-made—and garden images that are associated with that primal Garden in the Western Christian world, Eden.[1] In the novel, the story of the loss of Eden by Adam-Charles and Eve-Sarah becomes the arch antipastoral—the story, in Victorian dress, of humanity's Fortunate Fall. Of course, the *felix culpa* in this secular novel is not to be seen in theological terms but as an affirmation of freedom from religious tenets, as well as from social conventions and all those other restrictive orderings of reality that the individual—especially the Victorian male—has developed to deny both the internal and external complexities of reality.

Fowles's association of gardens, generally, with the imposition of order on nature, both human and natural, may be found most explicitly in *The Tree*.[2] Here, after commenting on the comparable impact on our perception of the mythic Garden of Eden and the indexing of nature by Carolus Linnaeus, Fowles speaks of "our endless efforts to 'garden,' to invent disciplining social and intellectual systems" to counter the rich "wild nature" of ordinary consciousness (37). Later he speaks of "the safe garden of civilization" (68). Finally he speaks specifically of the "constricting tenets and philosophies of science" as "that old *hortus conclusus* again," the "emblematic walled garden of civilization" (63, 72). His point is not a total rejection of order; Fowles makes clear the necessity for structure in life and literature. What is needed, however, is a balance of the external systematic mode of perception and the inner emotional, experiential vision, to counter the tendency to value the public system and to devalue the private experience. Accepted orderings of reality freeze into precepts rather than descriptions and are mistaken for reality itself. When this happens, the "garden of civilization" becomes a prison, more *conclusus* than *hortus*. The loss of such a garden, if painful, is nonetheless "fortunate," and its replacement by the individual's unfettered freshness of vision offers the possibilities inherent in "acting what one knows," as urged in the Arnoldian epigraph to the last chapter of *The French Lieutenant's Woman* (461). The novel presents the whole Victorian age as just such a garden, and one well lost.

Whereas the various settings of *The French Lieutenant's Woman* are presented as gardens of one kind or another, some fertile and creative, others restrictive and stultifying, perhaps the setting most crucial for charting Charles Smithson's growth is the explicitly Edenic Undercliff (67). Here Charles's confrontation with nature is ambiguously presented. Although some aspects of the pastoral experience are presented positively, these aspects are countered and undercut by Darwinian science. This opposition might even be considered the typical "dialectical, tensive structure characteristic of all worthwhile pastoral" were it not that the unpastoral, realistic element, evolutionary science, carries the day.[3] As a result, in the novel the conventional, pastoral sense of a oneness with nature is explicitly denied. In addition, whereas Charles's expeditions to the woods do effect a new consciousness—a typical experience for earlier visitors to Arcadian sites—this new consciousness is not acquired instantaneously, but only gradually through a further series of expulsions from a variety of Edenic enclaves. Furthermore, the quality of Charles's newly won consciousness is different from that of the traditional pastoral. Although the visitor to Arcadia usually acquires a vision of the ideal to take back to civilization, Fowles's protagonist acquires a vision of reality, the reality of nature in the broadest sense of the term, as it applies to both human beings and physical nature. Charles may enter the woods as an amateur paleontologist—a student of fossils—but he emerges a biologist, of sorts—a student of life in a much wider sense.

In the scenes in the Undercliff, Fowles draws together Jungian and Darwinian elements to chart the course of Charles's passage from the apparently cozy security of early- or pre-Marxian, pre-Freudian, pre-Darwinian society into the twentieth century, and the sequence of encounters there may be read as successive assaults on Charles's consciousness in all these areas. Of the five meetings Charles has with Sarah in the woods, the description of the first focuses on the natural landscape and Charles's Victorian response to it. The presentations of the next three focus on Charles and Sarah but in Jungian and Darwinian terms, featuring Sarah as anima and as victim of implacable forces. The final trip that Charles makes into the woods begins with a focus again on the physical world surrounding Charles—and his very different response on this occasion. By this time Charles has become fascinated by Sarah, has lost Winsyatt, and has made a crucial decision to ignore Dr. Grogan's advice. Charles's response to nature in the last of these scenes is thus a measure of his changed perceptions.

With the first presentation of the Undercliff, on the occasion of Charles's first foray into the woods, Fowles sets up a pastoral frame of reference and simultaneously undercuts it. His first description is "from the air," as if from an airplane: "If one flies low enough one can see that the terrain is very abrupt, cut by deep chasms and accentuated by strange bluffs and towers of chalk and flint, which loom over the lush foliage around them like the walls of ruined castles" (66). This description is pastoral "distancing" with a modern vengeance and is meant, no doubt, to further the present-past dialectic of the novel. It is worth noting, however, that aerial perspectives predate the twentieth century; *A Short History of Lyme Regis* contains a picture of Lyme that Fowles describes as an enlargement of "a mid-Victorian miniature drawing, and curiously shown from an aerial viewpoint"—curious only because necessarily imagined, as what a bird's eye might see.[4] Fowles's description quickly descends onto the land itself, as the Undercliff would impress itself upon a walking visitor—its isolation, its "botanical strangeness" and tropical climate so unusual in the English landscape and, above all, its virgin, untouched, "total wildness" (67). It is, as the narrator remarks, "an English Garden of Eden," but it is less the tended and walled garden of Milton's *Paradise Lost* than it is wild, primeval nature.

In contrast to Eden with its prohibition, the woods of the Undercliff are more seemingly Arcadian in their freedom, and that freedom is an ideal they are meant to convey in several ways. Fowles has commented, in *The Tree*, on the use of this setting in the novel:

> In the wood I know best there is a dell among beeches at the foot of a chalk cliff. Not a person a month goes there now, since it is well away from any path. But three centuries ago it was crowded every Sunday, for it is where the independents came . . . to hold their forbidden services. There are freedoms in woods that our ancestors perhaps realized more fully than we do. I used this wood, and even this particular dell, in *The*

French Lieutenant's Woman, for scenes that it seemed to me, in a story of self-liberation, could have no other setting. (74–75)

In *A Short History of Lyme Regis*, Fowles explains further that during the 1620s and 1630s, antiroyalist Puritanism flourished in Lyme, and after the Restoration the dissenters were the objects of violent persecution: "Unable to worship normally, the congregations were driven out into the open air, most famously at White Chapel Rocks. . . . A place in the Undercliff where Jones [a local royalist] is said to have spied on those going to the 'Mount Sion' of Chapel Rocks is still known as Jones's chair" (23).

In the first presentation of the Undercliff in the novel, it is further characterized by comparison with Renaissance art (68), one of the means by which the woods are given a Jungian frame of reference, as a place representing the unconscious—that is, a place associated with the mother. In *The Aristos,* Fowles calls the Renaissance an "Eve society," in which "the woman and the mother, female gods, encourage innovation and experiment, and fresh definitions, aims, modes of feeling."[5] Similarly, in *The Tree*, he has characterized trees as "protective, maternal, even womblike" (74). Jung, in *The Archetypes and the Collective Unconscious*, designates the woods as one of the symbols of the mother. In *Symbols of Transformation* he makes the connection by drawing upon myths of human origins in trees, the "maternal treetrunks" in the Osiris and Adonis myths, and the worship of female deities in trees—which Jung suggests may have led to the "cult of sacred groves and trees."[6] Here two significant details establish the Undercliff as figuring the maternal unconscious in Charles's behavior. First, ironically, Charles enters the woods because the sea, which has its own Jungian association with the mother archetype and the unconscious, has cut off his shoreline return to Lyme, forcing him away from the usual open path to civilization.[7] Second, as Charles goes up the wooded path, he finds that it forks and then forks again until he comes to the small clearing from which he sees Sarah on the ledge below. These paths are significant because they symbolize rather finely the exact stage of Charles's psychic development as described by Jung: "Where the roads cross and enter into one another, thereby symbolizing the union of opposites, there is the 'Mother,' the object and epitome of all union. Where the roads *divide*, where there is parting, separation, splitting, there we find the 'division,' the cleft— the symbol of the Mother and at the same time the essence of what the Mother means for us—namely cleavage and farewell."[8] The topography here implies that Charles is approaching not the usual, pastoral *locus amoenus*, or sacred place, which is almost always presented as the "epitome of all union," but instead a place where he will discover the need to leave the security and comfort of his Edenic nineteenth-century existence.

Charles does feel the appropriate pastoral nostalgia; the narrator, however, counters it immediately by recommending the contemporary existential response of appreciating the present moment as an alternative to Charles's regret that "I cannot possess this forever, and therefore am sad." The "desire to hold and the desire to enjoy," we are told, "are mutually destructive," although Charles cannot see this (69). As Fowles asserts in *The Tree*, to "hold" nature is to arrest it, substituting a static framework for its living reality and thereby destroying its essence, what prompted one's enjoyment in the first place (50–52). Thus we do not see in Charles's response to the landscape "the integration of man with his physical environment," which Northrop Frye in *The Stubborn Structure* mentions as a characteristic of the Arcadian landscape.[9] Instead, we see an alienation that proceeds from an attitude the narrator characterizes later in the novel as "pseudo-Linnaean"—that is, a perception aligned with the static, scientific categorizing of Linnaeus (Carl von Linné), whom Fowles in *The Tree* calls "the great warehouse clerk and indexer of nature" (24). Fowles explains that the result of Linnaeus's effort, although a useful tool for natural science, has been to narrow and constrict human vision. Aside from the possibility that our theories, serving us like a "camera view-finder," may in fact distort what we see around us, they also sacrifice "certain possibilities of seeing, apprehending, and experiencing" (27). So it is with Charles as he is presented during his first excursion, on the beach; the narrator tells us that although Charles considers himself a Darwinist, he has not really come to terms with the disruption of the Linnaean world order that Darwin's ideas entail. As a result, he misreads the natural information around him. Rather than seeing the "continuous flux" of reality and the possibility that if new species do appear old ones may become extinct, Charles sees instead "an immensely reassuring orderliness in existence . . . very conveniently arranged . . . for the survival of the fittest and best, *exempli gratia* Charles Smithson" (49).

At the end of Charles's subsequent venture into the woods, he encounters Sarah, who has the alluring, mysterious characteristics of a Jungian anima figure, here in the guise of Eve. However, because Charles is not at first the Darwinian he thinks he is but, instead, the Linnaean collector, he makes the erroneous assumption that "one cannot reenter a legend" (69). However, "the Garden of Eden is an impossible dream," as Fowles says in *The Aristos*, and "the Fall is the essential *processus* of evolution" (165). So the process of developing the "self-intelligence," which Fowles believes is "the essential factor in evolutionary survival" (164), is the most basic and universal legend of mankind. Jung calls this process the quest for individuation. Because the urge to change, to progress, to grow psychologically is experienced individually (by a male) through projection onto a female "other," the encounter with the anima—in Charles's case, with Sarah—is crucial, both in a man's development and in Fowles's fiction.

Sarah, in the role of Eve in an English Garden of Eden, is associated with a fall: the place she has chosen for a nap is a precarious ledge over the beach (70). She lies surrounded by flowers, like John Milton's Eve upon awakening after having been created. Charles's response is appropriately Adamic: he is attracted to her sexually, yet he also has a "strange feeling—not sexual, but fraternal, perhaps paternal, a certainty of the innocence of this creature."[10] The transfiguration of the image of Sarah into that of Charles's sister in his imagination serves to underline the exact phase of Charles's development after the fourth meeting (177). Carl Jung's brilliant pupil Erich Neumann, in *The Origin and History of Consciousness*, elucidates the appearance of the anima as sister. In the developmental stages of the male ego consciousness, between the undifferentiated unconscious, signified in myth as the Great Mother, and the full-blown emergence of the feminine component, the anima, the ego may often perceive the anima in nonsexual, nonthreatening terms of a sister, a helpful companion. Neumann explains that in myth the experience is embodied in stories concerning the rescue of a captive or a treasure from a monster, a magician, or wicked parents, but the subjective experience of a male is that of some "change in his relation to the female" so that he may establish a partnership with her. Neumann's description of the "captive" soul as "something that cries out to be rescued, set free, and redeemed" from the dragon is objectified in Sarah's situation both as an inmate in Mrs. Poulteney's house and as an inhabitant of the broader Victorian society, which has carefully built walls around her. The perception of the sister-anima is a crucial step in the development of the ego, as Neumann explains, because it enables a change in the male's relationship with the female; its experience frees the male's "living relation to the 'you,' to the world at large."[11]

The imagery of the Fall is a constant and increasingly intense element in the novel's scenes in the woods. In their second meeting, Sarah slips on the path and "falls," and she is described as like "a boy caught stealing apples from an orchard" (118). In the third meeting Charles feels he is on a "brink over an abyss" (145). In the fourth meeting, a dangerous climb—with its possibility of a fall—takes place;

Sarah, after telling Charles the story of Varguennes, says that it was as if she had thrown herself off a cliff; and the scene ends with Charles's feeling that he has "one foot over the precipice" (186).

Part of Charles's development through these scenes is stimulated by another antipastoral element, Sarah's presentation of her plight as social victim. Charles's efforts at "alarmed propriety," as well as Sarah's expressions of social injustice, continually inject the issue of class into what in the traditional pastoral would be a situation without class conflict. Educated beyond her class, Sarah finds herself in social isolation, and she sees, if somewhat imperfectly, that society would prefer to keep her safely and obscurely out of sight. Sarah's revelations of her oppressed situation perform the same function for Charles that the narrator's information about Mrs. Poulteney's servant Millie and the laboring peasants performs for readers: to strip away a facade and remind them that pastoral sentimentalizes and falsifies.

Sarah's reaction to her plight, however, reveals that she is hardly the postlapsarian Eve of biblical tradition, whose patriarchal law dictates the subordinate, inferior position of the woman who, furthermore, is blamed for the loss of Eden. Indeed, her story of Varguennes's temptation and her fall is an ironic reversal of the Genesis account of the Fall of man tempted by woman, as well as a symbolic portrayal of woman's vulnerable position in Victorian society. By making her story public knowledge, Sarah has refused to acquiesce in society's evaluation of women. As Dwight Eddins puts it in "John Fowles: Existence as Authorship," Sarah "is thus duping the Victorian age in an escape that is also a mockery of the age's imprisoning forces."[12] Also, ironically, as Sarah tells Charles the fabricated (yet symbolically true) story of her fall, Fowles has situated them at White Chapel Rock—the heart of his Eden and the place he felt to be the necessary setting for such "a story of self-liberation." However, he has seated Charles on a "rustic throne," a "better seat" reminiscent of "Jones's Seat," and thus Fowles casts Charles as the Victorian version of the Royalist oppressor of the seventeenth century.[13]

This ironic undercutting of the pastoral culminates through biological means, when Charles and Sarah stand watching Sam and Mary: Sarah's smile seems to say to Charles, "Where are your pretensions now, . . . where is your birth, your science, your etiquette, your social order?" (185). Here Sarah performs the function of the anima that Fowles has described "as fundamentally subversive and destructive of structures in society which have been created by males."[14]

If Sarah, in her role as animating force, is responsible for Charles's encounters in the Undercliff with the two unpastoral realities of "ubiquitous economic oppression" and "the terror of sexuality" (145), she also initiates his awareness of Darwinian evolution as an existential reality rather than a mere avant-garde theory (145). His growth in perception will require additional, personal experiences—the loss of Winsyatt, the offer of "trade" from Mr. Freeman, the episode with the London prostitute, the crisis at the church in Exeter, and the loss of Sarah herself. Yet, Sarah serves as catalyst in surroundings that thrust evolution into the forefront, so that it becomes in effect, as Robert Huffaker has suggested, the main subject of the novel.[15]

The presentations of the meetings in the woods are permeated with references to evolution, further undercutting the pastoral setting. The narrator himself points to this function when he says that Darwinism was responsible for "undermining . . . the Biblical account of the origins of man" (120). Later, during Charles's conversation with Dr. Grogan, the narrator speaks of Lyell's geological studies and calls the story of creation in Genesis a "six-thousand-year-old womb"—terms that link the Edenic situation with the mother (160). Charles at first goes to the Undercliff to look for the "tests," or echinoderms, which the narrator tells us were "one of the first practical confirmations of the theory of evolution" (46); and before Charles even meets Sarah, the narrator raises the subject of the pre-Darwinian cardinal principle *nulla species nova*—there can be no new species—as a "foredoomed attempt to stabilize and fix what is in reality a continuous flux" (49). The movement and constant change of the living world as described in evolutionary theory effectively negate the pastoral attitude, which desires a static, stable environment. As the narrator explains, the appearance of new species means the possible extinction of old ones, a destructive aspect of Darwin that Charles fails to understand fully. While Charles has successfully practiced one technique for survival, cryptic coloration—"survival by learning to blend with one's surroundings—with the unquestioned assumptions of one's age or social caste" (145)—Sarah's challenge of this technique implies that it may no longer be of use to him. The epigraph to Chapter 19, drawn from *The Origin of Species*, makes it clear that variation from the norm is sometimes the best means of survival: "any being, if it vary however slightly in any manner profitable to itself, under the complex and sometimes varying conditions of life, will have a better chance of surviving, and thus be *naturally selected*" (147).

The deterministic implications of evolution, which consistently intrude upon what might otherwise be Arcadian meetings, receive ironic emphasis in Charles's disquisition on free will immediately following his fourth meeting with Sarah, when Charles resolves to repress his attraction to Sarah. Later, however, after returning from Winsyatt and finding that Sarah is missing, Charles discards these resolutions and is forced to admit that "he had no more free will than an ammonite" (237). Still, this gloomy belief, although he reiterates it later in London, is no more accurate, Fowles would say, than is Charles's earlier, inflated overconfidence. Because free will is, to Fowles, the "highest human good," it is important to understand how it coexists with scientific determinism in his scheme. In *The Aristos*, he sees free will, like the afterlife, as a basically insoluble problem: It may be proved some day that "we do not, in some evolutionary or biological sense, possess any free will"; nevertheless, he continues, we do have times when "we *feel* . . . we choose freely." As in a chess game, we are bound by "a framework of set rules and prescribed movements," yet there are free choices to be made (68–69). Although the evolutionary process seems indifferent to the individual, he feels an assurance that "the whole is not in hazard" (28). Humans must realize that, "like every other form of matter, [they are] not necessary but contingent," but that they "can by exercise become—free to choose courses of action and so at least combat some of the hostile results of the general indifference of the process to the individual" (26).

Charles's problem in both the extremes he adopts is a misunderstanding of the individual's position and abilities. Although he cannot control the broad *processus* and thus is fighting a losing battle in denying his sexuality (and the possibilities of life that Sarah represents) through claiming, initially, a "higher" position on the scale of creation, he is not the powerless fossil he calls himself later. Whereas Charles the gentleman may in fact be a victim of social evolution, Charles the individual has a chance for "growth of experience, of intelligence, of knowledge, and this growth engenders moments of insight, moments when we see deeper purposes, truer causes, more intended effects." There is, as Fowles defines it in *The Aristos*, a chance for evolution (38).

Nevertheless, in Charles's fifth and last visit to the woods, despite his decision to trust his own intuitions about Sarah (which still are wrong, as he now sees her only as a frightened victim), Charles still feels intensely the hostility of the natural surroundings, "universal chaos, looming behind the fragile structure of human order" (240). Yet, there is a suggestion that Charles has made some progress; he is vitally aware on this visit not of phyla and species, but simply of *what is*.

Of all the presentations of the Undercliff area, this one seems at first to be the most pastoral. The narrator even refers to the scene as "a perfect world" after having provided a sensuous description: "Each grass-blade was pearled with vapor. On the slopes above his path the trunks of the ashes and sycamores, a honey gold in the oblique sunlight, erected their dewy green vaults of young leaves; there was something mysteriously religious about them, but of a religion before religion; a druid balm, a green sweetness over all . . . and such an infinity of green, some almost black in the further recesses of the foliage; from the most intense emerald to the palest pomona" (239, ellipsis in original). All the creatures present share "the same divine assumption of possession," all "mysteriously religious." Charles feels "a flood of warmth through him and seems to notice everything with an immediacy and distinctness that he has not sensed before—not unlike the singing bird or the staring fox." Indeed, what he is witnessing is true pastoral classlessness, an equality of species—the "universal parity of existence."[16] As Fowles explains in *The Aristos*, unlike the human being, the animal lacks the ability to compare, and this is what sets apart the human being, who alone has the consciousness that enables the perception of inequality. Eden—this "happy oblivion"—is thus closed off. "The enormous price of knowledge is the power to imagine and the consequent power to compare. The 'golden age' was the age before comparison; and if there had been a Garden of Eden and a Fall, they would have been when man could not compare and when he could: between Genesis 3:6 and Genesis 3:7" (60). The "parity of existence" that Charles witnesses, then, is one that precedes the Fall.

Thus Fowles's true Eden, we may see, is predicated on the evolutionary process; paradoxically, it necessitates its own loss, a "fortunate fall" into the recognition of reality, undiluted and unmediated by a pastoral myth that may inhibit the individual's personal growth. The spokesman for the *processus* here is the tiny wren, "a midget ball of feathers that yet managed to make itself the Announcing Angel of evolution" (240). The wren's aptness can also be explained in Jungian terms, in which, as delineated by Joseph Henderson, the bird can serve as a symbol of transcendence, the struggle to unite the conscious and unconscious contents of the mind that leads to the individual's realization of the potential of the psyche, or self. According to Henderson, the bird in primitive cultures is often thought to be the shaman, regarded in Jungian psychology as related to the magician or the trickster archetype, the master of initiation.[17] For Fowles, versed in Jungian theory, the wren signals a crucial stage in the evolution of Charles's consciousness; it is for him a moment of vision comparable to the scene of St. Hubert's conversion in the forest, which, the narrator reminds us, has been depicted by Antonio Pisanello: "He stood as Pisanello's saint stood, astonished perhaps more at his own astonishment at this world's existing so close, so within reach of all that

Tudor House, 16 Cheyne Walk, Chelsea, London. The architectural bay with ivy in the center of this 1870 photograph is the place where Charles discovers Sarah near the end(ings) of *The French Lieutenant's Woman*. Restored in 1994 (but not open to the public), 16 Cheyne Walk is well-known as the address where Dante Gabriel Rossetti and others associated with the Pre-Raphaelite movement in the arts lived between 1862 and 1871, implications of which are discussed by James R. Aubrey in "The Pre-Raphaelite 'pack of satyrs' in John Fowles's *The French Lieutenant's Woman*" (*Nineteenth-Century Prose*, 18.1 [1990/91], pages 32–36). Photograph courtesy of The Royal Borough of Kensington and Chelsea Libraries and Arts Service.

suffocating banality of ordinary day. . . . The appalling ennui of human reality lay cleft to the core; and the heart of all life pulsed there in the wren's triumphant throat" (240). For Charles, it is still a long way to the Rossettis' house in Chelsea—the last of a series of Edens from which he must be expelled—before he will understand more clearly, more personally, the relationship between the hazards of existence and his capabilities as an individual. Along his evolutionary way, the Undercliff has offered Charles a premonitory vision of actuality.

Like Wallace Stevens's "scrawny chorister," the wren in the Undercliff announces for Charles "a new knowledge of reality."[18]

Notes

1. John Fowles, *The French Lieutenant's Woman* (Boston: Little, Brown, 1969).
2. John Fowles, *The Tree* (New York: Ecco Press, 1983).
3. The quoted phrase is from Harold Tolliver, *Pastoral Forms and Attitudes* (Berkeley: University of California Press, 1971), page 5.
4. John Fowles, *A Short History of Lyme Regis* (Boston: Little, Brown, 1982), page 27.
5. John Fowles, *The Aristos: A Self-Portrait in Ideas* (Boston: Little, Brown, 1964), page 166.
6. Carl G. Jung, *The Archetypes and the Collective Unconscious*, trans. R. F. C. Hull, vol. 9, pt. 1 of *The Collected Works of C. G. Jung* (Princeton: Princeton University Press, 1970), page 81; *Symbols of Transformation*, trans. R. F. C. Hull, 2d ed., vol. 5 of *The Collected Works of C. G. Jung* (Princeton: Princeton University Press, 1967), page 219.
7. Also in *Symbols of Transformation*, Jung draws clearly the connection between the sea, the mother archetype, and the unconscious: "In dreams and fantasies the sea or a large expanse of water signifies the unconscious. The maternal aspect of water coincides with the nature of the unconscious, because the latter (particularly in men) can be regarded as the Mother or matrix of consciousness" (219).
8. Jung, *Symbols of Transformation*, page 371; italics in original.
9. Northrop Frye, *The Stubborn Structure* (Ithaca: Cornell University Press, 1970), page 126.
10. John Milton, *Paradise Lost*, 2d ed. (New York: W. W. Norton, 1993), Book 4, lines 449–51; Fowles, *The French Lieutenant's Woman*, page 71.
11. Erich Neumann, *The Origins and History of Consciousness*, trans. R. F. C. Hull (Princeton: Princeton University Press, 1970), pages 188, 195–203.
12. Dwight Eddins, "John Fowles: Existence as Authorship," *Contemporary Literature* 17 (1976), page 201.
13. Fowles, *The French Lieutenant's Woman*, page 166. In fact, topographically, Jones's seat is almost a mile east of Whitechapel Rock, which is north of the coastal path between the Whitlands Cliff and the Pinhay Cliff. This particular formation is referred to in the singular, whereas an area known as Whitechapel Rocks is just to the west.
14. Joshua Gilder, "John Fowles: A Novelist's Dilemma," *Saturday Review*, October 1981, pages 36, 39–40.
15. Robert Huffaker, *John Fowles*, Twayne's English Authors Series 292 (Boston: Twayne, 1980), page 109.
16. Fowles, *The French Lieutenant's Woman*, page 239. Although this phrase is found in the novel, the centrality of the concept to Fowles's thinking is indicated by its presence in the earlier *The Aristos*, where it is called "relativity of recompense" (59), and its almost identical representation later, in *Daniel Martin*, as "a mysterious yet profound parity in all existence" (273).
17. Joseph L. Henderson, "Ancient Myths and Modern Man," in *Man and His Symbols*, ed. Carl G. Jung and Marie-Louise von Franz (1964; reprint New York: Dell, 1968), pages 95–156.
18. Wallace Stevens, "Not Ideas about the Thing but the Thing Itself," in *The Collected Poems of Wallace Stevens* (New York: Alfred A. Knopf, 1954), page 534.

"Water out of a Woodland Spring": Sarah Woodruff and Nature in *The French Lieutenant's Woman*

SUZANNE ROSS

SARAH WOODRUFF IS THE ENIGMATIC FIGURE IN JOHN FOWLES'S 1969 novel *The French Lieutenant's Woman*, a mystery both to readers and to the other characters within the narrative framework itself. Is she a fallen woman, a victim of male concupiscence, or a wanton, a siren? Is she a woman ahead of her time, a feminist, or a madwoman, an hysteric? This is the Sarah that Charles Smithson rashly falls in love with, a mysterious woman he meets in the place she has been exiled to, a wild place beyond the bounds of Victorian society. Even the narrator himself asks: "Who is Sarah? Out of what shadows does she come?"[1]

She is a puzzle, as well, for other readers and critics attempting to come to terms with her meanings in their own transactions with the novel. Of recurring interest for many has been Sarah's potential for feminist interpretation. On the one hand, she has been called "a positive role model," who through the course of the narrative "develops a feminist consciousness." She has on the other hand been termed merely "a symbol, an ideal, a mythic figure, an Other"—thus, as a woman, absent and voiceless. Given the elusively multiple quality of this character, another critic has suggested that it might be fruitful "to understand Sarah herself as a text to be read" in that such a strategy would cast light upon the many Sarahs constructed by those around her, both within and external to the narrative frame.[2]

One thing we can know for certain of Sarah Woodruff is that she is associated with the natural world: she shares her surname with a small, aromatic woodland plant (*Galium odoratum*), commonly known as sweet woodruff. Her initial appearance in the narrative is as a lone, mysteriously cloaked figure who seeks out the windblown isolation of the Cobb at Lyme Regis. She seems "naturally" drawn to the wild landscape of the Undercliff and Ware Common. Given John Fowles's own interests in natural history—and his relationship with nature is the "key" to his fiction, he tells us in *The Tree*—we should not be surprised to encounter a character such as Sarah Woodruff.[3] Clearly, Sarah's link to the natural world is a central feature of her characterization, and it accounts in part for her appeal. Indeed, her connection to nature at first would appear to be a wholly unproblematic aspect of her femaleness. But is it?

Because John Fowles's interests in the natural world are becoming well known, it is worth noting that literary critics of his work, perhaps because of their own limited interest in nature, either have given little attention to the presence of the natural world in Fowles's fiction or have interpreted it in terms of symbolic references or stereotypical correspondences. One result has been an oversimplified view of Sarah Woodruff's connection to nonhuman nature. That Fowles might be saying something of significance about the distortions and limitations implicit in gendered representations of the relationship between human beings and the nonhuman world has rarely been addressed. Perhaps most critics have not been in a position to frame the necessary questions.

In recent years the traditional bond between women and nature has been the subject of lively discussion.[4] Many feminists, following Simone de Beauvoir in *The Second Sex*, have called for the liberation of women from being identified with nature, arguing that women's devalued status stems from their culturally constructed position closer to this devalued other.[5] However, contemporary *ecofeminists* claim that patriarchal culture's traditional linkage of women with nature underwrites the continued domination and exploitation of both. Ecofeminists do not call for the liberation of women *from* nature; instead, they cast their lot *with* the nonhuman world.[6]

Ecofeminists insist that it is neither through a transcendence of nature nor through the destruction of the bonds (whether culturally constructed or innate) linking them to nature that women will liberate themselves. Ecofeminism recognizes that the liberation of one is inextricably linked to the liberation of the other. The liberation of both requires not that the bond be broken but that it be refigured—in fact, that the whole system of oppositional and hierarchically ordered categories—culture *and* nature, man *and* woman—itself be reconceived. At the most fundamental level, according to Greta Gaard, ecofeminism offers an alternative understanding of the self not as defined by disconnection and separation but as "interconnected with all life" (1–2).

Such ideas as these today shape the efforts of female readers in particular to understand their relationship as women and as humans with the rest of nature. Such ideas may also be shaping recent readings of *The French Lieutenant's Woman*. Sarah's link to nature has become something to think about, and to think through. Now, approaching Sarah as a text to be read poses a new question: What are the stories of the connection between women and nature that this text of Sarah tells?

The reading of the text of Sarah Woodruff offered here is informed in large part by the insights of contemporary ecofeminism, which requires serious critical attention to Fowles's characterization of a female figure and how he represents her link to the world of nonhuman nature. This reading of Sarah's character sheds light on the varied, even contradictory stories of the connection between women and nature that our own cultural tradition tells. It will become evident that in *The French Lieutenant's Woman* Fowles casts a critical eye on such stories, explores their implications, and proposes an alternative.

* * *

In *The French Lieutenant's Woman*, John Fowles is clearly working with the sets of dichotomous conceptual pairs referred to above. The man Charles Smithson is linked to culture and the woman Sarah Woodruff to nature. Sarah's propensity for escape to the Undercliff, and her seeming "fittedness" for that place can be taken as signs of the inarticulable connection she feels for the nonhuman world. Charles's repeated recognitions of his own unfittedness and his interloper status on the Undercliff similarly signal the absence of that tie to nature for him, as a man. However, beyond merely reiterating patriarchy's construction of the woman / nature bond, Fowles's narrative framework exposes the system of values underwriting Charles's privilege and Sarah's oppression. In Sarah, specifically by means of the many possible readings of the text of Sarah, Fowles constructs a site where the work ecofeminists call for might imaginatively begin—namely, the work of refiguring this system of hierarchically ordered binary oppositions in order to reconceive of the self in terms of interconnection and interanimation.

Three characters within the narrative frame offer readings of Sarah that represent aspects of patriarchy's construction of the woman / nature bond. For Mrs. Poulteney, Sarah is a sexually licentious woman, apparently unrepentant of her sin. Against explicit instructions, she continues to frequent Ware Common, "a *de facto* Lover's Lane," the narrator informs us, a place through long tradition where young men and women have met to celebrate the summer solstice— and one another (90). To the puritanical Mrs. Poulteney, Sarah and nature together represent the immorality of uncontrolled sensuality and sexuality.

Dr. Grogan is a sympathetic yet ultimately condescending clinician in relation to Sarah. He believes that he understands her, insofar as she can be understood, or knows at least how to handle her as a case of disease. He has a label for her predicament: "obscure melancholia"; a diagnosis: she is addicted to her melancholy; and a suggested treatment: "a private asylum in Exeter," where matters are "conducted in an intelligent and enlightened manner" (154, 156, 227). Grogan tells Charles, "you must not think she is like us men, able to reason clearly, examine her motives, understand why she behaves as she does. One must see her as being in a mist" (156). For Grogan, Sarah the woman is irrational, like nature, without the capacity for self-awareness and reflection, motivated by elemental forces over which she has no control.

Ernestina feels both pity and distaste for Sarah. When in chapter 2 she and Charles encounter the mysterious, cloaked figure far out on the Cobb, Ernestina tells him that it must be "'Poor Tragedy.'" Sarah is also known locally as "'the French Lieutenant's ... Woman'"; the ellipsis indicates that Ernestina cannot bring herself to say "whore," but that is evidently how she views Sarah, for when asked if this French Lieutenant is a man Sarah has fallen in love with, Ernestina responds that it was "'worse than that'" (8–9). When Charles returns after his second accidental encounter with Sarah in the Undercliff, Ernestina, unaware of the aptness of her words, mocks him with accusations of "dallying with the wood nymphs" (88). She reveals here how she herself has been shaped by cultural expectations and fears, how diminished is her own experience of the natural world, how filtered through the sanitizing screen of classicizing art is her own knowledge. Ernestina is a woman of her times, her sensuality tamed.[7] She views Sarah from her own position within the constricting role approved for women by Victorian society. Uneasily, she looks out on Sarah as a wild outcast.

Through the persona of the novel's late-20th-century—to be exact, late-1960s—male narrator, Fowles offers an *apparently* positive reading of the text of Sarah and of Western culture's continued linkage of women to nonhuman nature. Early in the novel, Sarah and Charles's significant interactions occur out of doors in the Undercliff, a place about which she is knowledgeable, a place for which, the narrator implies, she is clearly fitted. He informs us of her uncanny talent for finding tests, the fossil sea urchins Charles prizes, and of her "genius" for finding secluded, wild places (164, 166). Fowles paints this picture: having decided to tell Charles the story of her relationship with Var-

Lister House, Lyme Regis. Formerly the residence of Joseph Lister, pioneer in antiseptics, the house served as the imagined model for Mrs. Poulteney's house in *The French Lieutenant's Woman* (interview, John Fowles Symposium, 11 July 1996). In the novel, Fowles describes her "large Regency house, which stood, an elegantly clear simile of her social status, in a commanding position on one of the steep hills behind Lyme Regis"; the chapter's description of the unpleasantness of life below stairs and its epigraph about how Victorians live above their own cesspools suggest that Fowles sees the house—and perhaps by extension the town, as opposed to the country—as a symbol of the age, as well, with its repression of wildness. Photograph by James Aubrey, 1996.

guennes, Sarah suddenly appears before him standing at the end of a dark tunnel of ivy through which he must pass to reach her, a sulfur-colored butterfly floating behind her (163). Her physical appearance and abilities are, we might say, "natural"—her loose, dark, sun-glistened hair and her nimbleness on difficult ground (165). Like a wild animal, she has "sharper ears" than Charles (121). In an important sense she *is* a wild animal, offering merely the appearance of tameness when enclosed within the invisible bars of Mrs. Poulteney's drawing room, in the large house—surrounded by traps—that Fowles makes a symbol of tyranny (18–20, 103). Real rest, authentic freedom Sarah finds only in the Undercliff—asleep on a precipitous grassy ledge in this "English Garden of Eden" (67–70). She is made to seem to belong in the natural landscape, outside the town of Lyme Regis.

Undercliff over Pinhay Bay. When Charles climbs to the Undercliff in Chapter Ten of *The French Lieutenant's Woman* he discovers Sarah asleep on a "little green plateau" like this one, which "opened out very agreeably, like a tiny alpine meadow" between himself and the cliff over the beach (page 69). Photograph by James Aubrey, 1996.

A social outcast, Sarah is profoundly lonely. When Charles first comes upon her in the Undercliff, asleep on that grassy ledge below him, the narrator describes his shock as he realizes that nothing short of despair "could drive her, in an age where women were semistatic, timid, incapable of sustained physical effort, to this wild place" (71). Incapable of coquetry or triviality, she is an acutely observant and insightful woman, disconcertingly direct, possessing, the narrator tells us, an intuitive, nonanalytical intelligence (52). What most defines her, however, is her sorrow, a sorrow that the narrator describes as welling out of her tragic face "as purely, naturally and unstoppably as water out of a woodland spring" (10).

The narrator's reading of Sarah—his descriptions of her appearance, her kind of intelligence, and her emotional state—is very appealing. Surely it has been so for many readers over the years. Yet, this reading of Sarah, just like the others, links her at once to traditional and contemporary patriarchal formulations of both the feminine *and* the natural world, the engendering site, according to patriarchy, of the devalued instinctual, nonrational capacities she possesses. The wild, lonely, elemental places Sarah is drawn to early in the novel are, the narrator implies, the physical correlatives of her psychic landscape and emotional weather.

Clearly, the Sarah the narrator describes is not like other women of her time and place, at least not others of the social class to which her education would attach her, not in appearance, not in behavior, not in essence. Repeatedly, if implicitly, the narrator contrasts Sarah with Ernestina. Sarah's physical appearance and capacities—her loose, unoiled hair and brown skin, her ability to climb difficult terrain, her apparent compulsion to be outdoors, her seriousness—all distinguish her from Ernestina with her fashionable clothing, her careful toilette, her frailty and pallor, her headaches, her triviality. Charles's proposal to Ernestina occurs indoors, in her family's conservatory; his encounters with Sarah are outdoors, in the Undercliff. We are reminded of the differences between the two women again when Sarah is recounting for Charles her story. The narrator reinforces this contrast, telling us that Sarah "seemed totally indifferent to fashion; and survived in spite of it, just as the simple primroses at Charles's feet survived all the competition of exotic conservatory plants" (167). Thus, while patriarchy's generalized connection between women and nonhuman nature is acknowledged, it is Ernestina who is the hothouse plant and Sarah who is, as Charles flippantly puts it in a conversation with Dr. Grogan, "the specimen of the local flora" (153). Through such implicit comparisons, the narrator reveals again and again that he takes Sarah's part along with the part of untamed nature. Through his descriptions of Sarah and his associations of her with the natural world, the narrator reveals as well his own values, preferences, and beliefs about women and nature both. Indeed, if Sarah is not a woman of her own time, the late 1860s, is the narrator perhaps telling an idealized story of women and nature from his own time, the late 1960s? It seems plausible.

Charles, in his efforts to come to his own reading of Sarah, shifts among all of the available readings—the Victorian perspectives as constructed by the three characters within the narrative frame as well as momentary intimations of the contemporary reading constructed by the narrator, his future counterpart from the late 1960s. Within each reading Charles adopts the appropriate male position in relation to Sarah. He tries on roles and attendant demeanors: the outraged moralist, the dutiful though socially distant Victorian gentleman, the sympathetic if perhaps condescending scientist, the hopeful lover. He can imagine at once both taking Sarah as Varguennes and saving Sarah from Varguennes (176). Charles is either drawn to or repelled by the Sarah constructed by each of these stories. He suspects her now of being half-mad, then of being more sane than any person he has ever before encountered. Even so, none of his readings satisfies him for long; Sarah's meaning (or meanings) continue to elude him.

As readers, we ponder along with Charles the plausibility of each of these Sarahs. Yet, and perhaps oddly, in an effort to read the text of Sarah from a fresh perspective—to enrich our understanding of her meanings—it may be Charles whom we must first consider, specifically his relation to women and to the nonhuman world. Thus, because patriarchal culture has constructed him as a man in oppositional terms to woman, Charles's inability to take a stable and dependable reading of Sarah leaves him unsure of who he is, who he should be. Because his culture links women *with* nature, devaluing both, his estrangement from the one is connected in the novel to his exile from the other. Entering into the Undercliff in order to meet Sarah is, for Charles, a passing beyond the pale, both a physical and psychological movement away from the constricting limitations—and the safety—of Victorian society.

With Sarah in the Undercliff, Charles steps out into a wild, primeval place, a place offering the potential for direct, unsublimated experience—sensual, sexual, emotional, physical. It is a place where, again and again, he has unsettling flashes of awareness, glimpses of a reality unlike the stable and rationally ordered one he believes he knows. The narrator explains the power of this place over Charles, a place that resembles Darwin's tangled bank: "the prospect before [Charles], the sounds, the scents, the unalloyed wildness of growth and burgeoning fertility, forced him into anti-science" (68). Charles does not at first realize the folly of his habitual approach to the natural world—collecting and classifying—what Fowles describes in *The Tree* as Victorian society's unwelcome gift, "the demand that our relation with [nature] . . . be purposive, industrious, always seeking greater knowledge" (33). Later, however, the song of a wren powerfully cuts through his and his culture's arrogant assurance of human rationality and dominion, revealing to Charles "a universal chaos, looming behind the fragile structure of human order" (240).

These moments of awareness are, tellingly, ones that reveal as well the manner in which his society's propensity for subdividing reality into hierarchically ordered, oppositional relationships has exiled Sarah as a woman *to* nature and exiled him as a man *from* it. Entering into the Undercliff and meeting Sarah there, Charles has his certainty about his own identity radically destabilized. Beyond the safe harbor of the male self that patriarchy constructs for him—defined by separation rather than by connection, power over rather than interdependence with—Charles is at sea.

The narrator's claim at the end of chapter 10 that, with Charles's first sight of Sarah asleep on that grassy ledge in the Undercliff, "the whole Victorian Age was lost" (63) is not an overstatement but an accurate assessment of the critical juncture Charles has reached in his life. As Thomas Foster puts it, Charles "is in danger, as the novel progresses, of becoming merely another pillar of the Victorian establishment" (76). He is in danger of reclining into the comfortable certainty of the "naturalness" of his privilege as a man, the finality of his separation as a human from the world of nature. Yet, in that moment, he apprehends within Sarah an irrepressible wildness as she struggles to be fully herself in the face of the limiting and conforming pressures of patriarchal society, a wildness he realizes is nearly lost within himself. Charles imagines that Sarah is the door—his access to his own inner green being—but he fears that he has no key (186).

This particular one of Charles's many images of Sarah, this reading—perhaps influenced by the narrator's late-1960s perspective on women and nature—has power and appeal. From this perspective, Sarah is indeed Charles's means to salvation, his link to the nonhuman world, the door to which he merely needs a key. Many readers have been content to imagine Sarah—and other women—playing the traditional role of mediator for man, connecting him to the world of nature from which he is exiled by his own link to culture. At some point, however, the limitations and denials implicit in such a reading surface, making it apparent that each of the readings of Sarah discussed so far is joined by a single ideological allegiance. It is not difficult to recognize the ideology that gives rise to the stories of Sarah and nature told by Mrs. Poulteney, Dr. Grogan, and Ernestina. It is less evident, however, that the same ideology produces the 20th-century male narrator's apparently positive reading of Sarah and her connection to the natural world. Nonetheless, although they differ in emphasis, each of these texts of Sarah does acquiesce in a belief in the innateness, or "naturalness," of the bond linking women to nature. Each acquiesces as well to the "naturalness" of the conceptual system that isolates and differentially ranks culture above nature, man above woman.

Surely it is that wren who insists that we open our eyes—that "midget ball of feathers," Fowles calls her, "the Announcing Angel . . . of a far deeper and stranger reality than the pseudo-Linnaean one" gripping Charles, continuing to grip us. It was the wren's song, "violent," "defiant," announcing "the priority of . . . ecology over classification" (240). In other words, that tiny wren cut through all the foolishness, challenging the whole system of hierarchically ranked oppositions—culture / nature, man / woman—and offering another, wiser story of "the universal parity of existence" (239). For Charles at that moment, "the appalling ennui of human reality lay cleft to the core; and the heart of all life pulsed there in the wren's triumphant throat" (240). In this wiser story, Sarah is no more exiled to the Undercliff than Charles is exiled from it.

It is through this wiser story that another text of Sarah emerges. In this story, Sarah finds herself as a woman in a position of exclusion from Victorian society. Socially and economically unable and clearly unwilling to be Ernestina—in other words, to inhabit the approved position that her society has constructed for her as a woman—she is pushed to the margins. Her apparent options are disturbingly narrow: governess, servant, prostitute. In becoming the French Lieutenant's Woman as well as in continuing to walk in Ware Common, she chooses her marginal position. In embracing her status as outcast, she astounds Charles with her "talk of freedom beyond the pale, of marrying shame" (175). Yet, only in this way does she begin to rewrite in positive and affirming terms the story of her own identity as a woman and of her connection as a woman with the nonhuman world. Sarah strategically embraces the position of woman as more closely connected to nature. The position has been created for her, but its meaning for her is not preexistent, awaiting only discovery. She must interpret the position and use it as a location, a point of departure for the construction of new and liberatory meanings.[8]

If we read the text of Sarah from the perspective of the wren's wiser story, we can see that her actions both acknowledge and deny the power of the ideological and discursive forces of her society. Her actions acknowledge that in part she is constructed as "woman" by those forces. Her actions deny, however, that she can have no hand in it. Sarah's actions to rewrite her identity as a woman deny as well that the category "woman" is necessarily closed and static, its meanings determined. Through her actions, she reveals this category instead to be open and dynamic, its meanings relational. Because *woman* is a relational term, Sarah's actions have the effect also of destabilizing the meanings of such other category labels in patriarchy's system of hierarchies as *man, nature, culture*. Finally, Sarah's actions open up to reinterpretation and revision the story of the bond linking women more closely to nonhuman nature. No longer is it evident that this story must be read in such a manner that both nature and woman are conceived of as the devalued other.

In such a reading of the text of Sarah, we note that she is pushed and pulled. Centripetal forces seek to spin her into the drawing room, into the confining roles and expectations of women that patriarchal society has written for her. On the other hand, her own desire, at first inarticulate, to speak in her own voice, spins her centrifugally outward toward the margins, away from the strictures of Victorian society and out into the chaos of wild nature—into the Undercliff. When she chooses to embrace her status of outcast, she acts to render herself as a speaking subject. She chooses to tell Charles her story, albeit *a* story, of her relationship with Varguennes. As she speaks, she pauses now and then. In the interstices of her story, we are told of the flight of a crow (169), a spray of blue-petaled milkwort (170), and the song of a missal thrush hidden in an ash tree, "wild-voiced beneath the air's blue peace" (172). The fabric of her story is threaded through with the stories of these others. Like the Green Man Fowles describes in *The Tree*, Sarah "speaks" the interconnection and interanimation of all life.[9] She is the Green Woman.

Who then *is* Sarah? Out of what shadows *does* she come? In other words, what is Sarah's "real nature"? In the final two chapters of the novel, this question hangs between Sarah and Charles. It is the question upon which the alternative conclusions of the novel hinge. In the second, "unhappy" ending, Charles finds in Sarah "a spirit prepared to sacrifice everything but itself . . . in order to save its own integrity" (465). She is a woman unwilling to be pinned down, unwilling to be read once and for all, summed up, fully known. In this ending, Charles reads Sarah's inability or refusal to love him "as a wife must" (463)— that is, from a position of subordination, as a revelation of her "real nature," as a selfishness surpassing, he believes, even that of Mrs. Poulteney. Significantly, whereas in this version Charles may be darkly satisfied with the accuracy of his reading of Sarah, it is a reading to which Sarah refuses to acquiesce. Willingly, though perhaps sadly, she watches as Charles walks out of her life.

Alternatively, in the earlier, "happy" ending, Sarah responds to the question by deferring to the superior explanatory powers of her little child, Lalage. It is Lalage, whose name means "to babble like a brook" (459), who, Sarah asserts, "will explain . . . my real nature far better than I can myself" (454, ellipsis in original). In this ending, however, Charles, in softly asking, "'shall I ever understand your parables?'" (460), accepts the inscrutability of the child's explanation and thus the ungraspability of Sarah's meaning, her "real nature." He abandons his need for a stable and dependable reading of Sarah, his need to classify and so possess her. It is upon Charles's acceptance of Sarah's otherness that they begin a transformed relationship.

In each version of this crucial encounter with Charles, Sarah either rejects or eludes his efforts to approach her purposefully. She refuses to be meaningful in the sense of being determined and known. She resists classification; she will not be collected. Sarah maintains—must maintain—her otherness, her mystery, her alienness. She says to

Charles, "'... I am not to be understood even by myself. And I can't tell you why, but I believe my happiness depends on my not understanding'" (452); Sarah thus acknowledges and accepts the green chaos within herself. Her resistance to Charles's purposefulness corresponds to the resistance of the natural world to all human purposefulness. Again, she is like the natural world, as Fowles describes it in *The Tree*: "It waits to be seen otherwise, in its individual presentness and from our individual presentness" (56).

Thus, although in *The French Lieutenant's Woman* Fowles acknowledges our own culture's stories of connection linking women to nonhuman nature, he opens up those stories to new interpretations. Specifically, he discloses ways in which they limit and distort our view not only of women but also of men, and of the rest of the natural world as well.

This brings me to my final point. Fowles has said, also in *The Tree*, that the actual place that inspired his descriptions of the Undercliff and Ware Common in *The French Lieutenant's Woman* is in fact a perfect place for "self-liberation" (75). He has not, however, been specific about whose liberation that might be. Why not imagine that it is potentially the site for the liberation of both Sarah and Charles, or of any woman and any man? In its fullest sense, it would be a liberation from a worldview founded upon dominance and disconnection. This worldview is realized through the maintenance of a dualistic conceptual system, which, in opposing culture to nature and male to female, offers a restrictive understanding of the self, a self characterized by alienation and defined through opposition. By calling the Undercliff "an English Garden of Eden" (67), Fowles indicates that he envisions it as a primal place, the site of a possible awakening to nature, to its dynamic wholeness, to the fact of human envelopment within it. Otherwise, as he explains in *The Tree*, "as long as nature is seen as in some way outside of us, frontiered and foreign, *separate*, it is lost both to us and in us" (78). In *The French Lieutenant's Woman*, the Undercliff—and the world of nature it represents—rather than a marginal location, to which Sarah as a woman is exiled and from which Charles as a man is excluded, is instead a central place, both geographically and psychologically—a green and immediate place, resonant with the green chaos in all of us.

Notes

1. John Fowles, *The French Lieutenant's Woman* (New York: Little, Brown, 1969), page 94.

2. Sarah is positive for Deborah Byrd, "The Evolution and Emancipation of Sarah Woodruff: *The French Lieutenant's Woman* as a Feminist Novel," *International Journal of Women's Studies* 7, no.4 (September 1984), pages 306–21. She is negative for Magali Cornier Michael, "'Who is Sarah?': A Critique of *The French Lieutenant's Woman*'s Feminism," *Critique: Studies in Contemporary Fiction* 28, no.4 (summer 1987), pages 225–36. Sarah's multiple identifications are discussed by James R. Aubrey in "The Pre-Raphaelite 'pack of satyrs' in John Fowles's *The French Lieutenant's Woman*," *Nineteenth Century Prose* 18, no.1 (winter 1990 / 1991), page 35. Her meaning is open "to be read" for Thomas C. Foster, *Understanding John Fowles* (Columbia: University of South Carolina Press, 1994), page 81.

3. John Fowles, *The Tree* (New York: Ecco Press, 1983).

4. Readers unfamiliar with ecofeminist thought will find that the following volumes provide a useful introduction: Diamond, Irene, and Gloria F. Orenstein, eds., *Reweaving the World: The Emergence of Ecofeminism* (San Francisco: Sierra Club Books, 1990); Greta Gaard, ed., *Ecofeminism: Women, Animals, Nature* (Philadelphia: Temple University Press, 1993); Carolyn Merchant, *The Death of Nature: Women, Ecology and the Scientific Revolution* (San Francisco: Harper & Row, 1983); Patrick Murphy, *Literature, Nature, and Other: Ecofeminist Critiques* (Albany: State University of New York Press, 1993); Judith Plant, ed., *Healing the Wounds: The Promise of Ecofeminism* (Philadelphia: New Society, 1989); and the special edition "Ecological Feminism" of the journal *Hypatia* 6, no.1 (spring 1991).

5. In an influential though controversial article published in the early 1970s, American anthropologist Sherry Ortner asks, "Is Female to Male as Nature Is to Culture?" in Michelle Rosaldo and Louise Lamphere, eds., *Women, Culture, Society* (Stanford, Calif.: Stanford University Press, 1974), pages 64–87. Ortner argues that women are devalued because they are viewed as closer to "nature"—that is, closer to whatever is implied by that conceptual category figured in opposition to the category "culture." Hence, women's devaluation stems from their culturally constructed position closer to the devalued other. According to Ortner, culture's readings of women's physiology, their social roles, and their psychic structure all place them closer than men to nature (71–74). She concludes that women's middle status, their mediating role, and their potential for ambiguous, even contradictory symbolic meanings "all are different readings, for different contextual purposes, of women's being seen as intermediate between nature and culture" (87), providing for men a link, as it were, to the natural world.

6. Contemporary ecofeminists tend to accept the accuracy of Ortner's analysis of Western patriarchy's construction of women's status (see note 5) but take her argument in an alternative direction. Arguing that patriarchal culture's traditional linkage of women to nature underwrites the continued domination and exploitation of both, they, unlike Ortner, do not call for the liberation of women from nature so that they may join with men on the culture side of the divide. Rather, they find common cause with the environmental movement as well as with other movements of liberation. Ecofeminists like Greta Gaard assert:

> the ideology which authorizes oppressions such as those based on race, class, gender, . . . and species is the same ideology which sanctions the oppression of nature. . . . No attempt to liberate women (or any other oppressed group) will be successful without an equal attempt to liberate nature. (1)

They conclude, as Rosemary Ruether (*New Woman / New Earth: Sexist Ideologies and Human Liberation*, New York: Seabury Press, 1975) has argued, that "within a society whose fundamental model of relationships continues to be one of domination," nothing short of "a radical reshaping of [that society's] underlying values" will do (204).

7. We learn early in the novel, at the end of chapter 5, how Ernestina's own sexual thoughts have been shaped by cultural expectations and beliefs, how she has learned to suppress and sublimate her own longings:

> ... she had evolved a kind of private commandment—... "I must not"—whenever the physical female implications of her body, sexual, menstrual, parturitional, tried to force an entry into her consciousness. But though one may keep the wolves from one's door, they still howl out there in the darkness. Ernestina wanted a husband, wanted Charles to be that husband, wanted children; but the payment she vaguely divined she would have to make for them seemed excessive. (29)

8. Feminist theorist Linda Alcoff's concept of positionality offers an illuminating framework within which to read Sarah's decision to embrace her status as outcast and the consequences of such a decision ("Cultural Feminism versus Poststructuralism: The Identity Crisis in Feminist Theory," Signs 13, no.3 (spring 1988), pages 405–36). Alcoff contends "that the very subjectivity (or subjective experience of being a woman) and the very identity of women is constituted by women's position." She further asserts, however, that women are not merely acted upon by the sociocultural forces that construct their position. They are also actors who "actively contribute to the context within which [their] position can be delineated" (434). She continues:

> ... the concept of positionality includes two points: first, ... that the concept of woman is a relational term identifiable only within a (constantly moving) context; but second, that the position that women find themselves in can be actively utilized (rather than transcended) as a location for the construction of meaning, a place from where meaning is constructed rather than simply the place where a meaning can be *discovered* (the meaning of femaleness). (434)

9. *The Tree*, page 38. By applying the status of devalued other to both women and nonhuman nature, patriarchy pushes them together to the apparently permanent and stable position of marginalized and alienated outsiders, separated from human males at the center. An alternative to this hierarchical conceptualization is the heterarchical recognition of what ecofeminist critic Patrick Murphy in *Literature, Nature, and Other: Ecofeminist Critiques* (Albany: State University of New York Press, 1995) calls "anotherness, being another for others." Framing his argument in Bakhtinian dialogics, Murphy contends that anotherness acknowledges "the ecological processes of interanimation—the ways that humans and other entities develop, change, and learn through mutually influencing each other day by day, age by age" (35). Anotherness allows us to conceive of the other in relational rather than oppositional terms. The other is another, a self-existent natural entity. Anotherness is positively identified, Murphy contends, "as non-alien, healthy diversity" (48). This leads to a realization of "interanimation, the mutual co-creation of selves and others" (49).

Landscape This Side of Landscape: Transcendence and Immanence in the Fiction of John Fowles

H. W. Fawkner

THE FICTION OF JOHN FOWLES IS HIGHLY INFLUENCED BY TWENTIETH-century Continental theory. Existentialism plays an important role in *The French Lieutenant's Woman* and *The Magus*, and most existentialist philosophizing in such works has roots in modern phenomenology.[1] However, Fowles rarely goes to the roots of phenomenology, to its theory of the immanent. Instead, he basically adopts late, modified phenomenology—a theory of nonimmanence, of the transcendent rather than the transcendental. The father of modern phenomenology, Edmund Husserl, theorized a new, utterly radical immanence—a "transcendence within immanence.[2] This extreme immanence has the power of beforehand sucking transcendence back into immanence. Each stepping-out is beforehand a receiving-of-stepping-out that does not itself step out. After Husserl, however, phenomenology became diluted, mundanized, and transcendence oriented. Martin Heidegger's popular concept of "being-in-the-world" belongs to this mainstream movement. Heidegger, Emmanuel Levinas, Jean-Paul Sartre, Maurice Merleau-Ponty, and others created a worldly phenomenology. By "liberating" phenomenology from undesirable idealism-essentialism, one could now present the illuminating truth that life is not revealed in an intimate-elect domain this side of man and this side of the world—for instance, in root affectivity. Instead, the heart of life is supposedly revealed in the human—the being who steps out, transcends, possesses a horizon, a history. Life is supposedly revealed in the world, in the "factic" sphere of human action, historical materiality, "authentic" involvement—preferably a deathward involvement.

This opposition in Continental theory between a phenomenological outlook that is transcendental, or immanent, and a phenomenological outlook that is transcendent, or mundane, is conveniently misrepresented in theory as a mere dichotomy, as the contradiction between idealism-essentialism and its other. However, the matter is more complicated. To hold the view that ultimate reality occurs this side of the world, and to theorize life's truth in Husserlian manner as so-called transcendental subjectivity is to be neither a Platonist nor a subjectivist. A phenomenological theory of extreme immanence does not view the mind that sports this extreme immanency merely as a "mind," merely as an entity in the world, a psyche, a subjectivity, an interiority. If we claim that the Undercliff in *The French Lieutenant's Woman* is an instantiation of an extreme immanence landscaping itself this side of the world, that assertion does not mean that the Undercliff belongs to some higher or ideal world. Nor does it mean that the Undercliff is less touchable than a worldly site. The meaning is quite the contrary—that that which is extreme-immanent is also extreme-sensual. It sports a hypersensuality, a touchability exceeding anything the senses can experience "in the world"—that is, in modern, three-dimensional, Renaissance-type, classic space.

On the level where imaginative and literary phenomena phenomenalize themselves as showings of the core life of the work, Fowles's imaginative landscape shapes itself spontaneously as a tension between landscape landscaping itself immanently as extreme immanence (as pure revelation without mediation) and landscape landscaping itself transcendentally as transcendence (as the world of classic reality, surveyable and mastered by men). Thus, landcape in Fowles is, on the one hand, a mundane territory, like the spaces typically possessed by the modern forces of white, male reason and representation. On the other hand, landscape in Fowles wants to be nonmundane, a not-territory, one in which the mapping and conquering narrator is more at home but from which the heart of the work's imagination is beforehand surreptitiously banished. The writer-narrator thus comes to be torn from himself by some master-narrator who perpetually seems to want to defer pure immanence, without world. However, the "without world" of pure immanence, like the sheer-extreme immanence of that which goes without world, is not merely that which sets up its fright in the master-narrator, a cogito that would find nothing to master if it had no world to master. The sheer-extreme immanence without world also sets up its secret and unacknowledged fright in a corpus of critics, in reviewers and commentators with a vested interest in understanding the work as a world and the writer as a being belonging to this world. Only such a work and such a writer can be ushered into standardized knowability as an identifiable and localizable "X."

✳ ✳ ✳

We can sight the ontological difference between immanent and transcendent landscape in Fowles by looking first at the standard, transcendent landscaping of landscape in his fictional works. The narrator, a work's "landscape architect," begins the job by effectuating reassuring moves that suggest to the reader that the narrator is where the reader as a being in the world is—that is, in the world. Standard landscaping in Fowles is masculine, possessive, mundane, transcendental, sure of itself, sweeping, self-conscious, arrogant, reckless, ecologically insensitive, humanistically suave. It is inwardly illuminated by the *systematic* spatialization of life into representation, availability, and measurability—that is, by the proud reason of Renaissance "humanism." Standard landscaping in Fowles is landscaping landscape as the sure, mundane worlding of a world, for transcendent landscaping is mundane. It is epistemological. Reason gives itself space as knowledge and gives itself knowledge as space. Woman, too, becomes part of this mundanization. She, too, is "landscape." She, too, is space. She, too, is "the world." She, too, is to be slyly "opened" (supposedly emancipated) by the humanist gentleman. She, too, is knowable—particularly as "the unknowable." To know the unknowable as knowable, and to know this unknowability as woman, this is the master intentionality of master landscaping, of world knowing, of trans/scending (stepping/out). All this is wrapped up, of course, as humanism, literary education.

Ironically, the transcendent narrator in Fowles—the one who landscapes everything as neoclassic master space and rational representation—does not seem to be aware of the fact that this type of appropriation has its roots in the Renaissance, a period the master-narrator in his innocence benevolently and conventionally interprets in *The French Lieutenant's Woman* as an epoch of beautiful emancipation, as "the green end of one of civilization's hardest winters. It was an end to chains, bounds, frontiers" (68). There seems to be no awareness that the Renaissance is precisely the time when the Western male emerges as crowning, hypermasculine ego-beast and master-predator. It is during the Renaissance—not in the Middle Ages—that witches are burned all over Europe. It is during the Renaissance that man becomes God—the very kind of god idolized in *The Magus* as intersection of rational knowledge and the mystical unknowable. It is during the Renaissance that Western man turns away from life as renunciation of world in order to find salvation in that very world, a world now understood for the first time as horizon, as subjectivity plus environment, as cogito plus milieu. It is during the Renaissance that perspective painting comes to the fore as token of the subjection of life to a linealization of experience into extension, and of extension into the pointlike "I" as command post of representability. This comfortable Renaissance sense of the spatialization of life, as mundanization of self into ego, is passed on to the reader in small units of world conquest that go more or less unnoticed. Reading *The French Lieutenant's Woman*, we may fail to notice how innocent units like "a bedroom overlooking the Seine" or "seeing the fine landscape the place commanded" (70) accumulate to make of the all-commanding narrator a creator of fine landscapes who, by the same token, is subjectivity as command post.

This master-narrator is of course subject to discursive irony in the text. Fowles is making a parody of a quasi–Victorian "omniscient narrator." Yet, whether writing is utilizing this narrator for the sake of parody or not, the master-narrator as transcendent narrator is a transcending command post of post-Renaissance subjectivity. When writing is not making a deliberate ironic object out of the narrator, this narrator, the Fowles voice as such, is distinctly the transcending command post of Renaissance and post-Renaissance mundanization. Even in the nonfictional works like *The Aristos* (the title is revealing), the one who speaks directly, informs, and educates is masculine-horizonal in outlook—a Captain Cook or Darwin-god of a globe quickly becoming mundane, quickly becoming a world.[3] As the world opens up for the famous world discoverers after Vasco da Gama, so in *The French Lieutenant's Woman* a landscape "opened up very agreeably" for Charles as the site "from which he could plainly orientate himself" (69). This is what the ideal narrator is in Fowles. The narrator is one who is orienting himself and the characters and who hopes to orient the reader, too, once his or her Darwinian education approximates near-completion. This orientation smacks of reason, of the standard, rationalistic outlook of the Cartesian cogito as ego point situated in the middle of a horizon to be reached, or on the verge of a frontier to be crossed ("opened").

It is only after the event of consolidating this sense of the Fowles world as an ontology of orientating, of Renaissance representing-as-possessing, that we fully come to gauge the acute masculinist poignancy of the moment in which space becomes the prey of the Fowles narrator as a moment of classic, Euclidian-type landscaping of affectivity: observing Sarah asleep in the Undercliff, Charles remarks, "It irked him strangely that he had to see her upside down, since the land would not allow him to *pass round for the proper angle*" (71, emphasis added). Here the transcendent narrator is at once ego point and horizon, the representing middle that ideally needs to move subjectivity full circle in order to totalize the appropriation of life as extension and surveyability. Woman is the middle point of this surveyability only insofar as she is thinkable as coextensive with the area of the surveyability, only when she is identical with the regard that fixes her as emblem of all possible and thinkable mundanization. Woman in Fowles is thus not (as many think) an object of desire but, on the contrary, a unit of horizon, reason, tellability, and surveyability. Moreover, this mundanization of women is no mere "idealization" or "objectification" of the feminine. We can have (as, for instance, in "primitive" fetish societies) a reification that is not a mundanization. Nor is the mundanization a simple "secularization." For I can secularize life without turning it into a world; I can be heretic and heterodox without projecting the accumulated totality experience onto extension and horizon.

In order now to deepen our understanding of the Fowles world as a landscaping world that landscapes life as transcendence (world) rather than as life (experience without world, without extension), we need to take account of the fact that the transcending or transcendent narrator landscapes not only space but also time. Put differently, time, too, is transformed into space and landscape in the landscape world of the Fowles transcendency. Here, again, the declared or undeclared reference point is the Renaissance, as in the vulgar foregrounding of the carpe diem motif—"I possess this now, therefore I am happy"— which is so pleasantly available to those illuminated, fortunate, humanistically-educated readers of *The French Lieutenant's Woman* who in addition have "the lessons of existentialist philosophy at our disposal" (69). Had the transcendent narrator been slightly less illuminated and Renaissance-like, he would no doubt sooner or later have stumbled on the more sophisticated intuition: that happiness in fact has nothing whatsoever to do with the "I" in the first place but only with happiness as such. The "I" is never happy. Only happiness is happy. The source of happiness is happiness, not the I-point, not humankind, the least of all Renaissance carpe diem male. However, this radically happy consciousness does not normally emerge in Fowles. It surfaces only inadvertently at points where the transcendent, nontranscendental narrator is so exhausted by his conventionalized, world-illuminating, existence-orienting superhumanism that he momentarily forgets his mundanizing mission as well as "the lessons of existentialist philosophy" that underpin them. Only then does experience in the Fowles fiction reach the acute pitch of the immanent.

The Renaissance—indeed rational humanism in general—transforms life into extension (*res extensa*) and experience into world, into landscape as three-dimensional "environment." Reason systematically destroys life as happiness without extension, life without landscape to survey. In order to do this, reason institutes the interval. The interval is elevated to a principle of principles (dialectic, difference, "différance," "the other," and so on). This installation of the interval also affects time. In rational humanism, life is time, time is extension, and extension is space. Thus, time itself is a form of space, is spatialized. Time becomes landscape, territory, firmly surveyable timescape. Nowhere in modern letters is this spatialization of time into landscape, this landscaping of time, more evident than in the works of Fowles, who follows in the footsteps of Aristotle, René Descartes, and Galileo Galilei. If we place Fowles in a historical context, we discover that his is the era in which man becomes the being who obsessively places things in their historical context. This placing is not simply a situating, it is a territorializing, a mapping, a making landscape of life. Is the placing in historical context of life itself "historical"? Perhaps it is not. In Fowles's case it is probably ontological. In that event the oscillation between the human-cultural habit of landscaping life and the human-cultural habit of refraining from such mundanization does not occur in "time" at all, least of all in landscape-time. Indeed, there are traces of such an originary nonoccurring in the fiction of Fowles.

Such a possibility is likely to exist for the simple reason that the installation of the interval as landscaping of time into world-as-extension, or milieu, is thematized. Anything that is thematized may be critiqued, turned into an object of irony, questioning, quasi-negation. The thematization of the spatialization of time in the name of Renaissance reason occurs in *The French Lieutenant's Woman* through the familiar device of contrasting Victorianism (or indeed the past in general) with modernity (the supposedly enlightened and supposedly emancipated present). Only intermittently in Fowles is there consciousness on the part of the writer-narrator that the present, which *includes the writer-narrator's judgments,* is the unenlightened, unemancipated pole in the opposition. Thus the distancing from the smugness of the narrator that occurs in *The French Lieutenant's Woman* as irony of narrator vis-à-vis author redeems the Renaissance pomposity of the writer-narrator only partially. In fact such partial, intermittent self-irony on the part of the narrator functions as an excuse, a carte blanche allowing him to wallow further in the Renaissance mission of educating readerly awareness—that is, of landscaping the reader. The warnings against the objectification of life provided by the writer-narrator do not prevent this selfsame writer-narrator from deepening the objectification, totalizing the mundanization. Thus, it is not the innocent Fowles reader who is the real victim of the Renaissance mundanization built into the ideology of Fowles fiction but, on the contrary, the "enlightened," ironic, "self-conscious" reader, the one who (guided by the author) "notices" that the writer-narrator is omniscient and for this very reason is all the more willing to swallow all the existentialist propaganda about life's "improvement" over the centuries. How fortunate we are to be superior to the likes of Mrs. Fairley and Mrs. Poulteney. Yet, are we? Mrs. Fairley is, precisely like the writer-narrator, a figure on the lookout, a landscaping cogito. Like the writer-narrator(s), she establishes herself in the novel as "spying" and as promoting a "network of relations" (61). Her interest in the *landscaping* of emotional facts is analogous to the writer-narrator's interest in the *landscaping* of historical, geological, medical, sociological, and sexual facts.

Looking out to sea, Sarah is "looking for Satan's sails" (63). However, this looking, whether it is implicitly condemned by a Victorian lady or implicitly lauded by an enlightened writer-narrator, is condemned and lauded by one who is in the process of understanding life as something that occurs in a space (*res extensa*) between self and horizon. Like his Victorian enemies, the writer-narrator understands the event of life as a landscape event. The contrast set up by the writer-narrator between himself and Victorianism, between enlightenment and bigotry—in short, between light and darkness, between knowing and ignorant backwardness—obscures a more fundamental trait they have in common.

We thus need to take stock of the fact that narratorial utterances—such as those contrasting "the difference between Sam Weller and Sam Farrow (that is between 1836 and 1867)"—do not, on an ontological level, primarily call attention to difference but to similarity and self-sameness (43). Throughout the entirety of *The French Lieutenant's Woman* an absolutely selfsame technique (indeed outlook) is programmatically forwarded: the Renaissance habit of understanding life as world through the installation of the interval that everywhere makes possible a landscaping of experience into measurable discrepancies—this versus that, early versus late, educated versus ignorant, close versus distant, frigid versus free, humanistically wise versus medievally narrow-minded. Landscaping in general is thus made possible by a system of signifiers—writing, thought, imagination, wishful thinking, ideology—that everywhere allows one set of differences to be translated into another. The space that opens up as interval, world, and Renaissance extension between the two Sams or the two Sarahs is likewise the space that opens up as interval, world, and extension between other landscaping poles. Each interval is by the same token another interval. Nothing escapes from these interval makings, not even the not-interval. It, too, fits nicely in somewhere, conveniently "illustrates" this or that "truth" shared between eagerly landscaping reader/self-educator and eagerly-landscaping writer/self-narrator.

Characters in *The French Lieutenant's Woman* are thus in essence not characters but intervals, almost ideas, ideas landscaped into "history" as time extension. The novel is thus "French" in the classic sense, in the way that the works of Jean La Fontaine and Jean Racine are French. Interval and reason mutually illuminate each other—being, in the final analysis, indistinguishable. The interval throws light on light. Light throws light on light as interval. Writing is landscaping, turning life into extension so that mind can govern life as the process in which it travels from one end of reality to the other with a measuring stick, a telescope, a microscope, and (for purposes of time) a medium-sized geology kit. Accordingly, the difference between Sarah and Ernestina is not essentially a character difference but an interval. Put another way, the difference between Sarah and Ernestina is space, is landscape.

We have a work of fiction, then, in which there is not first a landscape and then fictional characters discoverable within it, as in Thomas Hardy. On the contrary, we have landscaping-characters. Characters do the landscaping, not the landscape. A landscape in Fowles is in this sense never a landscape at all (something living) but a space that unfolds in Renaissance fashion out of the classicist process of thinking the interval. This thinking is ultimately not an imaginative act but precisely a thinking—which is why the cessation of the thinking (of the author's reasoning) is by the same token automatically a vanishing (or ceasing to appear) of the landscape. Outside the range of the operative, moral, stratifying range of thought's reasoning-landscaping, landscape in Fowles has no powerfully autonomous existence, no true life of its own, no real justification or forceful powers of spontaneous revelation. Landscape is there to make a point, to open an educative showing-surface.

* * *

The obsessive need to install the interval, to envision a horizon, and to turn life into existence—into the transcendent—is likewise the obsessive need to deny utter immanence, its very possibility. No doubt some future generation of scholars will need to question our late-twentieth-century habit of assuming the strict impossibility of pure immanence as such. The unthinkability of sheer immanence—the awe of the difficulty of the task of actually facing it—surfaces in Fowles as its repression. Immanence as such comes into view only when the writer-narrator is expressing himself despite himself, when he forgets himself, forgets the world and writing. There are such moments in *The Magus* and in *The French Lieutenant's Woman* when there is no longer a denial of the immanentist thesis that it is impossible for being not to be entirely present to itself. This denial, which shows itself as a comprehensive, intellectual translation of all manifestation into landscaping, is a battle against immanence for the sake of landscaping transcendence.[4] Life is time, time is landscape, landscape is extension, extension is measurability, measurability is reason, reason is man, and man is ego. Space is, of course, landscaped space. To be such space, as in *The French Lieutenant's Woman*, is to experience time as landscaped time, Heidegger's "spannedness."[5] In Fowles, as in mainstream critical endeavor in general nowadays, each nook and cranny of experience needs to be translated into twentieth-century truth, into spannedness, difference, stretch, landscape, horizon. This movement culminates in the apex notion of the landscaping phenomenology that is subsumed in Fowles's writing as ideological and existentialist framework for the educative novel: the notion of phenomenological distance (Merleau-Ponty). Every now is spanned within itself, cries Heidegger (269). In other words, the now can never lack an internal landscape, can never do without some stretch, extendedness, spacing out. The now is a landscape with a horizon because time is a landscape with a horizon, and time is a landscape with a horizon because time is not life (the immanent as such, pure affectivity, unmediated revelation) but world. All making-landscape in quasi-existentialist writing is in this sense ideological. Existentialism is a landscaping of life, a landscaping of phenomenology. Life without a horizon—without a world—becomes a joke, a metaphysical ideal abstractly embraced by the not yet illuminated. Original time, says Heidegger, father of existentialism, is "outside itself, it is the outside-itself itself" (267).

However, this is precisely what time normally is in Fowles, too. Victorianism is outside itself in *The French Lieutenant's Woman*. Woman is outside herself: she is in her gaze, which is the elastic, faraway gaze yearning for the world, "the other." Sarah is outside herself (the very name splits, bifurcates, self-contradicts). Love is outside itself, being the outside-itself, as such, sex. The narrator is outside himself, being the ongoing outside-himself of any thinkably immanent narrator. The world is outside itself, freedom is outside itself, and so on. Landscaping is thus no mere furnishing of pretty countrysides or ugly urban environments but a positive mundanization of life, the rendition of experience as extendability. Reality is now real only insofar as it is itself *and* other than itself, as Michael Henry would observe (71). Landscaping becomes a condition of possibility for appearing. Nothing can appear without having a landscape or mini-landscape *in which* to appear. Manifestation without landscape, without phenomenological distance, becomes a joke, a Platonic absurdity, a romantic dream entertained by those who are less hardheaded than the writer-narrator and his enlightened, materialist twentieth-centrury peers, all of them reassuringly far from Victorian, far from Romantic, and far from idealistic. Originary presence is always preceded and beforehand undercut by a sweetly melancholic originary remoteness. From this fashionable viewpoint, even that which lasts for a mere millionth of a second has a span, what Heidegger calls "breadth" (270). As long as he remains the familiar, reassuring materialist, an intellectually correct world-mentor, the writer-narrator will perpetually suggest with Heidegger that no now can be punctual and that no time-moment can be punctualized (264). Hence comes the relish the writer-narrator takes in giving a span and an extension to that which has lost span and extension. Originary intercourse between Sarah and Charles, which immanently for both of them *as experience* is extensionless and unspanned, is for the detached, knowing writer-narrator something that has an exactly measurable span and extension. "Precisely ninety seconds had passed" (304). On the one hand, love takes place this side of time and world in pure life; on the other hand, it does not. Love, too, has mundane extension, situatedness. It, too, is absolutely measurable representability.

This *ontological landscaping*, as reason's demand that the interval and the span be inserted everywhere *without exception*, betokens the metaphysical need in masculine rationalism during and after the Renaissance to interpret life as world and experience as manipulability, as natural resource. Fowles's manic preoccupation with classification does not disappear because the writer-narrator is able to turn the classifications of Carolus Linnaeus into an object of self-criticism and irony. The very act of *classifying* Linnaeus as one who classifies is part and parcel of an overall tendency toward excessive and relentless classifying in Fowles's writing. The "thought" that goes on in the works of Fowles is predominantly taxonomic. Even during a moment of immanentist revelation, in *The Magus*, when Conchis comes to self-understanding about the crippling nature of his "ornithological approach" to life (308), this moment is on a higher-order level no emancipation from classification but one more taxonomic instant, one more unit of intellectual landscaping. In the same way, the sweet talk in *The French Lieutenant's Woman* about existentialist insight into time as a now, as a "room" immanently all around us (320), is on the higher-order level one more item marking the life of the novel as a mundanized set of intervals, a classicist thought landscape where this "observation" is merely one more pencil mark in the firm adumbration of a world made of sober measurability and sure judgments of the distance between one point and another, one experience and another, one developmental stage and another, one truth and another, one insight and another.

Measurability and mundanizing availability thus go hand in hand with liberal relativization, the cornerstone of reason's all-conquering appropriation of world in terms of landscape and landscaping. The narrator of *The French Lieutenant's Woman* observes that "it was not, I am afraid, the face for 1867" (75). Physiognomy is measurable—understandable—not only for the "omniscient" narrator whose Victorianism is distanced into irony but for originary, classicist, taxonomic reason itself. A face is something that is placeable on a historical map that has a certain extension—not only in time but also in civilized taste, wisdom, certitude, and judgment. The face is *landscaped*. Its understandability is a world's, a landscape's understandability. The explicability, calculability, and manipulatability of the face—of anything—is a function of the fact that, in Fowles's world of reason, intelligibility is, beforehand, objective knowledge, and objective knowledge is, beforehand, either extension or something that can be brought within the precincts of extension.[6] The shrewd horse dealer's skills that the narrator attributes to Austen (52–53) are no less the shrewd horse dealer's skills of a rationalist author in Lyme.

* * *

The habit of landscaping affects the experience of near-presence. In Husserl's theory of immanence, near-presence is halo. In Heidegger's theory of transcendence, as well as later in Merleau-Ponty, near-presence becomes horizon. In general, then, halo is life; horizon is world. Halo is intimacy; horizon is extension. Halo is the unmeasurable quality of experience this side of the measurable; horizon is the sight of the promise of the measurability of all experience. As Michel Henry would observe, the one who travels, by means of landscaping, from near-presence as halo to near-presence as horizon travels from an originary domain of affectivity to the modern, post-Renaissance world of sensibility (463). Sensibility is reception of life as otherness—as distance, extension, measure, space, difference, interval, and landscape (463). Affectivity is reception of life as life, life's pretautological reception of itself *as itself,* without go-betweens.

In the experience of near-presence as halo, there is a middle and an aura. I am neither the one nor the other. In the experience of near-presence as horizon, by contrast, there is center plus horizon, identity plus environment, ego plus world, sensibility plus existence, cogito plus representation. This latter condition is the standard predicament of the Fowles hero. He is marooned in landscape. He is doomed to exist. He cannot live.

There are exceptions, however. There are moments in Fowles that are not moments, queer moments that occur this side of the line of demarcation between one moment and another. In these moments, the world (the horizon) is not being renounced. Rather it has been renounced already. Beforehand, before any "act" that could call itself an act of renunciation, the horizon is a halo and the world manifests itself as something other than a world, as life as such, the immanent. Here, too, the interval is beforehand swallowed by the near-presence of a nondistance that makes a joke of phenomenological distance, of all taxonomic gazing, of all reason. In this domain we do not make landscaping remarks like those of the narrator in *The French Lieutenant's Woman*, such as the one pointing out the "profound difference" between Mrs. Poulteney's God and Sarah's God (57). The self is no longer analogous to "a ship's captain when he comes out on the bridge" (62). We are no longer interested in making time coincide perfectly with space, as when we come to know with reassuring certitude that the "beavered German Jew" was "working" on "that very afternoon in the British Museum library" (12). In this way, the Undercliff is a region this side of regions, this side of the infinitely measurable space where intervals conveniently intersect in order to calmly constitute themselves as the familiar time-space continuum in which we can recognize ourselves as beings firmly situated in narrative-friendly situatedness. The Undercliff gives the promise of an escape from horizons. Here the near-presence of the unknown, without exactly being closer to the reader, is not sightable on a viewable horizon. Near-presence as halo—for example, "a distant woodpecker drummed in the branches of some tree"—must not too readily be harmonized with the localizability of a horizon: "When he turned he saw the blue sea . . . and . . . Portland Bill, a thin gray shadow wedged between azures" (68). The Undercliff, as a non-space this side of long-distance gazing over large world-spaces and large time-spaces, is a non-place where people "have been lost" for "hours" (66). The condition for this loss of bearings is a loss of horizons—ultimately a loss of world and transcendence. We argue then that the true arising of the immanent, life as such, is conditioned on the event of the withdrawal of the transcendent, a withdrawal that goes hand in hand with a vanishing of common sense, of the sense of the common, of reason as looking-measuring. *The Undercliff is not a landscape.*

✳ ✳ ✳

The Pasvik River between northern Norway and Russia. Conchis is rowed about eighty miles upstream from this point, near Kirkenes, to the fictional Seidevarre, where Henrik Nygaard talks to God from the tip of a shingle spit in the water—another of Fowles's sacred, extrusive landmarks in remote settings. Photograph by Nathalie Loubovitsky, courtesy of National Geographic.

Oddly enough, the foremost escape from phenomenological landscaping in the entirety of the fiction of John Fowles shapes itself as a physical landscape. This paradox is made possible by blindness. Without the blindness of the madman Henrik Nygaard, *The Magus* would not be able to reconcile the affectivity of the state of being this side of landscaping—the affectivity of pure immanence—with landscape. In other words, the landscape of northern Norway where Conchis meets Henrik and where Henrik meets God would be unthinkable as the affectivity landscape it is without the withdrawal from landscape made possible by Henrik's inability to perceive a horizon—to transform himself into ego, the immanent into the transcendent, life into existence. Precisely because he is unable to *exist*—that is, to occur in a landscaping of self as mundanizing of experience, Henrik can *live*— be alive in a way no other being in the novel can be alive. Henrik's inability to exist is his ability to unfold an affectivity affecting itself this side of the world.

Henrik's ability to touch things is not an ability to make contact with a world but a capacity to touch touching itself—to feel feeling. Henrik does not move through a world but through a feeling of being this side of the world, which is a horizonless feeling of absolutely large and sacred self-empowering: "After five minutes Henrik began to walk up towards the *seide*. Quite confidently, but feeling his way with the end of the staff" (305). According to Merleau-Ponty, the one who is blind is not familiar with remote simultaneity as such.[7] From the viewpoint of a mundane philosophy of transcendence, the simultaneity of the remote is itself remote, is itself in the world, mundane. For the philosophy of transcendence, remote simultaneity is horizon, the very horizon it presupposes. Yet, the immanentist implications of Henrik's blindness seem to deny this. Sounds, which always impinge immanently in reverberations setting themselves up in an intimacy this side of the transcendent exteriority that is their empirical origin, take the place of visual data so as to set up a remote simultaneity (God, madness, the visionary) that is not itself remote, not in the world: "Just as he passed us I heard high overhead one of the frequent sounds of the river, a very beautiful one, like the calling of Tutankhamen's trumpets. The flight cry of a black-throated diver. Henrik stopped . . . . He stood there, his face turned up towards the sky. Without emotion, without despair. But listening, waiting, as if it might be the first notes of the herald angels telling him the great visit was near" (305).

The phrase "without emotion" does not suggest a lack of affectivity. It is rather that emotion is in the world (it is mundane), whereas affectivity is not (it is mystical, religious, "mad"). There is emotionless affectivity just as there is horizonless life. The affective absence deepens the affectivity. The blind waiting enhances perception. Hence the "herald angels," although they may be "sighted" in an imagination that translates the dream of their voices into vision, cannot be apprehended by means of transcendence, phenomenological distance. Yet, this blindness to that which is seen, the sightless and horizonless sense of the real, also seeps into the perceptive apparatus of the one who sees: "Conchis" is no longer "conscious." Consciousness itself retreats to an unviewable zone this side of the conscious. This new zone is not "the unconscious." It is truth, God, in fact perception, phenomenon: "I arrived outside Henrik's hut at midday the next morning. It was raining slightly. A grey day. I knocked on the cabin door and stood back a few steps. There was a long pause. Then he appeared" (305). The attempt to mundanize the situation, to bring life straight back into world, reason, and sensible horizon quickly proves fruitless. "I explained that I was a doctor, that I was interested in birds . . . . I began to talk about modern methods of treatment for cataract" (306).

When Henrik now appears wildly swinging an ax, what is being once more annihilated is not so much reason as world, horizon. The world vanishes, and all that remains is a madman, a blind one. Just as the vanishing of emotion leaves us with a root affectivity that is greater than the emotive, so the vanishing of common sense and transcendent rationalism leaves us with a thinkable, mindful realm that is greater than reason, with thought more thoughtful than mere mind. "He must have known that I was watching him, for without warning he turned and swung the ax with all his strength into a silver birch just in front of him. It was a fair-sized tree. But it shook from top to bottom with the blow. And that was his answer. . . . He stared for a moment into the trees where I stood and then turned and walked into the hut, leaving the axe where it had struck. I went back to the farmstead a wiser young man" (306).

The phenomenality of the extreme north helps the reader to visualize a horizon *blindly*. Hyperborean light fills the sky with so much deep depthlessness that the sense of the luminosity of a horizon gives way to a visual sensation of a luminosity luminous enough to replace horizon with pure light—the irradiance of a faraway immanence startling us with the peace of an abundantly distanceless, irreal shimmer. "I went out of the barn to urinate when Gustav left. There was a brilliant moon, but in one of those late summer skies of the extreme north, when day lingers even in the darkness and the sky has strange depths. Nights when worlds seem always about to begin. I heard from across the water, from Seidevarre, a cry" (307).

What now is instituted is the interval. "Another cry came. It was dragged out, the cry of someone who is calling a great distance" (307). Henrik is calling to God. The interval here, precisely because Henrik dwells and moves this side of the world, is not itself in the world. It therefore lacks space. It is not an interval. Although it is first asserted that Henrik is calling "to" God, and although the cry seems "to stretch out" over forest, water, and starlight, "the two cries, with an interval between" (307) are pushed by the narrator toward a realm of suggestion where they are strangely ensphered within pure immanency, without intervals, spacings, distances, differences, or extensions:

> Henrik was standing at the very tip of the shingle spit, in about a foot of water. He was facing out to the north-east, to where the river widened. . . . As he watched, he called . . . as if to someone several miles away, on the invisible far bank. . . . Then we heard Henrik say one word. Much more quietly. It was "*Takk*" [Thanks]. . . . He . . . knelt on the shingle. We heard the sound of the stones as he moved. He still faced the same way. His

hands by his side. It was not an attitude of prayer, but a watching on his knees. Something was . . . visible to him. . . . He was not waiting for some certainty. He lived in it. (308)

There is a strange mixing here of the transcendent and the immanent. At first Henrik is still "facing." He still has a hypothetically viewable object of possible perception (a perceivable God-creature) outside himself in an exterior space of transcendent representability. At first the absolute is still faintly horizonal. Henrik's calls need to traverse the mists and cold stretches of an entire forest world to reach this godhead. Even when this horizon-God comes "very close to him," the *to* that assures this proximity and makes the absolute "visible to him" is a *to* that resembles the one of ordinary, human, transcendent perception: "as visible to him as Gustav's dark head, the trees, the moonlight on the leaves around us, was to me" (308). On the one hand, the narrator thus shares strange, momentary beauty—in fact, absolute revelation—with Henrik. Both are "blind," hyperimaginative. If we take the narrator to be Conchis as ontic personage and human character, the sharing is not an ongoing sharing between one radical imagination and another but a sharing of perceptual objects: the blind man sees units of blind vision *in the way* that the seeing man sees units of proper vision. On the other hand, however, the sharing is illusory. Conchis qua narrator cannot perceive what Henrik perceives for the simple reason that Henrik's perceived revelations have moved *so* close to his soul—the immanent as such—that no interval is thinkable (or indeed imaginable) between revelation and the act of revelation, between manifestation and the experience of manifestation. It is from this experience that the narrator—and by implication also the reader—is excluded.

* * *

In summary, then, analysis of landscaping in Fowles requires critical efforts that aim to account for the perimeters set up by transcendency and immanency. These perimeters are only marginally controlled by the writer-narrator. He is mostly unaware of the bias toward landscaping *as* a bias toward the ideology of the installation of the interval and *as* the equally rationalist bias toward the ideology of the landscaping not only of worlds but also of those rare and valued spaces that arise in modes of arising other than those recognized by the world. Nowadays, to be a writer means to be recognized by the world, as one who writes the world as world rather than as life. This recognizing and this writing ideology force a horizon and an interval on life everywhere. The best reader resists this violence by being this side of the world in reading. The reader waits patiently, like Henrik. When the reader says "*takk,*" the writer, insofar as he belongs to the world, cannot perceive or know.

Notes

1. John Fowles, *The French Lieutenant's Woman* (Boston: Little, Brown, 1969); *The Magus: A Revised Version* (Boston: Little, Brown, 1978).
2. Edmund Husserl, *Ideas Pertaining to a Pure Phenomenology and to a Phenomenological Philosophy*, trans. F. Kersten (Boston: Klower, 1982), vol. 1, page 133.
3. John Fowles, *The Aristos: A Self-Portrait in Ideas* (Boston: Little, Brown, 1964).
4. Michel Henry, *The Essence of Manifestation*, trans. Girard Etzkorn (The Hague: Martinus Nijhoff, 1973), page 291.
5. Martin Heidegger, *The Basic Problems of Phenomenology*, trans. Albert Hofstadter (Bloomington: Indiana University Press, 1982), page 263.
6. Henry, page 516.
7. Maurice Merleau-Ponty, *Phenomenology of Perception* (Atlantic Highlands, N. J.: Humanities Press, 1962), page 224.

The Geography of Ruins: John Fowles's *Daniel Martin* and the Travel Narratives of D. H. Lawrence

Lisa Colletta

JOHN FOWLES'S ADMIRATION FOR D. H. LAWRENCE IS DEEPLY FELT. IN HIS 1992 introduction for a limited edition of *The Man Who Died*, Fowles describes Lawrence as "lastingly significant," as "a peak in the Everest range," and in 1996 Fowles declared Lawrence to be, "with the possible exception of Joyce, the greatest writer of this century."[1] I believe that the basis for this admiration is Lawrence's relation with the landscape, for, more than any other writer since Lawrence, Fowles likewise uses the spirit of place to explore questions of identity and to map the terrain of twentieth-century psychological and political consciousness. From the enigmatic and very Lawrencean first sentence of *Daniel Martin*—"Whole sight; or all the rest is desolation"—to the bleak Palmyran landscape of the penultimate chapter, the characters in that novel are engaged in both inward and outward journeys, exploring the presentness of the past and finding their identities in their responses to place as they journey, Lawrence-like, amid the ruins of previous civilizations.[2] Particularly in the central chapter set in New Mexico, Lawrence's presence is felt by Dan: "It was my first visit, and like many people before me—most famously D. H. Lawrence, of course—I fell for the area almost on sight" (322). Even if Lawrence's ghost did not haunt the novel, Fowles would invite comparison to Lawrence by his similar, extraordinary sensitivity to the physical environment as context and cause.

Daniel Martin is informed by several closely connected themes: the importance of time and memory, the search for authenticity of self in the balancing of the intellectual and the instinctual, and an investigation of "Englishness." However, all of these themes are developed through Dan's response to his physical environment and his experience of travel and exile. In this sense Fowles can be seen to draw on the tradition of the travel narrative, specifically the modernist travel narrative, which employs the journey not merely to examine the exotic but as a means of self-exploration. For Dan "whole sight" is more a matter of coming into knowledge, not collecting it as his friend Anthony does, but moving toward it, almost traveling into it, and then exploring it like a place. There is no better guide to this kind of psychological journeying than Lawrence, whose "greatest contribution to the travel-writing tradition," according to Jeffrey Meyers, "was to shift the center of interest from the external world to the self."[3]

Lawrence's travel narratives are characterized by a sense of loss in much the same way *Daniel Martin* is. Throughout *Twilight in Italy, Sea and Sardinia, Mornings in Mexico,* and *Etruscan Places,* Lawrence battles with the modern tensions that occupy his life and work: the struggles between the intellect and the senses, between an anxious anticipation of the future and a nostalgia for the past, and between the longing to be part of a community while needing to remain intensely individual.[4] For Fowles, as for Lawrence, the twentieth-century is "overcomplex" (494), devoted as it is to capitalism and technology, and characterized as it is by loss—loss of the connection to nature and loss of the vital relationship between public and private life. The worship of the machine that Lawrence despises and sees, to his horror, invading the farthest corners of the globe is part of the same "stupid, one-dimensional age" that Dan tells Jane has "usurped everything . . . all our instincts" (610). The search to regain an instinctual or unselfconscious response to the world is the impetus for Lawrence's travels, just as Dan's journey into his past is prompted by a wish to regain an almost prelapsarian sense of "right feeling" (30). John Alcorn, writing about the concept of spirit of place, dubbed Lawrence a "naturist," as one who sees humanity as part of an animal continuum, reasserting the importance of instinct as a key to human happiness, tending to be suspicious of the life of the mind and wary of abstracts.[5] For naturist travelers, the travel narrative is "essentially a literary means of probing into nonconceptual and instinctive areas of human experience" (58). Clearly, the term *naturist* could be applied to Fowles as well, for he states in *The Tree,* "the key to my fiction . . . lies in my relationship with nature," and throughout his works Fowles comes down squarely on the side of the individual search for meaning, eschewing abstract systems of thought that can curtail the individual's true nature and freedom to choose.[6] Of course, both Lawrence and Fowles spend a good part of their works expatiating upon the very abstractions they dislike, and just as *Daniel Martin* was assailed by certain British reviewers for being too preachy, the *Times Literary Supplement* described *Twilight in Italy* as "a potentially fine travel book which has been spoiled by too much philosophizing."[7] However, the similar response to these two works adumbrates the connections between them and points to the comparable ways both authors use landscape and reaction to unfamiliar terrain to explore the nature of the individual's place and potential in the modern world.

Fowles locates several of the novel's significant moments in places that are redolent of D. H. Lawrence, and although many scholars have commented on this fact, no one has explored thoroughly the connections between Fowles's treatment of place and Lawrence's travel writing.[8] There is much in common. For many readers of *Daniel Martin*, the most memorable episodes in the novel rest on certain evocative landscapes, such as the opening harvest scene in Devon, the description of the New Mexico mountains, and the journey up the Nile. Of course, these images stand out because they are vividly depicted and lead to epiphanic moments, and this is the combination at the heart of modern travel writing. Norman Douglas wrote that "the reader of a good travel-book is entitled not only to an exterior voyage, to descriptions of scenery and so forth, but to an interior, a sentimental, a temperamental voyage, which takes place side by side with the outer one," and, as Michael Kowalewski notes in *Temperamental Journeys*, the most successful travel narratives generally blend outward, spatial aspects of travel with the inward, temporal forms of memory and recollection.[9] Representation of such an inward / outward journey is precisely what Fowles gives us in *Daniel Martin*.

Nearly half of the chapters in *Daniel Martin* have either place names—"Tarquinia," "Compton," "Tsankawi," "Kitchener's Island"—or directional names, such as "Westward," "North," "Passage," and "Forward Backward." Thus the novel shares with *Twilight in Italy* and *Mornings in Mexico* an episodic structure based on place and memory and not strictly on linear advancement. "Tarquinia" is the first of many chapters named for a place, and it describes the six-week holiday in Italy that Dan, Nell, Anthony, and Jane take after the end of their studies at Oxford. It is a "golden period" (104), in the summer when all four of the characters are young and about to embark on their married and professional lives. None has been to Italy before, and all four respond immediately to the spirit of the place, with its heat and disarray so antithetical to chilly and orderly Oxford. Paul Lorenz has noted that Dan's experience in Tarquinia is a profound moment of spiritual significance by which Dan measures the rest of his life; and Italy helps him to abandon the rigid, intellectual religion of his father, a cleric for whom being "demonstrative" was among the chief sins, as were the Platonic and Socratic thought patterns Dan had learned at Oxford.[10] Anthony, in his intellectual Catholicism, will move more and more toward such thought patterns, as Dan moves away. It surely cannot be a coincidence that, just prior to

Tarquinia, Italy. This panoramic view of Tarquinia is from a collection of photos selected by D. H. Lawrence for possible use in *Sketches of Etruscan Places*. In *Daniel Martin*, Dan feels the sacredness of the place as he and Nell, Anthony and Jane hold hands in a circle in the sea nearby: "It was a moment that had both an infinity and an evanescence—an intense closeness, yet no more durable than the tiny shimmering organisms in the water around us" (page 110). Photograph courtesy of The Bancroft Library, University of California, Berkeley.

their departure for Italy, the play that Dan gets accepted is called *The Empty Church*, a title that suggests Dan's break with his past and his eventual break with Anthony and Jane (108). In Italy, the churches are a source of humor. They represent the "sillier Catholic side of Rome," and even Anthony and Jane theatrically debate them "like a pair of gourmets over a Michelin guide"; the churches, like Imperial Rome, seem vulgar, and the travelers conclude that "all good lay with Lawrence and the Etruscans" (109). The architecture and landscape embody the struggle between the intellect and the instinct, and both Lawrence and Fowles prefer the "primitive," pre-Roman civilization that did not impose itself on the landscape but seemed an organic part of it. According to Lawrence, the Etruscans, in contrast to the Romans, lived and built on a natural, human scale, and their way of life was attuned to the rhythms of nature: "The Etruscans built everything of wood, houses, temples, all save walls for fortification, great gates, bridges, and drainage works. So that the etruscan [sic] cities vanished as completely as flowers. Only the tombs, like bulbs, were underground."[11] Lawrence's metaphor of a bulb reminds us of Dan's preoccupation, not only with flowers but also with orchids, and it implies that, like orchids, the secrets of past civilizations must be looked *for* and not *at*, intuited rather than merely observed.

Though Dan tries to discount the experience in Tarquinia as "playing pagan" (109), he finds the tombs deeply moving, and they connect him to nature in way he had not felt since his boyhood. Dan intuits what Lawrence writes about in *Etruscan Places*, and perhaps as Paul Lorenz waggishly suggests, if they had taken *Etruscan Places* as their bible instead of *Sea and Sardinia*, "it would not have taken Dan and Jane twenty years to understand what they felt in Tarquinia" (81). *Etruscan Places* is Lawrence's last travel book—he died before he finished it—and it represents the culmination of a lifelong search for the reconciliation of instinct and unself-conscious intellect. In the ruins of Etruscan civilization, Lawrence sees evidence of the balance between blood and mind consciousness. In their art and religion he finds "ease, naturalness, and an abundance of life," and unlike the conquering Roman gods and ultimately Christianity, there was no evidence of the need "to force the mind or soul in any direction" (19). Lawrence rejects the posturing and bulk of the Romans, just as Dan will reject the Egyptians, and finds in the Etruscans a sacredness in the ordinary, stating that "everything was in terms of life, of living" (19). In his description of the Tarquinian tomb paintings, Lawrence expresses what he believes is one of the most important aspects of Etruscan experience: a spontaneous, physical response to the world, which leads to comprehension of one's place in it. He explains the importance of this understanding in his description of "the mystery of touch" illustrated in a painting in the Tomb of the Painted Vases:

> On one end wall is a gentle little banquet scene, the bearded man softly touching the woman with him under the chin. . . . Rather gentle and lovely is the way he touches the woman . . . with a delicate caress. That again is one of the charms of the Etruscan paintings: they really have the sense of touch: the people and the creatures are all really in touch. It is one of the rarest qualities, in life as well as art. There is plenty of pawing and laying hold, but no real touch. (53–54)

For Lawrence being in touch meant not only personal connection with other individuals but a larger connection with nature, with humanity, indeed with the universe as a whole, all of which he believed the Etruscans experienced. Lawrence describes the mystery of touch

Tomb of the Painted Vases, near Tarquinia, Italy. This detail from the Etruscan Tomb of the Leopards illustrates part of a banquet scene that D. H. Lawrence describes in *Etruscan Places*. In *Daniel Martin* the tombs affect Dan, who sees something beyond historical contingency in this Etruscan place: "I think it was also the first time I had a clear sense of the futility of the notion of progress in art: nothing could be greater or lovelier than this, till the end of time. It was sad, but in a noble, haunting, fertile way" (page 109). Photograph courtesy of The Bancroft Library, University of California, Berkeley.

as something spontaneous, instinctual, and fluid, something that is lost to those who habitually seek and depend only upon objective knowledge.[12] A young German archaeology student, who accompanies Lawrence on his tour of the tombs and "looks as if he'd had vinegar for breakfast," is the embodiment of the kind of sensibility that fails to understand the significance of touch that goes beyond objective knowledge. Lawrence tells us that though the young man knows the tombs well, he "doesn't think much of them; is going to Greece and doesn't expect to think much of it either" (119). He explains many aspects of Etruscan life to Lawrence, but when asked the meaning of a particular tomb painting, he responds, "Nothing," and Lawrence states, "It meant nothing to him, because nothing, except the A.B.C. of facts, means anything to him. He is a scientist, and when he doesn't want a thing to have meaning, it is ipso facto meaningless" (122).

In *Daniel Martin,* Dan states that the tombs "spoke more deeply to me, even though Anthony knew far more about the Etruscans in scholarly terms" (109), just as Lawrence's German archaeology student did. In the chapter's culminating midnight swim, Dan experiences a "mystical unison" as the four hold hands and circle slowly in the water. The moment is "strangely uncarnal" and the focus of his attention isn't Jane but Anthony, describing him in Lawrencean language as "the brother I loved," whereas Anthony, the man who scientifically looks *at* orchids and not *for* them, misses the religious significance of the moment and sees Dan only as the "brother-in-law he liked." The moment of "intense closeness" that was an "infinity and an evanescence" is meaningless, a "midnight jape" to Anthony because it doesn't fit with his intellectual Catholicism (110). It isn't until he is on his deathbed that he realizes that his "blind obsession with things of the mind" has robbed him of eternal moments and ruined his marriage by suppressing the instinctual side of both himself and Jane (175). The Tarquinia memory goes back to the beginnings of the Dan/Anthony, instinct/intellect struggle that is one of the major concerns of the novel. So *Sea and Sardinia* is, after all, an appropriate travel guide for the couples; though it lacks the sense of reconciliation that pervades *Etruscan Places,* it deals actively with the struggle between the mind and the senses and suggests that mapping the geography of ruins offers a salutary look back at the psychic and historical past. Lawrence states in *Sea and Sardinia:* "So for us to go to Italy and to penetrate into Italy is like a most fascinating act of self-discovery—back, back down the old ways of time. Strange and wonderful chords awake in us, and vibrate again after many hundreds of years of complete forgetfulness."[13] It will be years later, amid the ruins of another civilization, before Dan and Jane fully explore and understand the lessons articulated in *Etruscan Places,* but *Sea and Sardinia* embodies the "forward backward" movement of self-discovery underway at the time.

"Tsankawi" takes place about twenty years later than "Tarquinia," and Dan again seems to be following a path beaten by Lawrence to his ranch near Taos. Dan's description of Sante Fe reads like a travel book, with its praise of "the Spanish Colonial adobe buildings with their pretty patios, the sweet-pungent incense of the *piñón* logs that pervades every New Mexican dusk, the marvelous light and air of the high desert, the cottonwoods, the old colonnaded shops around the sleepy central plaza, the cathedral bells chiming through the night . . ."

(322). However, it is the landscape and its geography of ruins that moves Dan, and he states that "Santa Fe could have been a far less attractive town than it is without seriously damaging my regard for the surrounding landscape" (322). At the abandoned "medieval" mesa sites of the Pueblo Indians, Dan's response to the spirit of place is Lawrencean, and he remarks on the "sense of some magical relationship, glimpsed both in the art and what little is known of their inhabitants' way of life, between man and nature" (323). Dealing as the chapter does with both Dan's past and his future, both his first and his third person selves, it is not surprising that he muses on the mysterious spirit of some places that exerts this deep personal attraction, why at them one's past seems in some mysterious way to meet one's future so that, as Dan says, one "was somehow always there as well as being there in reality. It is a feeling I had very strongly when I bought Thorncombe—that my real need for the place came from the depths of my unconscious . . ." (324). The views from the New Mexico mesas are described as "infinite," and the landscape seems to be a part of all history and all human culture; it reminds him at once of Dartmoor and Crete, and he finds the atmosphere strangely contemporary, as well as medieval, Etruscan, and Minoan.

Lawrence also speaks of the history that haunts the southwestern landscape, and he refers to "the curve of return," a cycle that leads from the present to the past and into the future, as his primary experience of the New Mexican desert. He observes in *Mornings in Mexico* that everything seems "to be slowly wheeling and pivoting upon a centre." The marketplace in Taos seems to be, similarly, a part of his psychic past, which, in its present concreteness, affords a "spark of contact" in the great centripetal flow of humanity and history. Commenting on the circular nature of experience, he finds it strange that Western culture "should think in straight lines, when there are none, and talk of straight courses when every course, sooner or later, is seen to be making the sweep round, swooping upon the centre. . . ." He states further that "the straight course is hacked out in wounds, against the will of the world."[14] Janik states that Lawrence's experiences in New Mexico changed his understanding of the relationship between civilization and precivilization and "with it the character of his own quest for meaning in life" (58). It is this sense of the circular, of the past informing and meeting up with the present, that Dan becomes conscious of at Tsankawi.

Like Lawrence, Dan's experience of the landscape "transcended all place and frontier" (325). He states, "It had [a] haunting personal familiarity . . . but a simpler human familiarity as well, belonging not just to some obscure Indian tribe, but to all similar moments of su-

Tsankawi, Bandelier National Monument, New Mexico. In *Daniel Martin*, as Dan prepares to describe Jenny's revealing lack of responsiveness to the place, Dan explains that he "fell in love with the abandoned 'medieval' mesa sites on the outliers of the Jemez mountains that face Santa Fe across the rift. Their atmosphere is paradoxically very European—to be precise, Etruscan and Minoan . . . that is, they are haunted by loss and mystery, by a sense of some magical relationship, glimpsed both in the art and what little is known of their inhabitants' way of life, between man and nature" (page 323, ellipsis in original). Photograph by James Aubrey, 1987.

preme harmony in human culture" (325). Tsankawi, though first described as haunted by mystery and loss, really represents for Dan a place where time is defeated, an eternal moment not unlike the midnight swim in Tarquinia. This is what both Abe and Jenny miss in the landscape there. Abe, the cynical modern man, can respond only by distancing himself from the intensity of the experience—different from Anthony's reaction at Tarquinia only in its wise-cracking mode (325). The sacredness of the place is missed, and Abe's constant joking is reminiscent of the amused tourists in Lawrence's *Mornings in Mexico*, who come to witness the Hopi snake dance, unmoved by the solemnity of the Indians who perform it. Imbuing the landscape with religious importance, Dan states that Abe was "treading on holy ground," but Abe can only joke about loving Indians in the movies, but "could he please cancel the reservation" (325). Similarly, in *Mornings in*

Mexico, the Western tourists who have come to watch the snake dance are requested to be silent and respectful, "as this is a sacred religious ritual of the Hopi Indians, and not a public entertainment. Therefore please, no clapping or cheering or applause, but remember you are, as it were, in a church" (138). The visitors listened to the admonition and looked around "with a grin at the 'church'" (145). In both works, the "tourists" see religion and life as distinct categories of experience and therefore fail to see the connection between humanity and nature.

Jenny, though clearly more receptive than Abe to the power of the landscape, also seems to miss the transcendent quality of the place. Dan states that she "did not sense the uniqueness of the place" (330), and he found her shard hunting "sacrilegious" (331). According to Dan, she should have sensed that she had no more right to the artifacts "than she would have had to those in a church or a museum . . . or someone else's house" (332). In addition, her insistence on interpreting the raven's cry as "Nevermore," against Dan's of "Evermore," echoes Lawrence's use of the same poem by Poe in the second chapter of *Mornings in Mexico*, where he complains of the Mexican peasants' suspicious response to himself and Frieda (27). For Lawrence, an overly instinctual and physical response to the world is as stultifying as an overly intellectual one, and according to him the intense physicality of the Mexican peasants is a fixed and finished thing, limiting them to only temporal existence. At Tsankawi Dan realizes that he and Jenny have no future together because of the intense presentness of her approach to the world. In the beginning of their relationship her simplicity and directness were a relief to him, but their different responses to the ruins at Tsankawi make him conscious of the presentness of the past, which creates the future. As Sue Park has noted, Dan's future cannot include Jenny because, to her, Dan's past is "something like an infidelity, something one has no right to remember or refer to . . . like a past mistress" (163). Jenny's desire to have sex on the cliffs is akin to her shard collecting, a self-conscious attempt to capture and fix the moment; it lacks Lawrence's "mystery of touch" that transcends the temporal. For her, reality is only of the moment, and she states that when they return to Los Angeles, "sitting here will be a thousand years away already. It won't seem real" (327).

Jenny's transitory response to the landscape is typical of the modern world, and Fowles, like Lawrence, writes of an alternative way of experiencing the world by piecing it together from the fragments of past civilizations. *Daniel Martin* shares with Lawrence's travel books a focus on the contrast between the modern and primitive worlds and between the modes of consciousness identified with each. These works set the primitive vitalism of past cultures against the arid intellectualism and ennui of the contemporary world, as well as against the protagonists' own modern prejudices, which both Fowles and Lawrence acknowledge with chagrin. Indeed, most of the characters in *Daniel Martin* resemble Lawrence's emotionally parched sightseers in *Mornings in Mexico,* who drive around the Southwest in automobiles experiencing ancient Indian rituals and ruins as tourist attractions. However, as Janik observes, *Mornings in Mexico* is not an attempt "to convince Western readers of the validity or preferability of the Indian way," nor even an attempt to explain the Indian ceremonies by comparing them with Western religion. Rather, the work tries to evoke, from the position of modern, intellectual humans, "the nature and significance of the Indian way, the way of the participation in the wonder of the earth's cycles" and to find in the geography of ruins a map for the living in the modern world.[15] In the essay "Democracy," Lawrence writes, "the great lesson is to learn to break all the fixed ideals, to allow the soul's own deep desires to come direct, spontaneous into consciousness. But it is a lesson which will take many aeons to learn."[16] It is a lesson that can be learned from past civilizations, for he states in *Fantasia and the Unconscious* that ancient civilizations had some kind of deep life-knowledge, and that "we are really far, far more life-stupid than the dead Greeks or the lost Etruscans."[17] Ultimately, this is the lesson Dan must learn. "Tsankawi," like *Mornings in Mexico,* does not represent the learning of that lesson, but it does provide a "spark of contact," furnishing Dan with a new awareness with which to further his journey into the demanding freedom of the individual seeking to make a life built on the past but made in the present.

In contrast to Dan and Jenny's trip to New Mexico, the journey Dan and Jane make to Egypt is also a voyage into their past, and as they uncover the past they move into the future. Inspired by their response to the landscape of ruins, their relationship progresses by furtive caresses and hand holding, which lead from their initial "spark of contact" to an eventual "mystery of touch," to use Lawrence's terms. Unlike the other tourists on the trip up the Nile, Dan and Jane are put off by the monumentality and cool precision of the Egyptian architecture, and Jane remarks on "how Roman it all is" (478). Dan's response, that every civilization needs its Etruscans, links this journey to their Italian one of twenty years ago and suggests that all empires, from the Egyptian to the Roman to those of "more recent dictators" (476), are vulgar, graceless, and grandiosely inhuman. Connecting the Egyptian pharaohs with the conquering Romans posits a contrast, not so much between past and present, but between an ancient way of life based on humanity's place in nature, as represented by the Etruscans, and a contrary way of life based on controlling nature, embodied in the great empires and the whole of Western tradition that they began.

This is precisely the contrast Lawrence writes of in *Etruscan Places,* and he argues that one feels for the Etruscans "instant sympathy, or instant contempt or indifference. Most people despise anything that isn't Greek, for the good reason that it ought to be Greek if it isn't. So Etruscan things are put down as a feeble Graeco-Roman imitation" (9). Lawrence's critique of the Graeco-Roman worldview runs throughout *Etruscan Places,* and he depicts ancient Rome, in particular, as a great negative force, reeking of repression, militarism, and materialism. Indeed, in his condemnation of Roman imperialism in the very opening lines of the work, Lawrence seems to be speaking to his English readers:

> The Etruscans, as everyone knows, were the people who occupied the middle of Italy in early Roman days, and whom the Romans, in their usual neighbourly fashion, wiped out entirely in order to make room for Rome with a very big R. They couldn't have wiped them all out, there were too many of them. But they did wipe out the etruscan [sic] existence as a nation and a people. However, this seems to be the inevitable result of expansion with a big E, which is the sole *raison d'être* of people like the Romans. (9)

In contrast, Lawrence finds among the Etruscan ruins a sense of warmth and humanity that still remains, though most of their architecture did not stand the test of time as that of the Romans did:

> Yet everything etruscan [sic], save the tombs, has been wiped out. It seems strange. One goes out again into the April sunshine, into the sunken road between the soft, grassy-mounded tombs, and as one passes one glances down the steps at the doorless doorways of tombs. It is so still and pleasant and cheerful. The place is so soothing. (19)

In his rejection of the massive stone Roman monuments for the graceful humility of Etruscan art, Lawrence also is critiquing the political ideology of empire building, which extirpates indigenous cultures and replaces them with a killing uniformity that is imposed from outside the culture rather than flowering naturally from centuries of interaction between the people, the landscape, and the cycles of nature. Thus, amid the fragments of past civilizations, Lawrence finds clues to an understanding of his own Englishness, which has little to do with being British. During his last visit to England in 1926, it is not the future of

Mexico or Italy that interests him, but of the English "common man." He writes to Earl Brewster: "Curiously, I like England again, now that I am up in my own regions. It braces me up: and there seems a queer, odd sort of potentiality in the people, especially the common people. One feels in them some old, unaccustomed sort of plasm twinkling and nascent. They are not finished."[18]

Fowles, like Lawrence, has stated that he feels himself in exile from England, yet both in his essay "On Being English but Not British" and in *Daniel Martin,* there appear to be certain characteristics of Englishness that he and his protagonist share, which he is careful to distinguish from the characteristics of the imperial British. Some English characteristics defined by Fowles in the essay are a tendency to be subversive and oppositional to authority, a moral perception that frequently leads to priggishness, and a furtiveness that can result in aloofness.[19] All of these things are at once strengths and weaknesses, and they make for delightfully eccentric travelers. Throughout the trip to Egypt Dan exhibits all of these traits: he continually complains about the food; he is critical of the hotel staff; he finds the other picture-taking tourists unimaginative; and both he and Jane do not participate in the organized tours, which are enthusiastically attended by the others. However, amid the landscape of ruins, he is educated to a new knowledge of the ancient Egyptian concept of the soul, and with this understanding he sees new possibilities for his public and private self in modern England. These possibilities lie in his comment that "every great civilization needs its Etruscans" (478), and Dan begins to see that a fulfilling life as an artist and as a partner depends upon the unity of "whole sight," which rests on intuiting a unity within and beyond duality or diversity.

Though the Egyptian architecture strikes the couple as elephantine and oppressive, hidden within the impersonal ruins are small expressions of humanity that transcend their historical moment and lead Dan a step closer to "whole sight." The first of these is a "delicately incised wall-carving of the ritual pouring of the flood waters of the Nile." Isis and Osiris, "brother and sister, husband and wife," face each other, pouring the water of the Nile in two crossing lines that form the arch of the world. The nurturing water of the Nile is depicted in cascades of "little loop-topped crosses," "the ancient keys-of-life" (477). Both Dan and Jane are deeply moved by this representation of the marriage of male and female principles, which together create the substance from which life flows. The second artwork is a bas-relief of the resurrection of Osiris by Isis, which reminds Dan of D. H. Lawrence and Frieda. The relief portrays Isis, "with strangely eager tenderness," massaging the penis of Osiris to bring him back to life, echoing the Persephone legend (502). It also is strikingly similar to Lawrence's description of the Etruscan tomb painting, quoted above. The bas-relief represents the physical manifestation of dual principles, portrayed in the forms of Isis and Osiris, but it also represents the unity that is beyond duality, depicted in the life-giving, "soft flow of touch."[20] Writing of the Etruscan tomb painting, Lawrence explains that "touch" does not unite to the point of sameness, but each thing retains its individual being: "Here, in this faded etruscan [sic] painting, there is a quiet flow of touch that unites the man and the woman on the couch, the timid boy behind, the dog that lifts his nose, even the very garlands that hang from the wall" (54). For Dan, the representation of the "mystery of touch" awakens a new understanding of himself, leading him to abandon his cranky, Englishman-abroad pose and show compassion to Jane, whom he resolves to "treat as she is" (483).

In the chapter appropriately named "The River Between," Dan begins to see a way of reconciling the dualities of existence that have kept him from "whole sight." From Professor Kirnberger, Dan learns of the ancient Egyptian concepts of *ka* and *ba*, or the dual nature of the human soul. *Ka*, the individual soul, is intimately connected to the body and cannot survive death except with it—thus the Egyptian fascination with preserving the body. *Ba* is also the individual soul, but it is not attached to the body, so after death it joins with the divine spirit. As Dan has quipped earlier, remarking on the bowdlerization of the bas-relief of Osiris and Isis, Western religion killed the body, something he now understands as killing a part of the soul, which, to be whole, must be dual and must include not only the physical and spiritual aspects of the individual but also the separate and communal aspects of existence. He concludes that instinct and intellect, artist and scientist, "would-be ambition" and "would-be selflessness" (513)— all are equally insufficient in themselves (513).

It is the reconciliation of duality evinced in the bas-relief that reminds Dan of Lawrence, for there are other amorous literary couples he could have mentioned if he was thinking only about their erotic behavior. In *Etruscan Places,* Lawrence not only comments on the ancients' understanding of the dual nature of the soul but also argues that comprehension of this is the fundamental characteristic of Etruscan experience. After visiting the Tomb of the Painted Vases, he descends into the Tomb of the Inscriptions, where he sees depicted on the walls images that suggest the Egyptian notion of *ka* and *ba,* as well as evoking the religious attitudes of the American Indians he so admired in *Mornings in Mexico:*

> The natural flowering of life! It is not so easy for human beings as it sounds. Behind all the etruscan [sic] liveliness was a religion of life . . . .

> Behind all the dancing was a vision, and even a science of life, a conception of the universe and man's place in the universe which made men live to the depth of their capacity. To the Etruscan, all was alive: the whole universe lived: and the business of man was himself to live amid it all. The whole thing was alive and had a great soul, or anima: and in spite of one great soul, there were myriad roving, lesser souls; every man, every creature . . . had its own particular consciousness. (56–57)

For both Lawrence and Fowles, the unity beyond the diversity of life is something that is intuited through the "touch" of each living thing. Relying exclusively on intellectual principles leads to a rejection of the diversity of life, whereby the force, power, and knowledge of both ancient, monolithic empires and modern, technological society are exercised for the sake of control rather than for the sake of life. Jane begins to realize the inadequacy of her political definition of the world when she is confronted with "two great puritanisms, the Marxist and the Muslim, in joint practice." She searches the Syrian landscape for "some redeeming feature," but she sees only "armed soldiers and army trucks . . . an air of enforced suppression" (581). The "drab grayness" that "hung over everything: buildings, people and shops" in Syria (581) is similar to the "khaki all-alikeness" that Lawrence excoriates in fascist Italy.[21] Both political systems represent an adherence to systems of thought that negate the individual and thus the duality of life.

For both Fowles and Lawrence, however, the power of the landscape resists the crushing uniformity of intellectually lopsided modern life. In *Sea and Sardinia,* Lawrence writes: "The spirit of place is a strange thing. Our mechanical age tries to override it. But it does not succeed. In the end the strange, sinister spirit of place, so diverse and adverse in differing places, will smash our mechanical oneness to smithereens" (103). Amid the desolation of the Palmyran ruins, Jane encounters a landscape outwardly sterile, analogous to a life lived solely according to intellectual principles, but the very bleakness of the landscape prompts her to reject the simple certainties of a strictly intellectual life and leads her to risk the uncertainties of "right feeling." Observing the architectural fragments of the past, Jane maps the analogous, inner ruins of her own wrong decisions and improper choices—and acts instinctively to build on those ruins a future with Dan. This dual geography of ruins not only reveals a dead civilization to Jane but also unearths a vision for her personal and political actions based on the duality of life and the "mystery of touch."

In *Daniel Martin* and Lawrence's travel works, both authors chart a psychological voyage from the sterility of the modern mechanized world back through the mystery and loss of ancient civilizations to a place where personal freedom and communal fulfillment can be glimpsed. And for both authors, an understanding of the importance of the journey rests on the power of the landscape to alter ways of seeing. Going up river to Kitchener's Island, at Aswan, Dan observes about the Nile:

> Its waters seemed to reach not merely back into the heart of Africa, but into that of time itself. This is partly the effect of the ancient sites, and of the ancient ways of life of the fellaheen villages and fields they saw as they passed: the minarets and palm-groves, the women with their water jars, the feluccas, the shadoofs and saqiyas—the great gaunt pole-dippers, the water wheels ringed with earthenware pots and driven by a donkey or an ox; but its origin lay in something deeper, to do with transience and agelessness, which in turn reflected their own heightened sense of personal present and past." (493)

The importance of the journey cannot be overestimated, for it is the outward analogue to inner, personal growth and the opening up of consciousness, just as the ruins and fragments of past civilizations are analogous to the individual's past-in-the-present. Lawrence's life, too, seems to suggest that self-knowledge cannot be realized without the experience of travel. In *Sea and Sardinia*, he says of his journey:

> Italy has given me back I know not what of myself, but a very, very great deal. She has found for me so much that was lost; like a restored Osiris. But this morning in the omnibus I realize that, apart from the great discovery backwards, which one *must* make before one can be whole at all, there is a move forwards. There are unknown, unworked lands where the salt has not lost its savour. But one must have perfected oneself in the great past first. (216)

Exploring backward in order to move forward, then, both Fowles and Lawrence use the geography of ruins to map their personal visions of past and present, individual and community, diversity and wholeness.

Notes

1. John Fowles, "Commentary on *The Man Who Died*," in *The Man Who Died*, by D. H. Lawrence (1992; reprint Hopewell, N. J.: Ecco Press, 1994), page 90; statement during a public interview at the John Fowles Symposium, Lyme Regis, United Kingdom, 11 July 1996.
2. John Fowles, *Daniel Martin* (Boston: Little, Brown, 1977), page 3.

3. Jeffrey Meyers, "Lawrence and Travel Writers," *The Legacy of D. H. Lawrence* (New York: St. Martin's Press, 1987), page 81.

4. Del Ivan Janik's thorough study, *The Curve of Return: D. H. Lawrence's Travel Books* (Victoria, Canada: University of Victoria, 1981), closely examines the unique treatment of these themes in Lawrence's travel writings. Among the many other works examining Lawrence's travel books, see especially Jeffrey Meyers, *D. H. Lawrence and the Experience of Italy* (Philadelphia: University of Pennsylvania Press, 1982); S. C. Rose, "D. H. Lawrence's Travel Books and Other Writings: Parallels in Themes and Style," in *Essays on D. H. Lawrence* (New York: St. Martin's, 1987); Mara Kalnins, "'Terra Incognita': Lawrence's Travel Writings," in *Renaissance and Modern Studies* 7 (1985), pages 66–77; Bridget Pugh, "Locations in Lawrence's Fiction and Travel Writings," in *A D. H. Lawrence Handbook*, ed. Keith Sagar (New York: Barnes and Noble, 1982); L. D. Clark, *The Minoan Distance: The Symbolism of Travel in D. H. Lawrence* (Tucson: University of Arizona Press, 1980). Paul Fussell has a chapter dedicated to Lawrence in *Abroad: British Literary Traveling between the Wars* (New York: Oxford University Press, 1980).

5. John Alcorn, *The Nature Novel from Hardy to Lawrence* (New York: Columbia University Press, 1977), page x.

6. John Fowles, *The Tree* (1979; reprint New York: Ecco Press, 1983), page 31.

7. Quoted in Janik, page 27.

8. Paul Lorenz's insightful article "Epiphany Among the Ruins: Etruscan Places in John Fowles's *Daniel Martin*" examines only the links between the novel and *Etruscan Places*. Sue Park's article "Time and Ruins in John Fowles's *Daniel Martin*" explores Fowles's use of time as represented in the ruins of past civilizations, but it makes no mention of Lawrence's travel writings. Indeed, most of the studies of *Daniel Martin* that include Lawrence focus on themes of nature or psychology and rarely, if ever, mention the trope of travel.

9. Douglas is quoted in Michael Kowalewski's introduction to *Temperamental Journeys: Essays on the Modern Literature of Travel*, ed. Michael Kowalewski (Athens: University of Georgia Press, 1992), page 9.

10. Lorenz, page 78.

11. D. H. Lawrence, *Sketches of Etruscan Places and other Italian Essays*, ed. Simonetta de Filippis (Cambridge: Cambridge University Press, 1979), page 13. Paul Lorenz presents a fairly detailed explanation of flower imagery in Etruscan mythology and suggests that flowers, representing the feminine, and birds, representing the masculine, symbolize both the duality and the essential unity of the cosmos. This symbolism certainly ties in nicely with Dan's interest in flowers and birds throughout the novel, symbolizing a balance of the masculine and feminine elements that is an essential part of "whole sight."

12. Janik, page 89.

13. D. H. Lawrence, *Sea and Sardinia* (New York: McBride, 1931), pages 215–16.

14. D. H. Lawrence, *Mornings in Mexico* (New York: Alfred A. Knopf, 1927), page 83.

15. Janik, page 68.

16. D. H. Lawrence, "Democracy," in *Reflections on the Death of a Porcupine and Other Essays*, ed. Michael Herbert (Cambridge: Cambridge University Press, 1988), page 78.

17. D. H. Lawrence, *Fantasia and the Unconscious*, in *"Psychoanalysis and the Unconscious" and "Fantasia and the Unconscious"* (New York: Viking, 1960), page 132.

18. D. H. Lawrence, *The Collected Letters of D. H. Lawrence*, ed. Harry T. Moore, 2 vols. (New York: Viking, 1962), vol. 2, page 933.
19. John Fowles, "On Being English but Not British," *Texas Quarterly* 7 (1964), pages 154–55.
20. *Sketches of Etruscan Places*, page 54.
21. *Sea and Sardinia*, page 164.

Greek Myths and Greek Landscapes in John Fowles's *The Magus*

Kirke Kefalea

In John Fowles's novel *The Magus*, narrator Nicholas Urfe feels caught between reality and fiction. At one point he expresses feelings of deep uncertainty: "Once more I was a man in a myth, incapable of understanding it, but somehow aware that understanding it meant it must continue, however sinister its peripateia."[1] Readers similarly feel unsure whether they are immersed in a realistic novel or a fantasy, and whether the manipulations of Nicholas are sinister or benign. Such ambiguities are, in part, generated by the author's own ambivalences. For Fowles, Greece is a theme in the novel, and the borders between real Greek experience and mythical, imaginative Greek experience are intentionally blurred.

John Fowles's wish to describe modern Greece in his novel does not prevent him from using archaic images, ancient legends, and references to mythology to enrich his representations, to make Greece again a kingdom of myths. Given the fact that Fowles had a traditional education in public school and university, one can reasonably assume that Fowles's later, firsthand experience of Greek landscape in 1952 was partly shaped by traditional ideas about classical Greece, carried with him as part of his cultural background.[2]

For Fowles, Greece is a special, even sacred place that he associates with Homeric sacred narratives of Greek history. For example, Greece is Circe, which implies that Greece is feminine and, perhaps, seductive and dangerous. Second, Greece can be symbolic, providing the time and space through which the hero moves but also allowing that journey to represent an inward "odyssey." Both aspects are present in Fowles's implied comparison of Nicholas to Homer's Telemachus, who undergoes a comparable process of initiation in *The Odyssey*.[3] Thus, in Fowles's novel, "myth" is both subject and structure, and the numerous references to ancient myth in *The Magus* not only represent Greece figuratively but also add a cultural dimension to the landscape and its spaces. With *The Magus*, then, Fowles has produced a new kind of "classical" literature.

Hotel Poseidon, Spetses, Greece. This hotel is the model for the Hotel Philadelphia in *The Magus*, where it is described as one of the town's "two eyesores," visible before landing: one is "an obese Greek-Edwardian hotel near the larger of the two harbours, as at home on Phraxos as a hansom cab in a Doric temple. The other, equally at odds with the landscape, stood on the outskirts of the village," the school where Nicholas will teach (page 50). The skyline in the photograph reveals the characteristic forest of "Mediterranean pines as light as greenfinch feathers" that Nicholas enjoys walking through on his way to visit Conchis' villa on the other side of the island. Photograph by Eileen Warburton, 1996.

It is worth noting that the place where the plot is set in *The Magus*, despite its exotic ambience and its apparent timelessness, very much belongs to the twentieth century, and the reader is constantly reminded of this through concrete details. The novel's action takes place on the island of Phraxos, a fictional name for the small Aegean island of Spetses, or Spetsai. The island described could be either the real island or the fictional one:

> Phraxos lay eight dazzling hours in a small steamer south of Athens, about six miles off the mainland of the Peloponnesus and in the centre of a landscape as memorable as itself: to the north and west, a great fixed arm of mountains, in whose crook the island stood; to the east a distant gently-peaked archipelago; to the south the soft blue desert of the Aegean stretch-

ing away to Crete. Phraxos was beautiful. There was no other adjective; it was not just pretty, picturesque, charming—it was simply and effortlessly beautiful. It took my breath away when I first saw it, floating under Venus like a majestic black whale in an amethyst evening sea, and it still takes my breath away when I shut my eyes now and remember it. Its beauty was rare even in the Aegean, because its hills were covered with pine trees, Mediterranean pines as light as greenfinch feathers. Nine-tenths of the island was uninhabited and uncultivated: nothing but pines, coves, silence, sea. Herded into one corner, the north-west, lay a spectacular agglomeration of snow-white houses round a couple of small harbours. (50)

This sensuous, general description of the island is vivid because Fowles borrows details from his experience, a technique that helps insure that Fowles's fictional world will seem real.

If Nicholas is like Telemachus, who must grow up, Greece is like Circe—a test for the hero. The novel is not schematic about such analogies, however. Alison, for example, though she is a constant lover, is not otherwise much like Penelope, and her reunion with Nicholas in England at the end of the novel may be, after all, a parting. Indeed, the parallels are so limited and the references to Greek mythology so scattered that one could say that in *The Magus* the process of mythologization is not fully integrated with the plot but, instead, works to establish a cultural atmosphere, in association with the landscape.

In *The Magus*, then, Greek myths have mostly given up their religious, truth-telling role and serve a more poetical function. This means that the myth no longer appears in its pure form, but instead it works as cultural background knowledge, in association with the landscape. In the novel, myths have two functions with regard to the presentation of Greece: a stylistic function and a hermeneutic one. Using references to mythology, the author establishes a stylistic level for his description of the landscape and, at the same time, helps to generate deeper impressions and feelings associated with the narrator-hero.

Some of the deeper correlations between mythic references and ancient archetypes can be traced among the images that some Jungian psychologists would say are embedded in our collective unconscious—for example, the idea that the sea is feminine, as are its islands—an idea that Fowles poetically connects to the mythic story of Circe. In Homer, various islands have qualities that might be deemed magical—even the realistically drawn isle of Scheria, where Odysseus meets Nausicaa in Book Six. Scholar Friedrich Hindermann explains how islands are aptly associated with ideas of transformation and enchantment: "Where the opposites touch each other, a sudden change can be completed: the magic of transformation lives on the islands. Circe with the sows, Ariosto's Alcina with their bewitched youngsters, the Sirens and Caliban, the island of Venus, symbolical archetypes that repeatedly emerge in the Centuries . . . ."[4] In his foreword to *The Magus*, Fowles says something similar: "The Greece of the islands is Circe still; no place for the artist-voyager to linger long, if he cares for his soul" (9). In Book Ten of *The Odyssey*, in our first introduction to this goddess, Odysseus recalls her as "Fair-braided Circe, dread god with a singing voice / The blood sister of destructive-minded Aietes" (136–37). For Fowles, the island of Spetses likewise evokes beauty and music; its pine forests he describes as "uncanny" in his foreword to *The Magus*, and he remarks that the novel's birth involves the sound of music from a harmonium, heard the first time he approached the Villa Yasemia in 1952 (8). That villa was, of course, the model and inspiration for Bourani, the villa of Maurice Conchis in the novel and most "sacred" place in the landscape of Phraxos.

At the same time Circe attracts, however, she also threatens; as many dangers faced by Odysseus are female—including Scylla, Charybdis, and the Sirens—Circe personifies temptation, seduction, danger, even possible death. Fowles tries to explain his own mixture of feelings in the same foreword, recalling his return from Greece to England: "I had escaped Circe, but the withdrawal symptoms were severe" (9). The author evidently identifies himself with Odysseus here, that earlier male who managed only with great effort to free himself from Circe and to leave her island. In representing Spetses metaphorically as the witch-goddess Circe, Fowles tries to account for the complex mixture of feelings he has about his experiences in Greece, and he makes similar attempts in *The Magus* as he explains the feelings of Nicholas:

> . . . I fell totally and for ever in love with the Greek landscape from the moment I arrived. But with the love came a contradictory, almost irritating, feeling of impotence and inferiority, as if Greece were a woman so sensually provocative that I must fall physically and desperately in love with her, and at the same time so calmly aristocratic that I should never be able to approach her.
>
> None of the books I had read explained this sinister-fascinating, this Circe-like quality of Greece; the quality that makes it unique. In England we live in a very muted, calm, domesticated relationship with what remains of our natural landscape and its soft northern light; in Greece landscape and light are so beautiful, so all-present, so intense, so wild, that the relationship is immediately love-hatred, one of passion. (49)

Nicholas's feeling of impotence and inferiority weakens him, as Greece steals his senses and bewitches him the way a beautiful and

Villa Yasemia, Spetses, Greece. This privately owned villa was Fowles's model for Bourani, the house of Conchis in *The Magus*. When Nicholas arrives for the first time, he stands on the red tiles in the shade and feels a mysterious resonance with the place as the architecture frames the Peloponesian mainland across the water, and seems to erase any sense of geographical or temporal distance: "I looked out over the tree-tops and the sea to the languishing ash-lilac mountains . . . a *déjà vu* feeling of having stood in the same place, before that particular proportion of the arches, that particular contrast of shade and burning landscape outside— I couldn't say" (page 78). Photograph by Kirke Kefalea, 1996.

seductive woman can bewitch a man. Nicholas finds himself repeatedly at a point where his enthusiasm turns to destructive feeling, through overexcitement. This paradoxical structure of his relationship with Greek landscape describes the earlier moment when Nicholas, "seduced" by the island, thinks of the girlfriend he left behind in England—that other island he has likewise abandoned—and realizes his unfaithfulness: "What Alison was not to know—since I hardly realized it myself—was that I had been deceiving her with another woman during the latter part of September. The woman was Greece" (39). Given the hero's feelings of incapacity, one should remember that Circe is a goddess and, as such, she is *ex principio* more powerful than men. The representation of the island of Phraxos as a feminist as well as a magical island makes it not only a seductive place but also a place where a male finds the normal rules—including the assumption of male superiority—to be suspended.

In Fowles's novel, the mythologizing and anthropomorphizing of nature through feminine forms merge with erotic enticements that are reflected in the Greek landscape. The step from mythologizing to eroticizing is a small one. At one point, Nicholas bluntly says, "I began to rape the island" (63). There are more subtle correspondences, fusions, and erotic attractions between the hero, Nicholas, who is surrounded by the feminine figures Julie / Lily and June / Rose (in their double roles), and the natural elements and their appearances. Sometimes nature is described in its most elemental forms and constituents: fire/the sun and water/the sea are typical, almost archetypical constituents of poetical descriptions of nature. Gaston Bachelard in his book *L'Eau et les Rêves* examines the psychoanalytical meaning of such images: "*Nous pourrons rendre compte du caractère presque toujours feminin attribué à l'eau par l'imagination naive et par l'imagination poétique*" (We can take into account the fact that the character attributed to water by the naive imagination and by the poetical imagination is almost always feminine).[5]

For Nicholas, water can have both a calming and an erotic effect: "I dived and seal turned on my back and looked up through the water at the blurred white specks of the stars. The sea cooled, calmed, silked round my genitals. I felt safe out there, and sane, out of their reach, all their reaches" (332). Later, he reflects, "The silence, the dark water, the brilliant canopy of stars; and my sexual excitement . . . . It was too erotic" (369). Similarly, the Aegean sun stimulates Nicholas: "The sun moved, came on me, and made me erotic" (77). The physical environment is thus personified in ways that reinforce the associations of landscape with both eroticism and ancient myth.

The hero's movement in this landscape involves other mythological considerations. Fowles considers his own Greek experience an existential phase of his life, when there were various problems and disappointments that he discusses in "Behind *The Magus*" (58–59). The author's situation led him from his homeland, abroad on a sort of odyssey, in search of new, external and internal experiences. Nicholas Urfe's journey to Greece likewise takes the form of an odyssey, modeled on a rite of initiation in three narrative stages: leaving London, one year in Greece as a teacher of English, and a return to London. This circular journey helps to mythologize Nicholas's experiences and the process of discovery so that he comes to understand what he has been told, earlier, by T. S. Eliot:

> "We shall not cease from exploration
> And the end of all our exploring

> Will be to arrive where we started
> And know the place for the first time." (69)

The Greek experience of Nicholas is associated with ancient legends and mysteries, which in turn are connected to initiation rituals, the basis of which are the Eleusinian mysteries with Demeter and Persephone as protagonists.[6] He goes through experiences that mirror pattern voyages of a hero—a metaphorical descent into the underworld, where a trial takes place, passage through a labyrinth, searching for the Omphalos, and so on. All these are mythic constructs, which, in their own ways, describe a confrontation with a foreign land as a search for the truth, as a psychologically risky, exploratory path to the self. Conchis, the magus-sorcerer-magician-Hades figure, Godlike, manipulates Nicholas into accepting role assignments and leads him into secretive, mysterious situations. Related to those situations are theatrical and, above all, sexual experiences that he undergoes. The hero's story unfolds in a radically de-structured world, made real in some instances by classical myths. Mrs. de Seitas, for example, is explicitly linked with Ceres, giving her an additional dimension in the novel (598, 626, 630). Similarly, perhaps, Ceres is given an additional dimension in the personal world of John Fowles by virtue of her representation as the only statue in his garden. In mental landscapes, the mythic and the real, the playful and the serious, fiction and nonfiction are not easily distinguished—and are not meant to be.

It is Circe in particular, however, in *The Magus*, who represents uniquely Greek space and who is seemingly the source of the island's magical dimension and attractive power. Fowles's use of a number of other mythological references symbolizes in a more abstract sense the stages of a journey that the hero must pass through. The protagonist is identified from time to time with mythical figures, such as Odysseus, Theseus, and Orpheus, in order to symbolize the complicated movement of the hero in psychological depth, or space, whose course is parallel to a process of discovery: "And yet as I walked there came the strongest feeling, compounded of the early hour, the absolute solitude, and what had happened, of having entered a myth; a knowledge of what it was like physically, moment by moment, to have been young and ancient, a Ulysses on his way to meet Circe, a Theseus on his journey to Crete, an Oedipus still searching for his destiny" (157). Fowles risks interfering with the novel's mythical "atmosphere" when the protagonist reflects on myth in such an abstract way, or when Nicholas remarks of the landscape, "The rest was sublimely peaceful, as potential as a clean canvas, a site for myths" (63). However, most readers seem not to mind.

It becomes clear that Fowles allows his own, modern Greek experience to fuse with ancient mythological experience to produce a kind of magical, classical realism. The result can be enjoyed as a residually classical image of Greece—as when a tourist enjoyably loses touch with Greek reality as he or she identifies with traces of Greek myth. In moments like these the foreign land of Greece is more than just a different national and ethnic reality, but deeply other—illusionistic, hallucinatory, and occult. Nicholas undergoes such an experience in the grip of the Greek landscape in *The Magus*, and readers undergo a similar experience in the grip of the literary landscape of Fowles's novel.

In the dialectic between myth and modernity, Fowles's experience in Greece during the 1950s merges with his background in Greek culture. As he represents this tension, a similar tension is created in the reader that influences his or her perception of the novel. On the one hand, the author provides an alternative to the traditional, philhellenic image of Greece with a mid-twentieth century version of it. On the other hand, he continues to update myths by blending classical motives and images with elements from his own experience. It is perhaps this productive contradiction that makes the reading of this ancient-modern novel about Greece, *The Magus*, so attractive and so exciting.

Notes

1. John Fowles, *The Magus: A Revised Version* (Boston: Little, Brown, 1978), page 381.

2. The first version of the novel was published in 1965, but Fowles had been working on it as "my first novel" since he left Greece in the early 1950s, according to both his Foreword to the 1978 edition (5) and his more recent essay "Behind *The Magus*" in *Twentieth Century Literature* 42, no.1 (1996), page 65.

3. Homer, *The Odyssey*, trans. Albert Cook, Norton Critical Edition, 2d ed. (New York: W. W. Norton, 1993). The first four books of *The Odyssey*, which focus on Odysseus' adolescent son, Telemachus, introduce as a theme his need to mature—as Part One of *The Magus* establishes a similar shortcoming in Nicholas (15–63).

4. Friedrich Hindermann, *Inseln in der Weltliteratur* (Zürich: Manesse Publishing House, 1988), page 403F. Translated by the author.

5. Gaston Bachelard, *L'Eau et les Rêves* (Paris: Librairie José Corti, 1942), page 20.

6. In a letter to James Aubrey, Fowles has acknowledged that the structure of the trial scene in *The Magus* is partly based on an article about the Eleusinian Mysteries that once appeared in *Eranos*, a Jung yearbook published in Switzerland. Aubrey identifies the article and discusses implications in "Eleusinian Mysteries in the Trial Scene of John Fowles's *The Magus*," *Journal of Evolutionary Psychology* 15, nos.1–2 (March 1994), pages 129–33.

The Landscape of Loss in the (Love) Poems of John Fowles

DIANNE L. VIPOND

> Cherish the poet; there seemed many great auks till the last one died.
> —John Fowles, *The Aristos*

JOHN FOWLES HAS REMARKED IN AN INTERVIEW, "THE TRAGEDY OF MY OWN life is that I am not a great poet."[1] Although he is indeed best known for his novels, not everyone shares his modest opinion of his poetry. Lawrence Durrell, for one, has described him as "a great poet."[2] Accolades such as his suggest that serious critical consideration of Fowles's poetry is long overdue.

The epigraph, above, comes from Fowles's book of philosophical observations, *The Aristos*.[3] The statement reappears with some changes in "Protect the Word" in Fowles's *Poems*:

> The best are not the most skilled.
> There seemed many great auks
> Till the last one was killed.[4]

The fact that these lines are repeated in two very different contexts—one prose, one poetry—is indicative of their significance for Fowles. Not only do they highlight the importance of the art of poetry to him, but they also warn against its potential diminishment or loss. In *The Lost Gods of England*, Brian Branston notes that "a curse of modern society is that it has a high mortality rate in poets: they get mashed up in the machinery. The Old English, on the other hand, held poets in high esteem with priests and kings. Great respect was paid to the art of 'finding sayings rightly bound.'"[5] Branston goes on to point out that they "looked on natural phenomena as a 'them' and not an 'it.' Their approach to nature was subjective . . . [and] intuitive . . . [they interpreted] the universe . . . by revelation which assumes form and body in myth. It is not to be wondered at that the myths are couched in verse, for poets were the instruments of revelation" (181–82). If the primary role of the ancient poet was to explain nature to the people, one of the major functions of the poet today is to elucidate internal *human* nature. In Nicholas Humphrey's terms, the poet, as natural psychologist, one who has learned the meaning of human experience through introspection, enables the reader to make sense of life by re-creating feeling through language and activating memory.[6]

Love, loss, and landscape—motifs central to Fowles's fiction—are no less relevant to an examination of his poetry. I have chosen to focus on four poems that illustrate how the landscapes and mindscapes of loss are represented by Fowles. Only one of these poems is a love poem in the traditional sense of the word, but part of what I hope to illustrate is how the other three also suggest different facets of the love motif that are central to so many of Fowles's essays and novels. In the poems, we are faced with physical and sociopolitical landscapes as well as psychological, intellectual, and emotional mindscapes that are economically crystallized in ways available only to poetic form. I have selected the poems for the way they span Fowles's writing career: "Apollo" (1952), "Crusoe" (1956), "Report from Starship 26" (1972), and "*Je fable*" (1994). In part because there is a continuum of content, these poems can be used to document shifts in nuance. The first three are found in *Poems*; the last appeared (along with another poem, "In the Middleyard") in the John Fowles special number of *Twentieth Century Literature*.[7] Fowles continues to write poetry and is planning to publish a new collection of poems; poetry will be an increasingly important genre in his oeuvre.[8]

My approach in this essay is something of an exercise in meta-intertextuality, a way of attempting to illustrate the seamless quality of Fowles's thought no matter in which genre he chooses to express himself, for the language of the poetry echoes themes and motifs prevalent in the fiction and expanded upon in his nonfiction—particularly in *The Tree*, "Behind *The Magus*," *Islands*, "The Nature of Nature," and *The Aristos*.

In 1945, T. S. Eliot wrote: "A poet must take as his material his own language as it is actually spoken around him. . . . The music of poetry, then, will be a music latent in the common speech of his time."[9] If a reader were to open *Poems* at random, he or she would immediately recognize that Fowles has taken this tack. Whereas Fowles's novels present the reader with highly visual, densely evocative text, perhaps best characterized as poetic prose, the poetry, especially the early poetry is marked by linguistic restraint. He exploits the lyric potential of flatness through the use of colloquial language. A passage from "At Llanvillo" provides an example:

> Until I hear voices, the voices
> Of friends from the village house.
> Hey, John! John?
>
> And I unbecome,
> Become their John. (64)

In many poems, the rhythms of everyday speech evoke the immediacy of overheard conversation filling the reader with a sense of "being there" that is reminiscent in kind, if not in style, of what he or she experiences while reading the novels.

The imagery, often nature or landscape imagery, also evokes a sense of immediacy. In the autobiographical essay *The Tree*, Fowles writes, "The key to my fiction . . . lies in my relationship with nature . . . ."[10] Although his "relationship with nature" is chronicled in various essays, the poetry provides further insight into this "key" to the fiction. In "The Nature of Nature," Fowles credits D. H. Lawrence with coming closest to capturing the "beingness, the existingness" in nature. "It is why I became a writer myself, always stumbling, despite being a novelist, after the poem. . . ."[11] Fowles's 1992 commentary on *The Man Who Died* elaborates on this quality of Lawrence's "isness." In that essay, Fowles quotes Cynthia Asquith's account of Lawrence: "He was 'preternaturally alive,' there was an 'electric elemental quality that gave him a flickering radiance.'"[12] Those who have met John Fowles will recognize that this description applies equally well to Fowles himself. In *The Tree*, Fowles writes: "What is irreplaceable in any object of art is never, in the final analysis, its technique or craft, but the personality of the artist, the expression of his or her unique and individual feeling" (46). In other words, the literary artifact is animated by the consciousness behind it. In the "Foreword" to *Poems*, Fowles admits to authentic self-revelation in the poetry: "The poem is saying what you are and feel, the novel is saying what invented characters might be and might feel" (viii). Both essays and poems, then, address and "translate" feeling respectively. In 1995, in "The Nature of Nature," Fowles returns to the role of feeling as it relates to literature, generally in a discussion of differences between art and science, feeling and knowing as they relate to C. P. Snow's *The Two Cultures*: "I see literature far more as an expression of feeling conveyed through poetry, drama and fiction than any sort of serious scientific statement about reality" (74). It is feeling that is behind the genius of his work. Nevertheless, Fowles has admitted, "Just as I wish I could have been an excellent poet, I also perhaps secretly wish I had been . . . a sort of philosopher."[13] Much of his writing has been devoted both creatively as well as discursively to a discussion of ideas, so it is not surprising that he chooses as an epigraph to "The Nature of Nature" related lines from Norman Mac Caig's "Equilibrist":

> Noticing you can do nothing about.
> It's the balancing that shakes my mind. (73)

Feeling balanced by knowledge yields the humanism that is the imprimatur of Fowles's writing.

One of the "Greek Poems," "A Kind of Philhellene," poses three questions that inform all of his work:

> Who art thou?
> Where from?
> Where to? (15)

Both in print and in talks that he has given, Fowles has often quoted Socrates' famous "Know thyself" as a summary statement of what his writing is about and what it is meant to help the reader learn to do. The seriousness in which he holds these questions is underscored in the stanza that follows them:

> All you who come to "write" or "paint"—
> God help you if you smile at this
> And find those questions merely quaint.

The road to self-discovery necessitates a revisiting and reassessment of one's past ("Where from?") and a careful consideration of where one is headed ("Where to?") based upon thoughtful selection of personal and social values. Nicholas Urfe and Daniel Martin are the protagonists in Fowles's fiction who most clearly demonstrate this questioning process; in fact, they may be profitably seen as incarnations of each other.[14] The process of self-creation is ongoing, never-ending, but like the blank page that faces the novelist or poet, the possibilities are infinite.

"Protect the Word," mentioned earlier in connection with the epigraph, contains two stanzas that warrant examination in any consideration of principles that are relevant to understanding Fowles's poetry (47–48). The title is a call for the preservation of the written word that has its origins in the oral tradition; its position as the first in the section called "Poems" is indicative of its importance. A sense of urgency gathers momentum in the first stanza and is sustained throughout the rest of the poem by way of defining "the word":

> At the beginning was the word,
> Before the image or the sound.
> In chaos, order is its heart.

The paradox in the last line implies the potential of language for making sense of chaos, no mere luxury, a survival quality if ever there was one. The poem continues:

> In order freedom is its soul.
> It is the art in which to feel
> Is not enough.

This fifth stanza clarifies the relationships among chaos, order, and freedom that are brought to consciousness through "the word." Anyone familiar with Fowles's work will immediately recognize the primacy for him of the concept of freedom. Despite the apparent undercutting of feeling in the second and third lines, the remainder of the poem elevates feeling above skill. Once again, the consistency of Fowles's thought is made evident over time and across genres, for thirty-five years separate the dates of composition of "Protect the Word" and "The Nature of Nature."

"Apollo," the last of the "Greek Poems" and the one that Fowles describes as especially relevant as a germ of *The Magus* and in registering the sense of loss he felt in having to leave Greece, catalogs elements of the Greek landscape: pines, sea poppy, shingle, shadow, stones, sun, sea, shrike, and silence (2, 18). It is a brief, twenty-line poem that accumulates meaning largely through reiteration, repetition of individual words and sounds, alliteration, and onomatopoeia. The sibilance of the recurring *s* sounds emulates the sound of water running over stones, the background noise of the sea, and an implicit whispering of wind "singing" in the pines. Entirely composed of visual and auditory images, impressionistic in spite of the spare sharpness of the individual images, the poem renders setting as primary. The chiaroscuro quality of contrasting darkness and light ("the shadow of pines" and the otherwise ubiquitous sun) is paralleled by the counterpointing rhythm of sound (singing, gurgling, screaming) and silence. The silence resonates beyond the piercing scream of the shrike at the end, a hovering echo, almost a lament. In his foreword to the revised *Magus*, Fowles reveals: "I had not then realized that loss is essential for the novelist, immensely fertile for his books, however painful to his private being. [It is an] unresolved sense of a lack, a missed opportunity."[15]

A deceptively simple listlike rhythm is achieved through the chronicling of landscape images, natural images that compose the domain of the god Apollo, god of the arts and intellect as well as of light, and appropriately so if one of the qualities of art is to en*light*en. The surface simplicity of the poem prefigures Fowles's novelistic technique by way of the space he leaves for the reader to recompose the elements, to fill in the gaps, to extrapolate from the artist's vision. One may also see the list operating as "notes" that re-create the atmosphere or feeling that fuels the fiction of *The Magus* by providing the writer with scope to compose the narrative. Setting is the impetus for the narration and thematic development of the novel. Again, in his foreword to the revised version of *The Magus*, Fowles writes:

> Away from its inhabited corner Spetsai was truly haunted, though by subtler—and more beautiful—ghosts than I have created. Its pine forests were uncanny, unlike those I have experienced anywhere else; like an eternally blank page waiting for a note or a word. In no place was it less likely that something would happen; yet somehow happening lay poised. I am hard put to convey the importance of this experience for me as a writer. It imbued and marked me far more profoundly than any of my more social and physical memories of the place. I already knew I was a permanent exile from many aspects of English society, but a novelist has to enter deeper exiles still. (8)

The pine trees may be literal, but they are also pregnant with symbolic meaning. These are the trees of the myth of Attis, Adonis, and Cybele, the regenerative fertility myth of ancient Greece. Here they are associated with the birth of the artist John Fowles, that is, with the writing of his truly first novel, *The Magus*. The yellow sea poppy is a reflection of the sun god Apollo and the necessary spot of color that subliminally reminds the reader of the title of the poem, "Apollo," the god of the arts—and very like the novelist who created his first fictional world in a novel with the working title *The Godgame*.

The last line of the poem, "I come," reverberates with a variety of meanings. Tacitly the speaker comes in response to the inspirational, natural landscape of Greece articulated by the awakening scream, the shriek of the shrike, a sea bird that oversees the island. In hearing the shriek as a summons, he is also responding to the bird as oracle and avatar—a reaction appropriate to a poet whose name is Fowles and who harbors a great fondness for birds. The call is implicitly, then, a call to the vocation of artist by the god of the arts for whom the poem is titled, Apollo. Finally, the word *come* can denote ejaculation of seed—reflecting the Renaissance idea of a parallel between literary and sexual generation—an idea that Fowles plays with in the novel *Mantissa*.[16] In "Apollo," Greece is the seedbed of a novel, the initial conception of what was to become *The Magus*.

Details of landscape identical to those in "Apollo" occur in *The Magus*: "its hills were covered with pine trees. . . . Nine-tenths of the island was uninhabited and uncultivated: nothing but pines, coves, silence, sea. . . . the rest was primeval pine-forest. . . . Its distinguishing characteristic . . . was silence" (50–51). Although the novel is best known for the magnetic pull of its narrative, its ability to enchant the reader must in part be attributed to the descriptions of landscape that are so appropriate to the purposes of the novelist as to be almost invisible at first reading. Their unobtrusive presence is a measure of their effectiveness in creating a setting that enhances the credibility of the narrative. The more a reader tries to imagine any of Fowles's fiction without its given natural setting, the more one recognizes just how much the landscapes are an intrinsic part of the magic of his writing, its mythopoeic quality.

Anyone familiar with *The Magus* might be hard pressed to see "Apollo," this imagistic paean to Greek landscape, as catalytic of such a rich, complex, intellectually ambitious novel. Yet, Fowles's 1994 essay "Behind *The Magus*," written some forty years after the poem and including an unretouched diary entry from that time, confirms the influence of the original poetic landscape images and provides a gloss on their "feeling": "A purity and simplicity of emotion, a kind of quintessential Mediterranean ecstasy, pervaded the air; the air infused with pine-resin and winter sharpness and the brine from far below."[17] This is just one sampling of the many descriptions in the essay. The resonance of the title of the poem "Apollo" is demonstrated by another passage from "Behind *The Magus*": "The Greeks see, feel, apprehend light not as others do, and from the beginning of history to its end. . . . Among other things it is all beauty and all truth. . . . It and its absence are life and death" (67). The "Greek Poems" and the essay operate in a dialectical relationship to each other, each giving voice to feeling through different genres but, read in tandem, each enriching and enlarging our understanding of the other. The reader begins to get a sense of how the searing light of Greece informs deeper meanings of the novel and of how Fowles's sacrosanct relationship with nature nourishes his creative spirit, his art. As he has written in *The Tree*, "Art and nature are siblings, branches of the one tree; and nowhere more than in the continuing inexplicability of many of their processes, and above all those of creation" (49). In some respects, nature is his muse.

Just as "Apollo" is inspired by the landscape of the real Greek island Spetsai, which becomes the fictional island of Phraxos in *The Magus*, "Crusoe" evokes another island, the imaginary island of Daniel Defoe's *Robinson Crusoe* and, more importantly, the island

(I-land) of the self (55). Although landscape is less apparent in the details of this poem than in "Apollo," the metaphorical island on which we are all stranded is ever-present as physical background imbued with symbolic meaning; thus landscape directs any interpretation of the poem. "Crusoe" is another short twenty-line, four-stanza poem, which underscores the psychic or psychological landscape embodied in the universal quest for identity through self-understanding and through relationship with the other. It is an existential recognition of the inherent isolation of the individual against a backdrop of the necessary but ever-retreating I-thou relationship, both inter-and intra-personally. "Crusoe" is a landmark poem in that it rehearses in poetic form what is behind the narrative of almost all of the fiction.

In the preface to *Islands*, a work of nonfiction that celebrates the ancient landscape of the Scilly Isles with the photography of Fay Godwin, Fowles writes: "This is much more about the Scillies of a novelist's mind; and beyond them, about the mysteries, symbolic and real, of all similarly situated small islands; about their silences, their otherness, their magi and their mazes, their eternal waiting for a foot to land."[18] *Islands* is a book of veiled literary criticism that discusses several of the texts that have been of particular interest to Fowles in his work as a novelist—for example, *The Odyssey*, *The Tempest*, *The Well-Beloved*. *Islands* illustrates what they mean to him and suggests ways in which he has incorporated aspects of them into his own novels—none of which should surprise us about a poet who is English, that is, an island poet, himself. *Islands* also reveals something about the way Fowles views his own creative process: "I have always thought of my own novels as islands, or as islanded. . . . the notion of islands in the sea of story. . . . The island remains where the magic (one's arrival at some truth or development one could not have logically predicted or expected) takes place; and it arises strangely, out of nothingness . . . in the writing" (30). The solitary act of writing provides an environment that fosters introspection, which in turn leads to islands of insight born of self-confrontation.

Framing the moment on the beach in *The Magus* where Nicholas finds the page marked with the four lines by T. S. Eliot, Fowles makes reference to Crusoe: "My first feeling was one of . . . a Crusoe-like resentment" (67), and after the discovery, "For the second time that day I felt like Robinson Crusoe" (70). The lines that elicit this reaction are from "Little Gidding":

> We shall not cease from exploration
> And the end of all our exploring

> Will be to arrive where we started
> And know the place for the first time. (69)

They operate as something of a proleptic coda for the journey to selfhood that Nicholas makes in *The Magus*. As Fowles points out in *Islands*, "Islands strip and dissolve the crud of our pretensions and cultural accretions, the Odyssean mask of victim we all wear" (105). Although the prototypically self-absorbed young man, Nicholas is rarely aware that what he is in pursuit of is his true self. The island setting throws him back upon himself, and Conchis' "islands in the sea of story" push him further in the direction of epiphanies of self-understanding, however partial they may prove to be.

The first stanza of the poem "Crusoe" documents our aloneness:

> Crusoes, all of us. Stranded
> On solitary grains of land. (55)

The pacing of the line breaks draws attention to the concepts introduced in the succeeding lines: we are like Crusoe searching for "the mystic print," the evidence of another. Here loneliness is equated with incompleteness, emptiness, a vacuum, a space that needs to be filled—not exactly loss, but a related concept that Fowles limns in *Islands* when he describes "the genesis of all art; the pursuit of the irrecoverable, what the object-relations analysts now call symbolic repair" (59). The print is described as "mystic" to suggest the mystery of the other and, to a certain extent, the mystery of the self. The print represents a Jungian *anima* or *animus* figure, a projected spiritual counterpart that nurtures the evolution of the self. The second stanza, which focuses on Friday, begins by emphasizing difference—the otherness of the other—but concludes with acknowledgment of a shared humanity. The line "Without a language we can speak" highlights the importance of communication while pointing out the very real difficulties inherent in any true communion. It is as if the shade of Ourika as later embodied in Sarah Woodruff lurks behind the language of this stanza—both victims of social alienation, more or less ostracized, certainly marginal figures in carefully circumscribed societies.[19] The verses in this stanza are straightforward, assertive, and definite. The first half of the poem is primarily masculine: "Crusoe," "Friday," "he."

The first three lines of the next stanza are reminiscent of Eliot's "Preludes," both in terms of rhythm and in the accumulation of quotidian detail. A transition takes place in the fourth line from the singular to the plural, from "I" to "we," suggesting some sort of potential individuation and integration, a step in the direction of wholeness. "That print, that sign" are blunt abstractions with room enough for the reader to fill them with symbolic significance. The word "loved" in the final line of the stanza intimates a vague female quality or presence, whether it be abstract femininity or an actual woman who is being addressed. The auxiliary verbs "could have" serve to indicate her absence, perhaps through loss or unrealized possibility.

The final stanza, consisting of three short lines repeating the first person plural pronoun, utilizes repetition of specific words and alliteration. Although there is no definitive resolution to the quest for completion established in the first stanza, there has been some movement toward understanding throughout the course of the poem. The seemingly elusive prizes of fulfillment, wholeness, and happiness, while not attained, have been articulated, and the means to their achievement implied. The title of the poem "Crusoe" alludes to the work of Daniel Defoe, one of the first English novelists whose inventiveness, narrative drive, and humanism Fowles admires.[20] Although it may be more like a faint negative than a sharp print, "Crusoe" contains the skeletal image of the search for selfhood narrative that is so evident in Fowles's fiction. Perhaps partly because of its position as the last word in the poem, as well as its conceptual centrality, the word *whole* reminds the reader of the opening line of *Daniel Martin*: "Whole sight; or all the rest is desolation."[21] As in Fowles's fiction, generally, perception is given a dominant role in the development of the self.

The island landscape apparent in both "Apollo" and "Crusoe" reappears in slightly altered form as an island in space, a planet, in the poem "Report from Starship 26" (111–113). The significance of this much longer poem lies in the sociopolitical landscape that it depicts. To summarize, a delegation from Earth is reporting on its visit to another planet, whose much older civilization seems based primarily on feminine principles. We are told of the "dominant role granted the mother," "the prevalence of gardens," advanced technology only in medical areas, simple social structures, smiles, lack of hostility, a female ruler, and the gesture of presenting the interlopers with a white wildflower in response to their "declaration of intent." Nature, nurture, simplicity, peacefulness—being rather than becoming—these are the characteristics of this female society.

One of the most striking attributes of the poem, the speaker's tone—an exaggeratedly superior attitude, harboring suspicion and relying on "proof"—is undercut by the poem's irony. The starship represents the prototypically masculine world of colonialism, imperialism, and empire that values technology, heavy industry, complex social structures, hegemony, competition, progress, categorization, self-congratulation, and self-absorption. It discounts the feminine. Understandably, the feminized planet does not respond to Mr. President's "eloquent offer of co-operation"; it refuses to be co-opted, to be colonized. The starship and the feminine community anticipate Fowles's 1985 novel *A Maggot*, in which a spaceship and its passengers appear to Rebecca, who subsequently gives birth to Ann Lee, founder of the Shakers, a religious community notable for its "striking feminism, simplicity, sanity and self-control."[22]

In a section of *The Aristos* designated "Adam and Eve," Fowles writes: "The male and female are the two most powerful biological principles; and their smooth inter-action in society is one of the chief signs of social health.... Adam is stasis ... Eve is kinesis.... All progressive societies are feminist." He further states that tolerance, an aspect of the female principle that is skeptical of violence, is of the greatest value to society and the most fundamental of all human wisdoms (165–67). Ezra Pound once proposed that "Poets are the antennae of the race."[23] What Fowles is pointing out here for the benefit of the human race is not that one set of traits is negative and the other positive, but rather, through his use of hyperbole, that our gendered tendencies are skewed toward the masculine. In the words of Robert Johnson, author of *Femininity Lost and Regained*, "If there is a better age—a millennium—to come, it would emerge out of [a] conscious appreciation of both values rather than from a violent swinging of the pendulum from one imbalance to the other."[24] Fowles would surely agree that men need to cultivate their feminine side and women to reclaim their masculine traits in order to achieve an equilibrium in psychic energy, to become more fully human.

Robert Graves has stated: "I cannot think of any true poet from Homer onwards who has not independently recorded his experience of [the White Goddess]. The test of a poet's vision ... is the accuracy of his portrayal of the White Goddess and the *island* over which she rules [emphasis added]."[25] In "Report from Starship 26," Fowles innovatively employs a science fictional space setting and, through defamiliarization, draws attention to what has been lost in the erasure of any trace of the matriarchal society that may once have prevailed in the primeval world. Although somewhat idealized in this context— for example, with the arcadian "prevalence of gardens"—the point remains the same: "symbolic repair" consists of ameliorating the potentially destructive qualities of a patriarchal society by balancing it with the addition of traits associated with a feminine community. When the ruler's daughter offers the male astronauts "a nondescript white flower," they can see only its biological commonness, not its symbolic value as a peace offering. We should not be blind to its further symbolism as a tribute to the White Goddess, Mother Nature, Mother Earth, but also of a relationship with the visitors that must be restored in the interests of peace and the survival of the planet Earth.

The juxtaposition of masculinity and femininity in a social context in "Report from Starship 26" is a logical extension of the personal process of individuation noted in "Crusoe." In both cases, self-discovery is realized through the search for the other, the other part of ourselves, the anima or animus. John Desteian, a Jungian analyst, describes the anima as relatedness (Eros) and the animus as the prevailing or essential spirit (Logos). "The anima introduces a man to his nature at a feeling level, while the animus provides the woman with an internal experience of her essential spirit."[26] He explains the process of individuation as the "*psyche coming into being in the conscious world*" (178), as "the struggle . . . to see the mirror images of ourselves in the world, and the world's mirror image within us. In the struggle to attain the wisdom of the symbolic life, we begin to create myth—for solutions to the inner and outer conflicts are just that, the myths of our lives" (179). Fowles readily admits the influence of Carl Jung, "whose theories deeply interested me at the time" (the 1950s), in his foreword to the revised *Magus* (6).

The last poem in this discussion of Fowles's poetry, "*Je fable*," actualizes the process of individuation through the persona's chameleon-like transformations of the anima. Fowles's note to the poem in *Twentieth Century Literature* reveals not only the dynamic, wild, or "green" quality of his creative process as he transmutes memory and imagination into art but also the close link between his poetry and his fiction:

> *Fabler* or *fabloiier*, to tell a story that is partly invented, occurs in Old French. This "poem" must seem as it first did to me: ridiculous. It tells of a character in a fiction that wasn't—and still isn't—even properly written; which I had never consciously conceived or willed, and indeed always felt it better (more shamanistic if less Christian) simply to harbour, to live with in secret, than to actualize. The elderly Alethia (Allie) flits past in twilit rags and tatters, much more a ghost than a fact. At least she has given herself a name. She thinks she is, among other things, a diplomat's divorced wife. I slowly comprehend from certain half-heard lines that she is related to my wife Elizabeth, who died of cancer on the first day of March, 1990. Eliz had neither a diplomatic lover, nor was she a botanist or a member of a resistance group, as my fabulous character appears to wish to present herself; but (as I've already hinted) Elizabeth remains the ultimate *revenante* in my green life, forever unable to leave each now. Though physically I know her to be mere cremated ash, she stays as alive to me, behind her mask, as she could never be in the other kind of reality. (8)

Without a doubt, this is a love poem and much more. It is the celebration of a muse, the honest, heartfelt tribute to a beloved wife, Elizabeth, as well as the evocation of a character, Allie. The headnote becomes a part of the poem that follows it by providing the reader with a glimpse of the transformative sliding panels of the imagination where stereoscopic vision yields a continually metamorphosing character. The infinitely mysterious powers of transubstantiation inherent in the creative process cause art and life to intersect as reality becomes the stuff of fiction and poetry, as the writer re-invents reality. The landscape of loss intrinsic to this poem is redeemed by love through virtual reality. As Conchis declares in the original version of *The Magus*: "*The dead live by love.*"[27] Although virtual reality is a term usually associated with cyberspace, it is also an appropriate designation for literary art when narrative—or in this case lyric—constructs an enveloping, simulated mental existence. The world of the imagination *is* virtual reality.

The speaker in this slipstream of a poem interrogates memory: "How could I forget, after so long?" Memory and mourning, that is, loss, have the same root in English. Memory yields images that are more than a series of cinematic stills; the accumulation of verbals suggests the dynamism of ongoing movement, that quality of Lawrencean "existingness" noted earlier. Specific images are associated with particular moments akin to Virginia Woolf's "moments of being": the way she walks, her style, the enthusiastic line of dialogue when she encounters a first bloom, the look, the little smile, her unchanging truth, her razor-edged reality, her shrug. These detailed images particularize the "you" of the poem, making her live in the imagination of the reader. On this level, the poem becomes a tribute to Mnemosyne, goddess of memory and mother of the Muses.

The unnamed female character in the poem is identified with various goddess figures but denies such apotheosis, at once confirming her simultaneous divinity and commonality, her universality. Her association with Astarte, Nerthus, and Freya, all of which are incarnations of the White Goddess, Mother Earth, and Aphrodite, the goddess of love, lend her an overarching timelessness. She exists against a natural background of "glades," "mountains," "meadows," "drowning in spring," all landscapes associated with the goddess figure, as is the fertility of spring. She is the personification of muse, beloved, and artistic creation. It is only in the note that she is identified with Allie or Elizabeth; in the poem she remains the unnamed "you," the other, the feminine archetype, the speaker's anima. However, she is not devoid of masculine qualities, as the images in the second half of the poem indicate. Ultimately, her "unchanging truth" asserts her freedom to be herself, thus suggesting the balance of male and female, the integrated personality, the realization of human potential inherent in the earlier poem "Crusoe."

Echoes of Gerard Manley Hopkins can be seen in the interplay of language in such lines as "made the dullest tat flash sudden all," as Fowles illuminates the inscape, the "fundamental intuitive sense of. . . being" that haunts his landscape of loss with such phantom loveliness in "*Je fable.*"[28] The last three lines achieve a kind of transcendence through fabulation; the poet transmutes the past into the ever-present now of art as time dissolves into a moment of stillness, of pure being.

In *The Double Flame: Love and Eroticism*, Octavio Paz has this to say about poetry: "Poetry lets us touch the impalpable and hear the tide of silence that covers a landscape devastated by insomnia. Poetic testimony reveals to us another world inside this world, the other world in this world. The senses, without losing their powers, become the servants of the imagination and let us hear the inaudible and see the invisible."[29] Paz describes how love implies sacrifice; implicit within the word *passion* is the concept of suffering concomitant with the mutability of nature. However, this suffering is freely chosen by the lovers; love becomes "freedom personified, freedom incarnated in a body and a soul" (181). He tells us that "love does not defeat death; it is a wager against time and its accidents. Through love we catch a glimpse, in this life, of the other life. Not of eternal life, but . . . of pure vitality" (273–74). Paz continues:

> Freud refers to an "oceanic feeling," that sensation of being enveloped in and rocked by all of existence. . . . the recovery of wholeness and the discovery of the self as a wholeness within the Great Whole. . . . Reconciliation with the totality of the world. With past, present, and future as well. Love is not eternity. . . . The time of love . . . is the perception of all times, of all loves, in a single instant. . . . the reverse and complement of the "oceanic feeling." It is not the return to the waters of origin but the attainment of a state that reconciles us to our having been driven out of paradise. We are the theater of the embrace of opposites and of their dissolution, resolved in a single note that is not affirmation or negation but acceptance. . . . the equation of appearance and disappearance, the truth of the body and the nonbody, the vision of the presence that dissolves into splendor: pure vitality, a heartbeat of time. (274–75)

Likewise in Fowles's (love) poems, the reader encounters loss of place (Greece), the self, a viable world, a woman, a character, and literary alternatives predicated upon artistic choices. Yet, behind each of these is the continuous awareness of the importance of being in the now, the irrecoverability of each passing moment. As Fowles has written in *The Aristos*, "All art is the attempt to transcend time" (189). The condensation that is essential to poetry lends itself particularly well to preserving the feeling that constituted the now of the poetic genesis. The poem becomes a linguistic artifact effectively stopping time through art that allows the reader to savor the now of the poem again and again, a timeless gesture in the face of inevitable, recurring loss.

As Nicholas Urfe contemplates his poetic aspirations in *The Magus*, he recalls "Emily Dickinson's great definition, her 'Publication is not the business of poets'; being a poet is all, being known as a poet is nothing" (57). As John Fowles transforms the landscapes of loss into mindscapes of "symbolic repair" through the "green" of his imagination, poetry infuses all of his work. He *is* a poet.

Notes

1. John Fowles and Dianne Vipond, "An Unholy Inquisition," *Twentieth Century Literature* 42 (1996), page 14.

2. Charles E. Claffey, "Lawrence Durrell: British Author of the Exotic Is Still Dazzling the Critics," *Boston Globe*, 25 April 1986, pages 12–13.

3. John Fowles, *The Aristos*, 2d ed. (Boston: Little, Brown, 1970), page 211. In the first edition (1964), the statement reads, "Cherish the *word*. . ." [emphasis added], page 161.

4. John Fowles, *Poems* (New York: Ecco Press, 1973), page 48.

5. Brian Branston, *The Lost Gods of England* (London: Thames and Hudson, 1957), pages 50–51.

6. Nicholas Humphrey, *Consciousness Regained* (Oxford: Oxford University Press, 1983), page 63.

7. John Fowles, "Je fable," *Twentieth Century Literature* 42 (1996), pages 8–9.

8. John Fowles, unpublished interview with the author, 23 April 1996.

9. Quoted in Donald Hall, "T. S. Eliot," *Writers at Work: "The Paris Review" Interviews*, 2d series, ed. George Plimpton (New York: Viking, 1965), page 108.

10. John Fowles, *The Tree* (1979; reprint New York: Ecco Press, 1983), page 31.

11. John Fowles, *"The Tree" and "The Nature of Nature"* (Covelo, Calif.: Yolla Bolly Press, 1995), page 92.

12. Quoted in John Fowles, "Commentary on *The Man Who Died*," in *The Man Who Died*, by D. H. Lawrence (1992; reprint Hopewell, N. J.: Ecco Press, 1994), page 95.

13. Fowles and Vipond, page 28.

14. Michael Barber, "An Interview with John Fowles" (London, 1977; rerecording North Hollywood, Calif.: Center for Cassette Studies, 1979), Audio-Text Cassette Number 38873.

15. John Fowles, foreword to *The Magus: A Revised Version* (Boston: Little, Brown, 1977), page 9.

16. John Fowles, *Mantissa* (Boston: Little, Brown, 1982).

17. John Fowles, "Behind *The Magus*" (London: Colophon Press, 1994; reprint *Twentieth Century Literature* 42 (1996), page 62.

18. John Fowles and Fay Godwin, *Islands* (Boston: Little, Brown, 1978), page 2.

19. John Fowles, foreword to *Ourika,* by Claire de Durfort, trans. John Fowles (New York: Modern Language Association, 1994), page xxix.

20. James R. Baker, "An Interview with John Fowles," *Michigan Quarterly Review* 25 (1986), page 667.

21. John Fowles, *Daniel Martin* (Boston: Little, Brown, 1977), page 3.

22. John Fowles, *A Maggot* (Boston: Little, Brown, 1985), pages 450, 453.

23. Ezra Pound, *The ABC of Reading* (New York: New Directions, 1934), page 81.

24. Robert A. Johnson, *Femininity Lost and Regained* (1990; reprint New York: HarperCollins, 1991), page 13.

25. Robert Graves, *The White Goddess* (New York: Farrar, Straus and Giroux, 1948), page 24.

26. John A. Desteian, *Coming Together—Coming Apart: The Union of Opposites in Love Relationships* (Boston: Sigo, 1989), page 57.

27. John Fowles, *The Magus* (Boston: Little, Brown, 1965), page 139.

28. John Fowles, "Commentary on *The Man Who Died,*" page 95.

29. Octovio Paz, *The Double Flame: Love and Eroticism,* trans. Helen Lane (San Diego, Calif.: Harcourt Brace, 1995), page 2.

Afterword

E*DITOR'S NOTE:* FROM JULY 10–12, 1996, THE JOHN FOWLES SYMPOSIUM brought fifty-four scholars from eight countries to Lyme Regis, England. Contributors to the present volume were among the participants in this symposium, which John Fowles reflects on below.

Those of you who were interested enough to come to the meeting at Lyme last July can't, poor devils, have avoided seeing me. I had some sympathy with the speaker who said he felt for the poor French infantry storming Wellington's grimly massed British cannon at Waterloo . . . though quite who was trying to face out who, in our battle, I'm not sure. On my side I tried to keep one rule; I would seldom argue the toss . . . seldom, since like all true Englishmen I know laws and rules are made only to be transgressed. They are always implicitly redundant; if they weren't, no Milton, no Shakespeare, no Keats, no Austen, no Brontës; elsewhere, no Newton, no Turner, no Samuel Palmer (it hurt me a little that that last was, I think, never mentioned in July). But I mustn't sink into one of those silly pothers where the subject blames his followers for not having spotted his peculiar secret tastes and quirks. Perhaps some of you (certainly if the some were male) will have noticed a certain rather bright young student from the Sorbonne at our meeting. Since she is French (and I'm one of those peculiar Englishmen who like France), and since she was also rather pretty (I begin to reveal disgraceful defects), and since I've just been in California staying with Dianne Vipond, and not least because I'm only too aware that my contribution to James Aubrey the symposiarch's distillation, his Calvados from the scrumpy of our session, is hideously overdue, I hope you'll forgive me if I appear to address just a one of you: Dominique from Dieppe . . . but only appear. This is intended for all.

Chère Mlle Lagrou, dear Dominique, Bless you for your recent letter, which managed in one charming (not foul at all!) swoop to convince me that I am not wrong to have put my money on two outsiders: "Europe" and "woman." In short, that like all decent socialists I am sure the destiny of this green iceberg lies with the continent from which it recently (a mere few thousand years ago) calved. We must learn to be European again, or dissolve into the dirty water whence we stemmed. Rather similarly but much more importantly we men, our whole gender, must come clean and admit our macho attitude to your sex has been grossly and barbarously wrong for at least three millenia . . . and please, we'd like to be allowed back into the marriage. (There may seem to be "cultural" reasons; but I don't think true humanism, except when brainwashed by "political correctness," ever admits them.) A sensitive and thinking male can't have felt innocent since the time of the Hittites.

As I say, Dominique, I've just been in Los Angeles, staying with Dianne Vipond and meeting your friend Lisa Colletta. I came back via New York, where, while having a first drink in the Algonquin with Katherine Tarbox and Eileen Warburton (who, brave woman, is coming here very soon to embark on my biography), I saw a not totally unknown face, who seemed also to vaguely remember me. This was Billie Whitelaw, Samuel Beckett's friend, muse and his great interpreter on stage. So the next day I am, thanks to her, in the Y, and hearing her marvelous voice and dryness recreate him and his work—no nicer transmigration back across the Atlantic. Still in New York I had met someone from the American stratosphere, who I hope shall soon become my New York agent. The problem for me is this: how can one bear the wretched stiffness and inflexibility of men, how can one not prefer the sinuosity of women? The U.S. is not just the world's leading democracy; I hope it becomes its first gynecocracy. Dianne, Lisa, Katherine, Eileen, Melanie, Circe in Athens, so many others, I pray you shall all one day rule the world.

Dominique, being under the spell of something is not me, is very un-English. I've always rejected the idea. So I now feel a bit like the ancient Circe's most famous victim; foolish, *idiot, niais*, soft in the bad sense. *Et trés jeune*, though sort of proud that what I term my "sense of being" (V. Woolf had another phrase for it) is still alive and keeps sweeping me off my feet. I can't be what convention or "correct behavior" or "the suburbs" or "academia" imagine I ought.

Academia. I like the sound of what you're proposing to do at the Sorbonne and will try to answer your questions when you come tomorrow. I'm not just blockishly against deconstruction, please believe me. I see there is something there; but for me it is both enough (certainly with Barthes and much of Kristeva) and yet not enough. I bought two books in Claremont, Dianne's charming and book-proud Los Angeles "village." Understand Lacan in half an hour, Baudrillard (rated almost as high as Foucault in the U.S.), ditto. Oh dear. If only these gods had a sense of humor. Dianne has one, so does Lisa; and so does Katherine, though you should see her bookshelves . . . not a deconstructionist classic missing. I sat beside her last summer on the banks of her lovely little Maine river, ferruginous and gently idyllic, so lovely. America is more than just the Atlantic away. Kristeva and Sollers, Foucault, Baudrillard and all the rest of them come to America and think they can snap-judge it. But they don't realize how physically *vast* it is; and how that explains its rampant excesses, its being very often so wildly toppling on the brink, and (incidentally) the way we Anglo-Saxons are so unable to communicate with each other humanly and emotionally. The French "expert" on America still to beat (to be bettered) remains de Tocqueville.

I used to blame various defects I saw in myself squarely on Oxford, I now think rather unfairly. Like most such barbed-wire fences erected between the ego and the world, they mainly come from personal temperament; in other words, from something far beyond simple remedies and solutions. I like *not* knowing, not being sure, the feeling that there is always room for change. The easy catholicity of taste and opinion in Oxford, even in 1945, that seeming license to follow one's nose and pursue private interests, made it seem almost a legitimate duty to do so. It was later to seem both oddly un-American, un-Victorian, freedom-obsessed, almost Rabelaisian (*Fais çe que voudras*). The war, and a spell of compulsory duty in the Royal Marines, didn't help me at all. Being able to read what one wanted and when one wanted . . . that was a sudden intoxicating bliss, mainly devoted in my case to discovering the existentialists (Camus much more than Sartre). I was also irremediably "perverted" by the life led in that time—perhaps still—by many of the dons. My own "moral tutor" at New College was Sir Isaiah Berlin. "I'm afraid I know absolutely *nothing* at all about morals." So used he happily—and very misleadingly—to burble (was ever anyone so patently created to define a rare verb?). The most useful thing I learned at New College, and for which it used to have a reputation, was a sort of Socratic skepticism. Some people take this for a twisted pessimism, a constant love of carping. But it isn't; at best it is a sincere belief in the virtues of doubt, and I have never unlearned it.

All this has left me in a familiar predicament for all those who have tasted, or tried to taste, as I suppose I have, too much of life. In one way we are left like Joan of Arc, in an *oubliette*, constantly squeezed between different periods, ages, times, schools, fashions, and thus condemned to live in any actual present only in a very minor way. Chronology, the actual time, *now*, only very rarely seems real and important. Speaking for myself I generally feel hopelessly scattered, disseminated, in absurdly too many places.

I wish happiness to all of those who came to the symposium and thank them for all they individually contributed to it. With my endless doubts about literature (that skepticism again!) and the constant neuroses of writing, I know I must seem difficult and uncertain. I rarely even know where I am myself, nor where I am going; but in that I am in part acting out what I sense my antediluvian existentialism has become, or becomes: a need both to feel and be continually free, always (though this sounds a pleonasm) to be being, both *still* and *in the now*. As I wandered last month around the two absurdly Roman Getty museums in California, through the dazzling Joshua Tree and Anza-Borrego deserts, as I stood beside Dianne, pursuing John Fante both on lovely Point Dume and macabre Terminal Island, or gawping at the superbly displayed archosaurs and pterodactyls (symposiast Kevin Padian's "field" at Berkeley) in the Manhattan Natural History Museum, I may seem to have hardly been there at all. But I was, I was just happily *being*; as indeed I was through the symposium. For years I have passed on a Zulu wish, *Go well*. Go well, and forgive me!

JOHN FOWLES

5 February 1997

List of Contributors

JAMES R. AUBREY is professor of English at Metropolitan State College of Denver, where he teaches British literature courses on such topics as the English novel, satire, and Jane Austen. In addition to publications on Shakespeare and Pope, among others, he is the author of *John Fowles: A Reference Companion* (1991) and of articles about Fowles in the *Journal of Evolutionary Psychology* and *Nineteenth-Century Prose*.

CAROL M. BARNUM is the author of *The Fiction of John Fowles: A Myth for Our Time* (1988), as well as articles on Fowles in *The Literary Review* and in *Texas Studies in Literature and Language,* and a personal interview, which appeared in a Fowles special number of *Modern Fiction Studies* (1985). She has also published articles about John Gardner and Joseph Campbell. Barnum received her Ph.D. from Georgia State University. She is a professor in the Humanities and Technical Communication Department at Southern Polytechnic State University in Marietta (Atlanta), Georgia.

LIZ-ANNE BAWDEN taught film studies at the Slade School of Fine Art, University College, London, from 1965 to 1985. Her principal publication is the *Oxford Companion to Film* (1976). She was national president of the Association of University Teachers from 1980 to 1981. She took early retirement to live in Lyme Regis, Dorset, where since 1988 she has been honorary curator of the Lyme Regis Philpot Museum.

PATRICIA V. BEATTY, professor of English at the University of West Alabama, teaches twentieth-century British literature, twentieth-century British and American poetry, the English novel, and women's twentieth-century fiction. She has published articles on John Fowles and Harry Crews in *Ariel, South Atlantic Quarterly,* and *Critique,* and she has read conference papers on Fowles, Crews, Joan Didion, and Thomas Pynchon. Works in progress include a book-length study of Fowles, focusing on the pastoral and the Edenic archetype.

LIST OF CONTRIBUTORS

CLARK CLOSSER is an associate professor of English at Southwest Missouri State University. A collection of his poetry, *His Times*, was published in 1997.

LISA COLLETTA is a doctoral candidate at the Claremont Graduate School, where she is completing a dissertation on comedy and social satire in the twentieth-century British novel. Her other research interests include the travel narrative and postcolonial writers. She is associate editor of *Women's Studies: An Interdisciplinary Journal* and has recently guest-edited a special issue of the journal, dedicated to women and travel.

H. W. FAWKNER is professor of English Literature (chair) at Stockholm University. His publications include *The Timescapes of John Fowles*, *The Ecstatic World of John Cowper Powys*, *Deconstructing "Macbeth," Shakespeare's Hyperontology*, and *Shakespeare's Miracle Plays*. He is currently researching interfaces of transcendental phenomenology and Buddhism.

KIRKE KEFALEA was born in Athens, Greece. She received her Ph.D. in comparative literature from the University of Saarbrücken, Germany (1994). Her book *The Land of the Greeks: The Perception of Greece in the Contemporary European Novel* was published by Königshausen & Neumann (1995). She has edited and translated into Greek a volume of short texts by John Fowles entitled *The Greek Experience*, published by Olcos (1996). Kefalea held the position of researcher in literary matters at the Institute of Mediterranean Studies in Greece from 1994 to 1996. Since October of 1996 she has been a lecturer in comparative literature at Athens Polytechnic and lecturer in German at the Air Force Academy of Greece.

BARRY N. OLSHEN is professor of English and humanities at York University, Toronto. His work on John Fowles includes *John Fowles* (1978) and the co-authored *John Fowles: A Reference Guide* (1980). His other main research and teaching interests are represented by the co-authored *Approaches to Teaching the Hebrew Bible* (1989) and the co-edited *Terms of Identity: Essays on the Theoretical Terminology of Lifewriting* (a special issue of *a / b: Auto / Biography Studies*, spring 1995).

KEVIN PADIAN is a professor in the Department of Integrative Biology and curator in the Museum of Paleontology, University of California, Berkeley. His research interests lie in large-scale patterns of evolutionary change, with a focus on the origin of major adaptations and major groups of animals. Most of his work is on dinosaurs, pterosaurs, and other fossil reptiles. His side interests include the history of evolutionary thought, particularly in Victorian paleontology and evolution.

SUZANNE ROSS is an associate professor of English at St. Cloud State University in Minnesota. Her research and teaching broadly concern our understandings and representations of the natural world. She teaches courses at the undergraduate and graduate levels on nature literature, women and nature, nonfiction nature writing, and wolves. She has presented her work at a number of conferences, and it has appeared in *ISLE (Interdisciplinary Studies in Literature and Environment)*. She serves on the executive council of the Association for the Study of Literature and Environment. An avid birder and walker, she recently walked the 110-mile Cleveland Way around the North York Moors National Park in England.

KATHERINE TARBOX teaches twentieth-century British literature at the University of New Hampshire. She is the author of *The Art of John Fowles* (1988) and numerous articles in her field. She is currently working on a new book, *Love Stories at the Millennium: British Postmodern Fiction*, which views contemporary British writers through the lens of cognitive anthropology. She lives in Maine with her husband and four children.

HUGH S. TORRENS is a geologist by training but a historian by inclination who has taught for thirty years at the University of Keele, in England. Keele was set up as the first "new" university in Britain, with the aim of being proudly interdisciplinary in both its research and its teaching. However, Research Assessment Exercises now imposed on British universities have killed off the whole idea, to his great regret, because all faculty members must now be assessed under only one "Unit of Assessment." Such academic attempts to cross the Two Cultures ocean, following the lead of John Fowles, are now forbidden.

LYNNE S. VIETH received her doctorate in comparative literature from the University of California, Berkeley (1992), and has been teaching at Stanford University since then, in the Program in Literature and the Arts. Her most recent article, "Photomechanical Tendencies in Giorgio De Chirico's Melancholy Vision," appeared in *The European Legacy* (January 1997). Having explored intersections between painting, photography, and graphics in John Fowles's nonfiction, she prepared a presentation on Alfred Hitchcock's *Vertigo* and Walter

Benjamin's film theory for the First International Walter Benjamin Congress, which was held at the University of Amsterdam in 1997.

DIANNE L. VIPOND is professor of English at California State University, Long Beach. She is guest editor with James A. Baker of the John Fowles special number of *Twentieth Century Literature,* in which her interview with Fowles, "An Unholy Inquisition," appears. She is co-editor of *Literacy: Language and Power* and has published articles on English education and on the work of Woody Allen, Margaret Atwood, Lawrence Durrell, and Flannery O'Connor. She is currently compiling an anthology of interviews with John Fowles.

EILEEN WARBURTON, of Newport, Rhode Island, is an independent scholar and freelance writer. She is at work on the first book-length biography of John Fowles.

Index

About the Woodcuts, 83–84
Acanthostega, 168n 16
Adam, 23, 71, 76, 169, 174
Adonis, 172, 243
Adorno, Theodor, 46
Aegean Sea, 232, 235
Aeolus, 55
Africa, 227. See also Egypt
Aietes, 233
Alain-Fournier, 22
Alcina, 233
Alcoff, Linda, 194n 7
Alcorn, John, 213
Alethia, 249–50
Alhambra, 37
Allie. See Alethia
All Saints Church, 103
Allsop, Kenneth, 19
Alpers, Svetlana, 86n 18
American Indians, 225. See also Anasazi, Hopi Indians, Pueblo Indians
Amleth, 98
Anargyrios School, 21
Anasazi, 27
Anderson, William, 96
Anglo-Saxon, 256
Anima-Animus, 174, 246, 249, 251
Anza-Borrego, 257
Apollo, 63, 243
Apollo, 239, 242–45, 247
Aphrodite, 250
Arcadia, 100, 169–70, 173, 176
Arcas, 100
archetype, 88–90, 93, 96–97, 101, 108, 172, 250. See also Anima-Animus, Magician-Trickster, Mandala, Mother, Wild Man
Arden, 29
Arethusa, 120
Ariadne, 55, 124
Ariosto, 233
Aristotle, 200

Armada, 52
Armorel of Lyonesse, 48
Arnold, Matthew, 24, 62, 68
Art of Describing, The, 86n 18
Arta, 120, 129
Asquith, Cynthia, 240
Astarte, 250
Aswan, 27, 37, 227
Atget, Eugène, 70
Athens, 21, 231, 255
Atlantic Ocean, 57, 256
At Llanvillo, 239
Attis, 243
Aubrey, James R., 67, 179, 193n 2, 237n 6, 254
Aubrey, John, 51
Austen, Jane, 48, 205, 254
Avalon, 71
Avon, 19
Axminster, 144
Axmouth, 152n 9

Bachelard, Gaston, 235
Bakhtin, Mikhail, 194n 9
Bandelier National Monument, 36, 220
Baring-Gould, Sabine, 48, 152n 9
Barns, Norman, 38, 146, 152n 6
Barnstaple, 30
Barnum, Carol, 38, 64–65
Barthes, Roland, 51, 65, 67–68, 80, 255
Bartók, Bela, 135n 4
Basford, Kathleen, 101
Baudelaire, Charles, 77
Baudrillard, Jean, 255–56
Bawden, Liz-Anne, 39
Beatty, Patricia, 39
Beauties of Lyme Regis, The, 141
Beauvoir, Simone de, 182
Beckett, Samuel, 255
Beer, Gillian, 158
Bel, 63–64
Belle Epoque, 48

Belmont House, 16, 18–20, 34, 42 n 19
Bembo, Pietro, 82
Benjamin, Walter, 70, 72–73, 78
Berkeley, 257
Berlin, Sir Isaiah, 256
Besant, Walter, 48
Bewick, 82
Bible, 84, 176
Bindon Cliffs, 28, 145
Birds, Beasts and Men, 15
Bittaford, 22
Bluebeard's Castle, 135 n 4
blue lias, 146–47
Bombadil, Tom, 98
bonne vaux, 29, 52, 90, 108, 127
Book of Ebenezer Le Page, 27
Borough, The, 111 n 6
Botticelli, Sandro, 24–25
Bourani, 90–91, 233
Bow, 101
Branston, Brian, 238
Breasley, Henry, 69, 109–10
Brewster, Earl, 224
Bristol Channel, 16, 19
British, 223–24
British Isles, 27, 159. *See also* England, Scotland
British Museum, 206
Brittany, 18, 109
Brontë sisters, 254
Brooks, Peter, 44
Brown, Rowland W., 141, 153 n 13
Brownian motion, 167
Buckland, William, 144, 152 n 3
Buckland, Mrs. William, 152 n 3
Buddhism, 78, 80, 82, 83
Burderop Park, 21
Burgess Shale, 165–66
Byrd, Deborah, 193 n 2

Caliban, 233
California, 257. *See also* Berkeley, Claremont, Los Angeles, Stanford University
Calvados, 254
Calypso, 55
Camus, Albert, 256
Carslake's Barn, 115–16
Carson, Rachel, 15
Catherine, 37, 60, 62–68, 127
Catholicism, 214–15, 218
Catullus, 119

Celts, 70–71, 89, 101, 109–10, 157
Ceres, 17, 20, 236
Charmouth, 147, 149
Charybdis, 233
Chasm, the, 144
Chelsea, 179
Cheng-ming, 79
Cherwell River, 125
Chesil Bank, the, 14–15
Cheyne Walk, 179
Chimney Rock, 143
China, 78, 83
Chordata, 165
Christianity, 96, 98, 109, 164, 169, 216, 249
Circe, 55, 230, 232–34, 236
cities, 16, 18, 23, 40. *See also* Athens, London, Los Angeles, New York City
Clare, Angel, 164
Clegg, Frederick, 17–18, 87, 91, 118, 128
Clegg, Stewart, 47
Closser, Clark, 37
Coastline, 16
Cobb, the, 16–18, 34, 139, 157, 162, 164, 181, 184
Coëtminais, 108, 110–11
Colletta, Lisa, 40, 255
Compton, 214
Conchis, Maurice, 21, 92, 108, 119, 204, 207, 210, 233–34, 236, 246, 250
Confucianism, 83
Continent, the, 98
Conybeare, W. D., 141, 146
Cooper, Pamela, 64
Cooper, Susan, 998
Cornwall, 33, 50. *See also* Land's End
Courbet, Gustave, 60
Crabbe, George
Cretaceous, 149
Crete, 27, 219, 232, 236
Crowcombe, 102
Crusoe, 239, 244–47, 251
Crusoe, Robinson, 26, 245–46
Cumberland, George, 139
Cumberland Terrace, 92
Curve of Return, The, 228 n 4
Cybele, 243
Cyclops, 55

Dairy, the, 141–42, 149. *See also* Underhill Farm
Dartmoor, 21–22, 26, 32, 81, 219
Darwin, Charles, 13, 24, 39, 88, 90, 154–56, 158–62, 164, 166–67, 168n 18, 170–71, 173, 176, 188
Dawson, William, 141, 144–46
Defoe, Daniel, 26, 247
Deleuze, Gilles, 48
Demeter, 17, 19–20, 120, 236
Democracy, 222
Descartes, René, 200
De Seitas, Julie, 235
De Seitas, Lily, 236
De Seitas, Rose, 235
Desteian, John, 249
Devon, 15, 16, 18, 22, 30, 32, 35, 38, 75, 101, 112n 14, 126, 128, 138, 140, 142, 144. *See also* Barnstaple, Bittaford, Dartmoor, Dornafield Farm, Exeter, Ipplepen, Newton Abbot, Undercliff
Diana, 100
Dickens, Charles, 156
Dickinson, Emily, 252
Dieppe, 254
Distracted Preacher, The, 153n 9
Dollin's Cave, 26
Donkey's Green, 141
Donne, John, 26, 62
Dopp, Jamie, 75–76
Doric, 231
Dornafield Farm, 30, 35, 128
Dorchester, 138
Dorset, 16–17, 101, 137–39, 147, 153n 9, 161. *See also* Charmouth, Dorchester, Lyme Regis, Portland
Double Flame, The, 251
Douglas, Norman, 214
Dowlands, 143
Draper, Jo, 138
Drexler, Lynne, 57
Druids, 100
Durbeyfield, John, 162
Durbeyfield, Tess, 162, 164
Durrell, Lawrence, 238

Earth, 133, 154–55, 249
Eau et les Rêves, L', 235
Ecclesiastes, 60, 67
Ecco Press, 75, 82
ecocriticism, 13, 15
ecology, 15, 96, 101
Eddins, Dwight, 175
Eden, 16, 23, 29, 67, 93, 115–16, 123, 127–28, 140, 169–70, 172–76, 178–79, 185, 192
Edwardian, 231
Egdon Heath, 137–38, 163–64
Egypt, 37, 40, 130, 216, 222, 224–25. *See also* Aswan, Kitchener's Island, Nile River
Eleusinian mysteries, 17, 19–20, 120, 135n 7, 236, 237n 6
Eliot, T. S., 91, 235, 239, 245–46
Ely Cathedral, 100
Emblems, 44
Emma, 63–64, 67
Empty Church, The, 215
End of the World, The, 130–31
England, 17, 23, 26, 39–40, 70, 93, 97–98, 101, 104, 108–9, 111, 112n 6, 127, 133, 140, 143, 148, 155, 159, 174, 185, 212, 223, 225, 232–34, 243, 254–55. *See also* Cornwall, Devon, Dorset, Isle of Wight, London, Norfolk, Oxford, Scilly Isles, Somerset, Steep Holm, Sussex, West Country, Wiltshire
English Channel, 18, 142, 147
English language, 250
English oak, 80–81
Epiphany Among the Ruins, 228n 8
Equilibrist, The, 241
Eranos, 237
Erato, 100
Etruscan Places. *See Sketches of Etruscan Places*
Etruscans, 84, 215–20, 222–26, 228n 11
Euclid, 198
Europe, 70, 78, 98, 197, 220, 254–55
Eurydice, 91, 120
Euston Road, 99
Eve, 23, 71, 91, 169, 172–75
Evolution and Emancipation of Sarah Woodruff, The, 193n 2
Exe River, 144
Exeter, 134n 2, 176, 184
Exeter Cathedral, 101
exile, 32

existentialism, 195, 257
Exmoor, 26, 30–31, 90, 108

Fairly, Mrs., 201
Fall of Man, 169, 173–75, 178
Fantasia and the Unconscious, 222
Fante, John, 257
Farrow, Sam, 158, 163, 175, 201
Fawkner, H. W., 40
Femininity Lost and Regained, 248
Finnmark, 15
Flax, Jane, 47
Florence, 84
Forest of Paimpont, 108
Foster, Thomas C., 64, 189, 19n 2
Foucault, Michel, 255–56
Foulke, Robert, 87
Fowles, Elizabeth, 16, 142, 249–50
Fowles, John, Works: *The Aristos*, 148, 172–73, 177–78, 180n 16, 198, 238–39, 248, 252; *Behind "The Magus,"* 17, 235, 239, 244; *The Blinded Eye*, 15; *The Chesil Bank*, 14; *Cinderella*, 134n 2; *The Cloud*, 37, 61–64, 67, 69, 127; *The Collector*, 17–18, 26–27, 35, 87, 91, 118, 128, 135n 4; *Daniel Martin*, 17, 21–22, 27, 30, 35, 36–37, 39–40, 52, 60–62, 71, 90, 92–93, 96, 101, 104, 108, 112n 14, 121, 124–26, 128–29, 131, 133, 136n 16, 180n 16, 212–15, 217–18, 220, 221–22, 226, 247; *The Ebony Tower*, 18, 24, 26, 37, 60, 69–71, 89, 104, 108–10, 118, 224, 228n 8; *Eliduc*, 89; *The Enigma*, 26, 29, 64; *The Enigma of Stonehenge*, 18, 31; *The French Lieutenant's Woman*, 16–17, 23–26, 30, 38–40, 43n 36, 60–62, 64, 67, 87, 90, 92–93, 106, 108–9, 114–15, 122, 137, 139–40, 142–43, 146–48, 150–52, 154–66, 169–72, 179, 182, 185, 192, 195–206; *A Greek Legend*, 120; *Hardy and the Hag*, 123–24, 129, 132; *Islanders*, 26; *Islands*, 26, 37, 44–52, 56–57, 62, 70–73, 80, 82, 86n 14, 88, 239, 245–46; *Land*, 73–75, 82, 88; *A Maggot*, 18, 26, 30, 31, 91, 95, 108, 113n 21, 248; foreword to *The Magus*, 242; *The Magus*, 250; *The Magus: A Revised Version*, 21, 26, 40–41n 9, 43n 37, 64, 67, 89–93, 108, 118–19, 121, 151, 195, 197, 202, 204, 207, 230–34, 237, 243–46, 249, 252; *Mantissa*, 93, 100, 121, 243; introduction to *The Man Who Died*, 212, 240; *The Nature of Nature*, 16, 47, 49, 52, 56, 69, 78, 81–82, 87, 90, 132–33, 239–42; *On Being English but Not British*, 101, 104, 108; *Ourika*, 134n 2; *Personal Note*, 89; *Poems*, 26, 238–40; *Shipwreck*, 26, 69–70, 73, 76; *A Short History of Lyme Regis*, 171–72; *Swan Song of the European Wild*, 15; *The Tree*, 14, 15, 26, 32, 38, 69, 71, 75–78, 80–83, 85, 88–89, 94, 104–8, 110, 169, 171–73, 182, 188, 191–92, 194n 9, 213, 239–40, 244; *Weeds, Bugs, Americans*, 15; *The Woman in the Reeds*, 136n 16
France, 18, 60, 111, 133, 156, 202, 254, 256. *See also* Dieppe, Poitiers
Frazer, James, 98, 100
Freeman, Ernest, 158, 163, 176
Freeman, Ernestina, 114–15, 146, 149, 156–58, 160, 162–66, 184, 187, 189–90, 194n 7, 202
Freud, Sigmund, 24, 90, 104, 106, 126, 132, 156, 170, 251
Freya, 250
Friday, 246
Frye, Northrop, 173

Gaard, Greta, 182, 193n 6
Galapagos Islands, 26
Galilei, Galileo, 200
Galium odoratum, 181
Gama, da, Vasco, 198
Gardner, John, 13
Garland, the, 98
Genesis, 175–76, 178
genius loci. See spirit of place
Germany, 217–18
Getty, John Paul, 257
Gibson family, 70
Glasinnis, 71
Glotfelty, Cheryll, 13
Goat Island, 28, 144–45, 149, 152n 6
Godgame, The, 243
Godwin, Fay, 38, 53, 70–76, 78, 80, 82, 245
Goldberry, 98

Golden Bough, The, 98
Golden Cap, 147
Golding, William, 48
Golem, 98
Gothic, 100, 162
Gotland, 44
Gould, Stephen Jay, 159, 165
Graeco-Roman, 223
Grand Meulnes, Le, 22
Graves, Robert, 112n 6, 157, 248
Great Bindon, 144
Great Chain of Being, 156
Great Mother, 174
Great Whole, 251. *See also* Mandala
Greece, 17, 21, 40, 70, 90–91, 100–101, 119, 135n 6, 222, 223, 230–37, 243–44 , 251. *See also* Athens, Peloponnesus, Spetses
Greek, 71
Green George, 98
Green Knight, 98, 100
Green Man, 39, 88, 96–110, 111–12n 6, 113n 21, 191
Green Man, The, 98
Green Mansions, 98
Green, Miles, 43n 30, 100
green movement, 13, 15, 97
Greenpeace, 16
Green Woman, 191
Greenwitch, 98
Greenwood, 98, 104, 108
Grey, Miranda, 17, 26–27, 91
Grim Reaper, 73
Grimsditch, H. B., 163
Grogan, Dr., 16, 115–16, 171, 176, 184, 187, 189
Guattari, Félix, 48
Gugh, 72

Hades, 236
Hamlet, 98
Hampstead, 17
Hampstead Heath, 27, 29, 35
Hanged Man, 113n 21
Hardy, Thomas, 39, 123, 137, 152n 9, 155–66, 202
Harvest, The, 60, 126, 131
Heidegger, Martin, 195, 203–4
Henderson, Joseph, 178
Henry, Michael, 203, 205
Hermes, 55

Hesperides, 71
Highgate Cemetery, 134n 2
Hindermann, Friedrich, 232
Hitler, Adolf, 160
Hittites, 255
Hollywood, 108
Holmes, Frederick, 64
Holy Ghost Church, 102
Holy Mother Wisdom, 94
Homer, 230, 232
Hopi Indians, 220–21
Hopkins, Gerard Manley, 96, 251
hortus conclusus, 169–70
Horvat, Frank, 75–78, 80, 82, 84
Hotel Philadelphia, 231
Hotel Poseidon, 231
Hudson, W. H., 98
Huffaker, Robert, 14, 176
Humbert, Humbert, 48
Humphries, Nicholas, 239
Husserl, Edmund, 195–96, 205

I Come, 243
Ice Age, 72
Ichthyostega, 168n 16
Iliad, The, 84
In the Middleyard, 239
Inversnaid, 96
Ipplepen, 30, 112n 14, 128
Isis, 224–25
Islands of the Blest, 71
Isle of Wight, 27
Isolation: To Marguerite, 24, 62
Italy, 40, 215, 217–18, 224, 227. *See also* Etruscans, Florence, Rome, Tarquinia

Jack-in-the-Green, 97–98, 100
James, Henry, 13
James, William, 22
Jameson, Frederic, 47, 49
Janik, Del Ivan, 219, 222, 228n 4
Japan, 80
Je fable, 239, 249, 251
Jefferies, Richard, 21, 77
Jeffrey, Ian, 73
Jemez Mountains, 220
Joan of Arc, 256
John, 240
John Fowles: Existence As Authorship, 175
Johnson, Aaron, 69, 81, 83, 85

Johnson, Robert, 248
Jones, 172, 175, 180 n 13
Joshua Tree, 257
Joyce, James, 61
June Eternal, 94
Jung, Carl G., 38–39, 88–90, 94, 106, 132, 171–72, 174, 178, 180 n 7, 237 n 6, 246, 249
Jurassic, 146, 149
Jurassic Park, 14

Kaplan, Stephen, 22
Keats, John, 254
Kefalea, Circe. *See* Kefalea, Kirke
Kefalea, Kirke, 40, 135 n 6, 255
Kelly, Alison, 91–92, 119–20
Kenwood House, 27, 35
Keraunos, 56
Kilvert, Francis, 48
Kind of Philhellene, A, 241
King of the Wood, 98, 100
Kirkenes, 207
Kirnberger, Otto, 225
Kitchener, Horatio Herbert, 37
Kitchener's Island, 27, 37, 90, 93, 108, 214, 227
Klein, Melanie, 106
Knight, Henry, 165
Kore, 120
Kowalewski, Michael, 214
Krauss, Rosalind E., 72
Kristeva, Julia, 68, 255–56

Lacan, Jacques, 106
Lady Chapel, 100
Laestrygonians, 55
La Fontaine, Jean, 202
Lagrou, Dominique, 254–55
Lalage, 164–66, 191
Land of the Blest, 71
Land's End, 71
landslip, the, 28, 143–45
Lapp, 43 n 37
Large white cloud near Bilsington, Kent, 73–74
Latin, 71
Lawrence, D. H., 16, 40, 56, 212–27, 228 nn 4 and 8, 240, 250
Lawrence, Frieda, 221, 224
Leaf Man, 98, 101
Lee, Rebecca, 94–95, 248
Legg, Rodney, 42 n 21

Lesbia, 119
Levinas, Emmanuel, 195
Lewes, 26–27
Lincoln Green, 98
Linnaeus, Carolus, 169, 173, 204
Lister, Joseph, 185
Lister House, 185
Little Bindon, 144
Little Gidding, 91, 245
locus amoenus, 29, 172. *See also* sacred place
Loftus, Elizabeth
Lolita, 48
London, 15–18, 24, 26, 29, 35, 92, 97–99, 135 n 4, 163, 166, 177, 179, 235. *See also* Chelsea, Cheyne Walk, Cumberland Terrace, Euston Road, Regent's Park, Hampstead, Hampstead Heath)
Lord of the Flies, 48
Lord of the Rings, The, 98
Lorenz, Paul, 214, 228 nn 8 and 11
Los Alamos, 133
Los Angeles, 221, 255
Lost Gods of England, The, 238
Lotus Eaters, 55
Loveday, Simon, 64
Lyell, 160, 176
Lyme Bay, 147
Lyme Regis, 12, 16–18, 23, 27, 34, 48, 73, 86, 101, 116–17, 133, 137, 139, 144–45, 147, 149, 171–72, 181, 185, 205, 254. *See also* Belmont House, Lister House
Lyonesse, 71

Mac Caig, Norman, 241
MacFadyen, W. A., 145
MacPhee, 155
Magician-Trickster, 178
Maine, 44, 57, 256. *See also* Monhegan Island
Mallory, Anthony, 124, 126, 130, 213–15, 218, 220
Mallory, Jane, 121, 124–27, 130–31, 213–16, 222, 224, 226
Man Who Died, The, 56, 212
Mancuso, James, 46, 48
Mandala, 90. *See also* Great Whole
Manhattan Natural History Museum, 257
Mansfield, Katherine, 61

268 INDEX

Mantell, 165
Markovian, 155, 167 n 5
Martin, Daniel, 30, 37, 40, 93, 108, 124–29, 131, 212–22, 225–27, 228 n 11, 241
Marx, Karl, 24, 156, 170, 226
Mary, 158, 163, 175
May Day, 98, 111
May King, the, 98
McNeil, Jenny, 220–22
McSweeney, Kerry, 64
Mediterranean Sea, 119, 133, 231–32, 244
Mehalah, 48
Melanie, 255
Merleau-Ponty, Maurice, 195, 203, 208
Mesozoic Era, 162
Mexico, 221, 224
Meyers, Jeffrey, 213
Michael, Magali Cornier, 193 n 2
Micraster, 150, 152, 153 n 12
Middle Ages, 197
Mighty Landslip of Dowlands and Bindon, The, 143
Millie, 175
Milton, John, 171, 174, 254
Minoa, 219–20
Mnemosyne, 250
Modern Etiquette, 48
Monhegan Island, 44–45, 57
Monmouth Beach, 147
Monmouth, Duke of, 147
Monsieur Nicolas, 29
Montgomery, Lily, 119, 121, 235
Montgomery, Rose, 235
Monumenta Britannica, 51
Mornings in Mexico, 213–14, 219–22, 225
Mother archetype, 172. *See also* Great Mother, Mother Earth, Mother Nature, White Goddess
Mother Earth, 249–50
Mother Nature, 75–76, 249
Mount Sion, 172
Mumbry, Dennis, 54
Murphy, Patrick, 194 n 9
Muses, 250
Muslim, 226
mystery, 21, 26, 87, 90, 94, 109

narrative, 23, 37, 47, 48
Nathan, Abe, 220–21
National Trust, 141
Nausicaa, 232
Nazi, 46
Nemi, Temple at, 100
Nerthus, 250
Neumann, Erich, 174
New College, 256
New Mexico, 27, 35, 40, 133, 212, 214, 218–20, 222. *See also* Bandelier National Monument, Los Alamos, Santa Fe, Taos, Tsankawi
Newquist, Roy, 135 n 4
New Statesman, 15
New World, 52
New York, 255. *See also* Manhattan
Newton Abbot, 35, 128
Newton, Sir Isaac, 254
Nietzsche, Friedrich, 48
Nile River, 27, 37, 130, 214, 222, 224, 227
Norfolk, 114
Norman Conquest, 46
Norway, 15, 26, 207. *See also* Finnmark, Kirkenes, Oslo, Seidevarre
Nygaard, Gustav, 209
Nygaard, Henrik, 41 n 9, 207–11
Nymet, 101
Nymph, 101
Nympton, 101

Oak January Derbyshire, England, 80
Oak-queen, 100
Odysseus, 44, 46, 51, 52, 55, 232–33, 236
Odyssey, The, 46–47, 54–55, 70, 86 n 14, 230, 233, 237 n 3, 245
Oedipus, 75, 106, 126, 132, 236
Okebourne Chase, 21
Old English, 238
Old Man of Gugh, The, 72
Olshen, Barry, 39, 60, 64, 67, 75–76
Omphalos, 236
On Being English but Not British, 224
Ong, Walter, 49
Ophelia, 65
Orient, 131
Origin and History of Consciousness, The, 174
Origin of Species, The, 88, 158–60, 162, 164, 167 n 11, 176
Orpheus, 120, 236

Ortner, Sherry, 193n 5
Osiris, 172, 224–25, 227
Oslo, 15
Ourika, 246
Ouse River, 27
Oxford, 27, 62, 124–25, 127, 133, 136n 16, 214, 256. *See also* New College
Oxford English Dictionary, 153n 13
Oxford University, 125

Padian, Kevin, 39, 257
Pair of Blue Eyes, A, 165
Paleozoic Era, 164
Palmer, Samuel, 254
Palmyra, 27, 93, 108, 130–31, 133, 226
Paradise Lost, 171
Park, Sue, 221, 228n 8
Parnassus, 49
Paston, George (G. P.), 35
Pasvik River, 43n 37, 207
Paul, 65
Paz, Octavio, 251
Peloponnesus, 231
Penelope, 55
Pennsylvanian Period, 161
Permian Period, 162
Persephone, 225, 236
Peter, 63–68
Phaestos, 27
phenomenology, 40, 195–96, 206–7
Phillida, 127
Photographic Conditions of Surrealism, The, 72, 74
Phraxos, 26, 90–91, 231–34, 244
Pikaia, 165–66
Pinhay Bay, 137, 139–40, 146, 186
Pinhay Cliffs, 141, 180n 13
Pisanello, Antonio, 116–17, 178
Plato, 84, 196, 203, 214
Playing and Reality, 106
Pleistocene Era, 161
Point Dume, 257
Poitiers, 18
Poland, 160
Pole, Sir W., 145
Portland, 162
Portland Bill, 206
Poulteney, Mrs., 23, 146, 174–75, 182, 185, 189, 191, 201, 206
Pound, Ezra, 248
Preludes, 246

Pre-Raphaelite Brotherhood, 134n 2, 179
Pre-Raphaelite "pack of satyrs" in John Fowles's "The French Lieutenant's Woman," The, 179, 193n 2
Primavera, La, 24–25
Principles of Geology, 160
Protect the Word, 241–42
Pueblo Indians, 219
Pulman's Weekly News, 144
Punch, 48
Puritanism, 172, 183

Quarles, Francis, 44, 82
Queen of the May, 98

Rabelais, François, 256
Racine, Jean, 202
Raglan, Lady, 100–101, 111n 6
Randall, Nell, 126, 214–15
Raup, David, 165
Reason, 88
Reed, Nancy, 30, 127–29
Reid, Neil, 142
Regency, 185
Regent's Park, 91–92
Renaissance, 24–25, 78, 86n 18, 100, 115, 172, 196–97, 199–202, 204–5
Rendell, Stan and Joan, 42n 21
Report from Starship 26, 239, 247–49
Restif de la Bretonne, 29, 90
Return of the Native, The, 137–38
Revenge of Hamlet, 98
Riddle, The, 156
Rima, 98
River Between, The, 225
Roberts, George, 143
Robertson, Carolyn and James, 69, 81
Robin Hood, 98, 104, 107–9, 111–12n 6
Rogers, Randolph, 20
Romanesque, 100
Romans, the, 100, 164
Romantic, 204
Romanticism, 47–48
Rome, 131, 215–16, 222–23, 257
Ronsard, 25
Rose, Gilbert, 122–24, 132, 135n 14
Ross, Suzanne, 39
Rossetti, Dante Gabriel, 134n 2, 179
Rossetti, Elizabeth Siddal, 134n 2
Round About a Great Estate, 21

270 INDEX

Rowe, A. W., 145, 153n 12
Royalists, 175
Royal Marines, 256
Ruether, Rosemary, 193n 6
Russia, 15, 207

sacred combe, 27, 29, 93, 109
Sacred Combe, The, 129
sacred place, 21, 32, 105, 108, 172, 215, 220. See also *bonne vaux, locus amoenus*, sacred combe
Saint Agnes Island, 49–50. See also Troytown
Saint Hubert, 116–17, 178
Salisbury Plain, 18, 26, 163
Sally, 63–64
Santa Fe, 218–20
Sartre, Jean-Paul, 195, 256
Satan, 31, 201
Saxo Grammaticus, 98
Saxon, 153n 11
Scheria, 232
Scholar Gypsy, The, 62
science, 14, 16, 23, 47, 87, 96, 105, 154, 158, 170, 225
Scilly Isles, 33, 44, 51–52, 54, 60, 62, 70–71, 80, 245. See also Gugh, Saint Agnes
Scotland, 111n 6
Scylla, 54, 233
Sea and Sardinia, 213, 216, 218, 226–27
Second Sex, The, 182
Seidevarre, 26, 41n 9, 43n 37, 108, 207, 209
Self, 88
Seven Thuja [Juniper] Trees, The, 78, 79
Shakers, 94, 248
Shakespeare, 26, 49, 55–57, 98, 254
Shangri-La, 29
Sherborn, C. D., 145
Sheriff of Nottingham, 104, 106
Sideros, 56
Sidmouth, 144
Silent Spring, 15
Siren, 52, 233
Sir Gawain and the Green Knight, 98
Sketches of Etruscan Places, 213, 215–18, 223, 225
Small History of Photography, A, 72

Smithson, Charles, 16, 24–25, 30, 39, 43n 31, 62, 87, 91, 114–19, 133, 134n 2, 137, 140, 146–48, 150–52, 154–58, 162–66, 169–92, 194n 7, 198
Snow, C. P., 240
Socrates, 214, 241, 256
Sollers, Philippe, 44–45, 49, 54, 256
Sollisch, James, 64
Somerset, 31, 51, 102. See also Crowcombe, Exmoor, Taunton
Southwest, the, 222
Spain, 46, 218
Spencer, Herbert, 160
Spetsai See Spetses
Spetses, 21, 26, 231–32, 234, 243–44. See also Anargyrios School, Hotel Philadelphia, Villa Yasemia
spirit of place, 20, 23, 219
Stanford University, 69
Steep Holm, 16, 19
Steep Holm: A Case History in the Study of Evolution, 42n 21
Steep Holm: The Story of a Small Island, 42n 21
Stevens, Wallace, 180
Stonehenge, 18, 26, 31, 49, 51, 91, 94
Stubborn Structure, The, 173
Sunday Times, 16
Sussex, 27, 128. See also Lewis
Sutton Benger, 103
Switzerland, 89, 237n 6
Symbols of Transformation, 172, 180n 7
Symposium, John Fowles, 12, 86n 14, 113n 21, 134n 2, 135n 6, 185, 254
Syria, 40, 131, 226. See also Palmyra

Talbot, 147
Taoism, 83
Taos, 218–19
Tao te ching, 84
Tarbox, Katherine, 36, 76, 255
Tarquinia, 27, 90, 93, 108, 214–18, 220
Taunton, 31
technology, 47. See also science
Telemachus, 230, 232, 237n 3
Temperamental Journeys, 214
Tempest, The, 26, 44, 49, 56, 245
Terminal Island, 257
Tess of the d'Urbervilles, 161–62, 164
Theseus, 236

Thomas Hardy after Fifty Years, 123
Thomas Hardy's England, 138
Thoreau, Henry David, 13, 15–17, 151
Thorncombe, 27, 93, 108, 127, 129, 219
Time and Ruins in John Fowles's "Daniel Martin," 228n 8
Times Literary Supplement, 213
Timing Her, 165
Tocqueville, Alexis de, 256
Tolstoi, Leo, 13
Tomb of the Inscriptions, 225
Tomb of the Leopards, 217
Tomb of the Painted Vases, 216–17, 225
Torrens, Hugh, 39
Tower Rock, 19
Tradition of Eighteen Hundred and Four, A, 153n 9
Tranter, Aunt, 149
Treece, Henry, 98
Triassic Period, 162
Trichoptera, 132
Trickster. *See* Magician-Trickster
Tringham, Parson, 162
Troytown, 49–50
Two Mile Oak, 35, 128
Tsankawi, 27, 36, 90, 93, 108, 214, 218–22
Tudor House, 179
Turner, J. M. W., 254
Tutankhamen, 208
Twentieth Century Literature, 94–95, 239, 249
Twilight in Italy, 213–14
Two Cultures, The, 240

Ulysses. *See* Odysseus
Undercliff, the, 16–17, 23–24, 26, 28, 30, 38–39, 43n 36, 90–91, 115–16, 137–41, 144–45, 149, 150–51, 153n 9, 163, 170–72, 175–76, 179–82, 184–89, 191–92, 196, 206
Undercliff National Nature Reserve, 138, 141, 143
Underhill Farm, 17, 141–43, 145, 146. *See also* Dairy, The
Understanding John Fowles, 193n 2
United States of America, 46, 48, 154, 255–56. *See also* California, Hollywood, Maine, New Mexico, New York
Universe, 161

urbanization, 47. *See also* cities
Urfe, Nicholas, 91–92, 118–20, 230–31, 233–37, 241, 245, 252

Varguennes, 147, 175, 184, 187, 191
Venus, 232
Victorians, 48, 114–15, 134n 2, , 147, 151, 152n 9, 155–58, 163, 165–66, 170–71, 174–75, 181, 184, 185, 187–91, 198, 201, 203–5, 256
Vieth, Lynne, 37–38
Villa Yasemia, 21, 233–34
Vipond, Dianne, 40, 132, 254–55, 257
Vision of St. Eustace (?), 117

Wanklyn, Cyril 144
Warburton, Eileen, 39, 255
Ware Cliffs, 141, 145–46, 151
Ware Common, 141, 143, 146, 149, 181–82, 190, 192
Ware Fields, 141, 143
Warmwell Heath, 138
Washington Post, The, 123
Waterford, 82
Well Beloved, The, 123, 245
Weller, Sam, 201
Wessex, 137
Wessex Tales, 153n 9
West Country, 18, 24, 26, 40, 93
Weston-super-Mare, 19
Whales, Dolphins and Seals, 15
White Goddess, 248–50
White Goddess, The, 157
White, Hayden, 104
Whitechapel Rock(s), 30–31, 38, 43nn 36 and 37, 139, 141, 146, 172, 175, 180n 13
Whitelaw, Billie, 255
Whitlands Cliffs, 139, 141, 180n 13
Whitsuntide King, 98
Wild Man, 104, 107. *See also* Green Man, Green Woman
wildness, 16, 18, 20, 23, 52, 54, 87–88, 90, 96, 101, 104, 107, 110, 133, 169, 184, 186
Williams, David, 24, 110
Wilson, Angus, 61
Wiltshire, 103. *See also* Salisbury, Stonehenge, Sutton Benger
Winefred, 152n 9
Winnicott, D. W., 39, 106–7, 109, 123
Winsyatt, 171, 176

Wistman's Wood, 26, 32, 76, 81, 85, 108
Wonderful Life, 165
Wonders of Geology, 165
Woodruff, Sarah, 26, 30, 29, 39, 43n 31, 48, 60, 91, 114–17, 121, 134n 2, 137–38, 146, 149, 150–52, 153n 13, 156–57, 161–62, 166, 169–70, 172, 174–78, 181–92, 193n 2, 198, 201–3, 206, 246
Woolf, Virginia, 27, 61, 250, 255
Wordsworth, William, 48

Y (Young Men's Hebrew Association), 255
Yolla Bolly Press, the, 69, 84

Zen, 14, 80, 82. *See also* Buddhism
Zhengming, Wen, 78, 79–80
Zito, Tom, 123
Zulu, 257